Ella L. Randall McDougall

From side streets and boulevards

A collection of Chicago stories

Ella L. Randall McDougall

From side streets and boulevards
A collection of Chicago stories

ISBN/EAN: 9783741181603

Manufactured in Europe, USA, Canada, Australia, Japa

Cover: Foto ©Andreas Hilbeck / pixelio.de

Manufactured and distributed by brebook publishing software (www.brebook.com)

Ella L. Randall McDougall

From side streets and boulevards

FROM SIDE STREETS AND BOULEVARDS

A COLLECTION OF CHICAGO STORIES

BY
PRESERVED WHEELER

CHICAGO
R. R. DONNELLEY & SONS COMPANY, PRINTERS
1893

COPYRIGHT
BY PRESERVED WHEELER,
1893.
ALL RIGHTS RESERVED.

DEDICATED TO CHICAGO.

"But, truly, for mine own part, if I were as tedious as a king, I could find it in my heart to bestow it all of your worship."

CONTENTS.

A VAGABOND FOR A YEAR,	9
ALL ON A CHRISTMAS EVE,	165
A PIECE OF LAND,	281
POEMS:	
GRANDMA,	337
THE FROST UPON THE PANE,	342
COMING HOME,	344
RETURNED,	345
FOR ONE DAY,	346
ROSE HILL,	348
FORGET ME NOT,	350

A VAGABOND FOR A YEAR.

VAGABOND FOR A YEAR.

In the year 1858 lived in a diminutive cottage, on the outskirts of one of our large eastern cities, a small family in rather reduced circumstances. This family differed from the thousands similarly situated in the misfortunes leading to their present condition. The father was one of the younger sons in a wealthy English family; he had been scrupulously taught the manly accomplishments appertaining to his station in life, received a liberal education, particularly in the art of spending money, and on reaching his twenty-fifth year fell in love with a handsome, highly educated girl, the daughter of a minister; this lady brought to her husband no larger dower than her beauty and devotion. All might have been well if the young husband had not already formed that taste for ardent spirits which has been, and is, the blight of so many hearthstones.

The father of this young man, whose name was Trevanion, remonstrated with him gravely on his faults; he encouraged the attachment which resulted in his son's marriage, under the impression that this tie might prove a powerful lever to work against his son's besetting sin. For a few months these hopes bade fair to be realized, as young

Trevanion's happiness and absorption in domestic life kept him from the gay companions who helped to lead him into excesses. This was not to last, however, for when a baby girl was born to him he seemed slowly but surely drifting back to his old debaucheries—the entreaties of his family, the prayers of his young wife, appeared powerless to save him.

Young Mrs. Trevanion held anxious consultations with her father-in-law concerning what had best be done to try yet the reclaiming of her husband. She thought, reasonably enough, that entire separation from the companions of his youth, the associations of his orgies, new scenes, new people, necessity for greater exertion in the care of his family, might break up the old habits and all would end happily yet. At length it was decided that the little family would leave their fair English home to "adventure all" in a new land. With many kind farewells from friends, and hopes for their future prosperity, they sailed from that old world they would never see again, and entered on the new life. How hard, how strange the new life was at first—but those first couple of years hope sang beside the door, whilst joy companioned her, for the husband and father was so kind and thoughtful; drink—that nightmare of their lives—remained behind upon that English soil. Could this have lasted—poverty, anxiety, even sickness, would have seemed to them but light calamities.

It did not last; by slow degrees their beloved was falling into his sodden ways again. So long as his circumstances permitted, old Mr. Trevanion had given his son pecuniary assistance; now, with increasing years upon him, a large and expensive family, and this son across seas, these allowances began to dwindle, then ceased completely. After many reverses this little family had been living for the last two years in the modest cottage where our story finds them. Trevanion's education, combined with some literary ability he possessed, sufficed to provide for their wants during his spells of sobriety; but those terrible periods in between, when books, clothing, furniture, even food, was pawned by him to satisfy his insatiable thirst — who can tell what his family suffered at those times? Trevanion's oldest daughter, Christine, was now approaching her fourteenth year. She was plump in figure, quite womanly looking for her age; this child was really the light of the household — the gayety of her spirits never flagged, her hopefulness remained undaunted through all reverses. They called her Crissy — no severer appellation would have suited the merry child-face and figure.

Crissy shared faithfully the cares of their precarious lives. When her father's excesses drove her mother to the very verge of despondency the young girl would cheer the broken-hearted woman with the fancies of what pleasant things their future might yet hold in store for them — with promises of what she would try to do to lighten her mother's burden. Crissy was intellectually precocious. Her father, in the happy weeks of sobriety which broke his long debaucheries, read with and instructed the child; the little cottage was visited by many persons of a literary, also a theatrical, tendency, newspaper men, playwrights, many people of this ilk. Trevanion wrote for papers and magazines, reviewed the latest works of fiction — in fact, turned his hand to anything where paper, pen and ink came into requisition. In addition to his other capacities he was an able accountant, but, owing to his erratic habits, could not retain such positions of trust for any length of time. In such a country as the United States of America a man of Trevanion's capabilities could readily have secured a competence had his habits been steady; even as it was he managed in those short intervals when he abstained from drink to collect some comforts, even luxuries, about his hearth. Crissy never lacked for books, for in the little parlor stood two well-filled book cases, busts and statuettes adorned the room, upon the walls a few good pictures bore testimony to Trevanion's taste. Thus the young girl, brought up in poverty, sorrow, anxiety, was in contact with tastes beyond her condition; she listened for many hours to brilliant conversations between men of exceptional talents, who, like her father, had in most cases ostracised themselves from culture and wealth by their own excesses. It could not be a matter of surprise that this girl, who was more familiar with the latest novel, the newest play, the opera just out, than most girls of her age would be with their French grammars, drawings or water-colors, should imbibe tastes of a decidedly dramatic tendency. Crissy therefore wrote poems at the mature age of ten, recited Shakespeare acceptably at twelve, astonished her friends by the exuberance of her fancies in prose at fourteen; she could at all times do what was far more indispensable to the family comfort—control her father in his wildest conditions; she was always helpful, always hopeful, invariably cheerful, yet many a time, as she sat apparently absorbed in some favorite book, she was really in serious thought. This girl idolized her mother—her dream by day and night was what she could do for her mother, that sweet, patient mother who bore hard fortune so uncomplainingly. She had heard these people who called upon her father tell of young girls—poor like herself—who had essayed to make their way upon the stage, who had secured plaudits, but, better still, fine incomes, had helped indigent friends to comfort, even to independence—why should *she* hesitate? Those who heard her recite praised her, prognosticating, with kind looks, bright things for her future; her father's editorial friends published her little poems, calling her a genius; such praises have misled older heads than Crissy's many a time. After weeks of secret thought, Crissy astonished her mother and shocked her father by openly declaring a desire to go upon the stage.

The first shock of such an idea is something like the first plunge into cold water—a couple of shivers then it's all right; such at least was the effect upon Mrs. Trevanion. Her husband regarded Crissy's fancy much more seriously, expressing very decided disapprobation. He realized more fully than his wife what it was to let a child in her fourteenth year essay the "battle of life" in such an arena; but, alas! his fatal habit conquered him just as his hand was needed at the helm.

One night in the fall of the year 1858, Crissy and her mother sat in earnest conversation in one of the chambers of their unpretending home; they spoke in hushed voices that they might not disturb the children sleeping near them. "Yes, mother," Crissy was saying, "Mrs. Burton has promised to take every care of me, to teach me all relating to the profession. Mrs. Burton and her husband have been upon the stage so many years that they know all that can be known in theatricals—you'll come with me to-morrow to sign the papers, then next day we'll be on the road." "Oh, Crissy dear," said the poor mother, "my heart fails me now! you are so young! and yet—" here she looked proudly at the girlish face beside her, "I can't help thinking you will do well, you have such talent! such perseverance!" After a long pause she turned upon the girl a searching gaze, then said: "One thing troubles me, dear. You will be thrown in contact with so many men, young men, who will flatter you and try to steal your heart away; be careful when they talk to you—never encourage the attention of any man unless he asks you to be his *wife*." Here the mother's voice trembled, it was so hard to say just what she wanted to the child, who looked at her with such large, innocent eyes. "Remember," she continued, more firmly, "that any man who behaves in a *lover-like* manner to you, without asking you to be his *wife*, *insults* and would degrade you; if that happens and your heart fails you, proving weak, recall your mother's words, and then run away from him." The girl listened silently, apparently without paying much attention, yet many months after, this advice recurred to her with startling distinctness.

At this time Trevanion was on one of his wildest sprees. Poor Crissy couldn't even say good-bye to him—she dared not venture to do so. She and the mother hastily completed their arrangements for the journey, talking hopefully together like two big children; these simple souls knew not the gravity of their undertaking, what dangerous shoals, what quicksands would lie along Crissy's path; to them it was a few months of study and experience on Crissy's part, then approbation and quick reward. The papers between Mrs. Trevanion and the Burtons had been duly signed and witnessed, to the effect that Miss Crissy Trevanion, in consideration of her professional services, should receive from the Burtons six dollars per week, as well as adequate instruction in the theatrical profession, also one benefit every six months, the proceeds of such benefit over and above its expenses to be placed in the hands of the beneficiary; in addition to this, that her traveling expenses and living expenses would be paid by said Burtons for a term not exceeding one year from date. The mother tremblingly implored Mrs. Burton to be careful of the child, then with many tears the final separation took place. It must be confessed that as Mrs. Trevanion walked slowly home her feelings partook more of anticipation and triumph than actual sadness; she had such faith in Crissy's powers—this child was to lift them all from the "slough of despondency" into which the father had plunged them. Crissy had little time for homesickness, as she was put to studying a part at once, being told by Mrs. Burton that she had better study it during the railroad journey, the better to be ready for rehearsing the next day. Crissy had no need to be told twice; she was charmed to begin her duties—everything delighted her, the bustle of starting for their destination, the bustle of getting to it, the being packed tightly, like sandwiches, into an omnibus and driven to an hotel, then, after a night of such intense repose as falls only to the young—to sit shyly beside Mrs. Burton at the long breakfast table as that lady told her in whispers that such a young man sitting on the other side of the table, the one with red hair, was their " walking gentleman," that the fat person farther down, with the good natured face, was their " heavy villain," that the extremely cadaverous, melancholy gentleman, with long legs, who was dressed in seedy black, was their " first comedian." Crissy surveyed these persons with astonishment, also some trepidation—the comedian, in particular, inspired her with awe, he took his food with such an air of overpowering dejection; when Mrs. Burton called out a morning salutation to him, he looked ready to weep, only responding with a melancholy wave of the hand. Crissy, whose appetite was excellent, soon became too much occupied with her breakfast to take more notice of these people; at a later hour—the ten o'clock rehearsal, she was introduced to them all in form; the feeling of dislike with which the comedian inspired her was not lessened when she noticed him looking at her in a disparaging manner, and remarking that she was much too young and small to be entrusted with the part Mrs. Burton had assigned her. Crissy inwardly wondered if it always made men cross and sad to play comedy. Her wonder increased when a diminutive, very young-looking person with a sweet child-like face, was pointed out to her as the comedian's wife; a greater contrast than this pair presented, could not be imagined. Crissy longed to talk to this pretty little woman at once, but was too bashful to do so; she was unable to note her companions longer as the rehearsal of her part claimed pretty thorough attention. On her way back to the hotel with Mr. and Mrs. Burton, she heard the former say to his wife that he feared the town had not been thoroughly "billed." Crissy was puzzled as to the meaning of this. Burton added, that the result might be a "slim house." The place itself was a lively country town where they intended playing only one night, appearing the next night in a town some distance beyond. That evening, after a hasty supper, they repaired to the large hall dubbed by courtesy a theatre. Here in the dressing room Mrs. Burton initiated Crissy into the mysteries of the "make-up;" having darkened Crissy's eyes after the conventional manner, rouged her cheeks and lips, and so forth, she proceeded to beautify herself, keeping up a continual flow of conversation as she did so. "I hope, Crissy," she said, "that you'll not suffer from stage fright, tho' it is an understood thing that the harder the stage fright a woman has, the better actress she is sure to turn out." "What does it feel like?" asked Crissy, "did *you* ever have it?" "Oh, yes!" responded her instructress, "I suffered dreadfully from it; you see it acts differently with different people, some forget their lines the instant they set foot upon the stage, being hardly able to get out a word, even when prompted; others tell me that they have a feeling of deadly faintness and sickness when they first stand behind the footlights. But, dear me," exclaimed Mrs. Burton, "it's getting quite late, here we are all dressed, yet I hear no stir at all!" Just then came a tap upon the door, Mr. Burton thrust in his head with a very rueful countenance: "Turned out as I half-feared Lizzie,--we didn't bill the thing long enough ahead. I'll be hanged if there's any audience! so change your gowns and come home." "Dear me," said Mrs. Burton, as the door closed upon her retreating spouse, "just to think that we wasted all this paint and powder!"

As they trudged back to the hotel Crissy thought it all over—it was such an astonishing thing that they should have no audience. That night in her dreams she was always coming on the stage with rows of empty benches in front of her and the powder partly washed from her face. The next night in the new place they met with better success; a large and very enthusiastic crowd—judging from the noise they made—greeted their efforts. The comedian came out in full force—one look at his woe-begone countenance as he stepped toward the footlights would provoke the wildest hilarity, incessant laughter greeted his every word; when he stalked off at the stage exits his saturnine face would become more unprepossessing than ever, as shouts of merriment followed his departure.

Crissy told Mrs. Burton that she didn't see how

he could do it; the latter laughed and said, "That was acting!" Crissy did so well in the rôle she filled that the Burtons bestowed warm praises on her. Then the poor child went to bed tired but happy; her last thought as she fell asleep was of her mother. Three weeks passed in this manner, the company never sojourning longer than two nights in one place; varying success met their labors. All this time Crissy wrote home frequently, giving lively descriptions of their surroundings and successes. Of their failures she never wrote; child-like, she looked always upon the bright side, paying little attention to the occasional mishaps which overtook these poor actors; notwithstanding, she noted many things. She had been wont to associate the idea of theatrical life with something superior, feeling quite sure that the people who devoted their time to it must be more intellectual than the ordinary run of mortals—now she discovered them to be for the most part quite commonplace. They interlarded their conversation with slang and strange phrases, rather repellant to her unaccustomed ears, they seemed so incongruous; the oddities and contradictions of that abhorred comedian appeared to be repeated to a modified extent in almost all the rest. Mrs. Burton and her little daughter, a child of eight years, realized Crissy's ideals more closely; the former was a finely educated woman who in early girlhood made the mistake of running away from a comfortable home to marry a talented but poor actor. This woman, in spite of her environments, the many hardships she had passed through, preserved her gentleness and a purity of manner not always found in women of her condition. The child, carefully reared by such a mother, was a lovely being; with her sweet voice, golden ringlets and pretty features, she was very engaging. Crissy became close friends with her at once. The mother encouraged the affection between these children, thrown by such chances of fortune into each other's companionship. Crissy in spare hours talked with, walked with, invented plays and toys for the little Leoline.

By the end of the third week of their wanderings Crissy made another discovery. She didn't know exactly *why*, but she had been under the impression that Burton had some means with which to push his enterprise; from a portion of a conversation she heard between him and his wife she was now led to the conclusion that this was not the case. Crissy was such a silent girl that people seldom noticed her proximity; thus it chanced that they often spoke quite unreservedly in her presence. One day she heard Burton saying: "I've been lucky today—struck a fellow with lots of money, and as green as a leek! he's perfectly stage-struck! talked to me about my company and said he reckoned there was heaps to be made in the show business, and said he'd like to be part proprietor in such a show as mine. Well, I kind of led him on and sure enough the fellow had lots of cash, for he showed it to me; so we struck a bargain. He puts in all he has against my brains and experience; he will act as our agent, going ahead to advertise and make all the business arrangements. He may be pretty good at *that*—in fact," added Burton, reflectively, "that's about *all* he is good for; he has no more understanding of theatricals than the 'man in the moon,' but it's a fine thing for us; the new partner comes in to-morrow." The partner alluded to was not seen by Crissy for a week subsequent to this conversation.

One Sunday evening, as she sat in the private parlor with Burton and his family—by the way, this was previous to the time that the public had learned to ask for Sunday performances—Crissy, who sat near the door, which was slightly open, became conscious of a penetrating and somewhat disagreeable odor. There was a gentle tap upon the door; to the summons of "Come in!" a lank, ill-dressed man appeared; every feature of his face proclaimed him what is called "low," his retreating brow, puckered lips, eyes set close together, produced anything except an agreeable impression. When Burton greeted him by name, asking him to be seated, Crissy knew at once that this must be the new partner; at the same moment, too, she became thoroughly cognizant of the odor which offended her—it was decidedly *horse*. The man sat talking with Burton for an hour. Crissy saw that during the interview, which related principally to advertising and general business of the concern, this man never looked anyone in the eyes. His orbs, which were dark and narrow, seemed to be playing hide-and-seek with everybody in the room; some fascination drew Crissy's gaze frequently to his face, but he never looked squarely at her, though she was aware that he regarded her with covert glances. After he left the room, accompanied by Burton, Mrs. Burton asked her how she liked Mr. Smith. "Not at all!" answered Crissy decidedly, "he is horrible! He smells so of horses!" "Well," exclaimed her preceptress, in surprise, "I never noticed that! However," she added with a smile, "he is not pleasant in either look or manner."

As a couple of weeks passed by Crissy noticed another peculiarity of Mr. Smith's—he was very seldom seen by any of the company of whom he was the financial head; he did not stop at the same hotels with them, he seemed to shun speech with any one except Burton. Owing to these oddities remarks of an uncomplimentary turn concerning him could frequently be heard from members of the company. One day the comedian, who never withheld unfavorable criticism against any one, was heard saying: "That fellow Smith behaves like a mean, miserable, slinking *hound*, going about the way he does. I came upon him unexpectedly on the street the other day, and I'll be hanged if he didn't dodge around the first corner to avoid me,—actually looked *scared* at the sight of me!" This statement produced a general smile, for the comedian's countenance was built upon a plan so lugubrious that it might by a very slight effort of the imagination be supposed to strike terror—or sentiments approximating to that—into anybody.

There was another thing which began to press upon Crissy's conceptions—this was that there seemed something out of the way with Burton himself. In appearance he was a tall, handsome man, with aquiline features; he belonged to the class which in those days was denominated "down-easter." He had the quick, nervous manners of his race, energetic and keen; he was a fine actor, especially in his rendition of Yankee character—not the Yankee of these days, but the "stage Yankee" of thirty-four years ago, the one all spring and sharpness, who came before the footlights in a pair of striped pants tightly strapped down, a long-tailed coat, an impossible hat; whose dry jokes convulsed with laughter an audience always appreciative of them, whose "local hits" always hit just right—a delightful and good-natured caricature of the typical Yankee; this character is rapidly disappearing, if not altogether obsolete, from the modern stage. Burton was a man nearing middle age when Crissy was put in his care; somewhat brusque, yet kind in his manners, he treated Crissy as he did his own child, taking pains in her instruction, firmly correcting her stage faults.

Crissy became conscious of a vague anxiety in her observations of him; first she felt this through seeing the glances his wife sometimes cast upon him—searching, yet fearful, long looks, which trembled in the balance between hope and dread; she had observed her mother looking at her father thus, hundreds of times. A thought presented itself which caused Crissy to shudder; could it be that she had left misery and despair at her own fireside only to find herself afloat again upon that dreadful sea which wrecks home, honor, life itself? These fears soon became confirmed, for, during a rather stormy interview held between Smith and Burton in the private apartments of the latter, it became unmistakably evident that Burton was intoxicated. That Crissy was so often present on these occasions was because Mrs. Burton kept the girl always near her, for, as Mrs. Burton truly and bitterly remarked to her husband, "the mere fact of Crissy being an *actress* would expose her to continual insult." The afternoon of this particular day in question Mr. Smith was urging Burton to move the company on more rapidly, saying that in the West they could play to big houses—that these eastern towns didn't pay. Burton angrily denied this statement, calling to witness the excellent houses they played to in this very town, where they had been two days. Smith, who was generally very reticent, being what is termed a "slow talker," became rather excited and anxious in advancing his views on the moving westward at once. When he found that Burton would not do it, he exclaimed coarsely, "It's easy to see why I can't get you to listen to reason, you're drunk!" Burton sprang to his feet with clenched hands and flashing eyes, his wife ran to his side to quiet him; just then there was a commotion at the door, heavy footsteps, loud voices, Smith turned deadly pale, running as if by instinct to the window, which he endeavored to raise; the door was thrown violently open, two stalwart policemen entered, with them a little man shabbily dressed, who held a written document in his hand. The little man called out, "Smith, alias Henly, I arrest you for horse stealing." The policemen came each side of Smith, who, turning with a savage look upon his sullen face, fronted the occupants of the room. "This is *your* fault," he said to Burton; "if you had gone on as fast as I *wanted* you to, they could not have caught me; you can take your company where you please now! to hell if you like. I've stolen horses right along to keep your d—d expenses paid! you've lived *well*, too," he added, with a sarcastic grin, giving a last defiant look at Burton as he was led from the room. The woman and Crissy listened to all this in silent terror. Burton ank into a chair, almost sobered by the shock. After a few minutes his wife said pointedly, "One needs to keep a clear head in this business; you'll have to look into things at once, Burton. Here we are living in the most expensive hotel in town; a good-sized company, two days' board for all may be a serious matter if unpaid; you can't tell what position this man has left you in. For my part," she continued, "I would much prefer that right along we had stopped at second or even third-class houses, and avoided so much expense." "It couldn't be helped!" said Burton desperately. "Smith was bound to have it so! He said living in style, hiring carriages, and all that sort of thing, would create a favorable impression and bring in *trade*, as *he* called it!" He said this last with a grimace. Burton found his wife's words prophetic. Mr. Smith had ordered for all the best that the place afforded; being nabbed before he had time to dispose of his last venture in horse-flesh, he had not liquidated these little bills.

The landlord, being quickly apprised of the state of affairs, came at once to Burton's room to have speech with him upon the subject; the corridors were filled with groups of people talking excitedly over the affair. Crissy felt her cheeks burn with shame as the stout, coarse, but good-natured landlord said to Burton, "You're in a pretty fix now, with this horse-thieving fellow; you'll have to see what can be done about what's owing *me* and others unless you have plenty of money by you to straighten out these things." Burton was obliged to admit his inability to do so, Smith had managed both receipts and expenditures. "The only faculties," Burton said, angrily, "Smith had, seemed to be those of managing money and stealing horses, though, of course, the last accomplishment no one but Smith himself had been aware of." Then Burton and the landlord summoned the members of the company into the room and held a consultation on "ways and means." Crissy sat sadly in a corner, listening to this curious confab; the degrees of impecuniosity confessed by all of these poor actors was astonishing; in fact, their impecuniosities appeared measureless! The good-natured landlord looked from one to another in perplexity. "Well!" he exclaimed at last, "there's only one thing to do; the longer I keep you here the worse off I am. I could keep your baggage, of course, but I opine that it wouldn't be worth much; so just go right on and play to-night, perhaps when the proceeds are divided up you'll have enough to carry you out of town; if there's any over," he added, with a twinkle in his eye, "just let me have it on account, that's all."

This being on the whole a very kind arrangement for the landlord to make, all acceded to it joyfully. After that functionary left the room they all with one accord fell upon Burton with violent vituperations. Why had he—Burton—been so short-sighted? Wasn't the man Smith a scoundrel on his very face? Here had Burton decoyed them from their homes, perhaps from better engagements, to strand them in a far-away place; what excuses could he offer for treating them this way? The comedian was the fiercest of them all. He stalked up and down the room uttering the most dreadful denunciations; poor Crissy fairly trembled under his wrath. When the excitement consequent upon these recriminations had somewhat subsided Burton told them calmly that as they felt so aggrieved, the best thing for them to do would be to cancel their engagements with him and go their separate ways; they knew that all along they had been playing to very poor business; there was little hope for any better; let them then divide what they would take in this night, and separate. Two of them declared their intention of sticking by Burton, the rest grumblingly closed with his proposition. Fortunately for the stranded actors they had a good house that night. At the end of the performance they all met by arrangement in Burton's apartments, where the results of their last appearance together were evenly divided; each one looked rather sharply after his or her share, but the wrangling of the afternoon seemed done away with. Had Burton been more reliable, they would probably, at least the greater portion of them, remained by him; as it was they felt that they were leaving a sinking ship and had the right to do so.

The two exceptions, both men, declared openly that they intended going on with him to the Far

West; a young man named George, a callow youth, was one of them. He was a good-hearted, loud, enthusiastic talking fellow, full of hope, and really sorry for the position Burton's indiscretions had placed his family in. This ingenuous youth reasoned with himself thus: "There's poor little *Crissy*, too! what is likely to become of her? I guess I'll stick by them and see this thing through."

The other exception was a middle-aged man, a musician, one of the orchestra Burton had attached to his company. This man had apparently no domestic ties to trouble him, and said merrily that he could *afford* to take his chances.

The ensuing morning all started. The animosity they had previously exhibited to Burton had quite gone now; the careless souls, living, as they did, "from hand to mouth," thought of this only as one of the incidentals of their lives. The remainder then hastily arranged their plan of campaign. "There's only one thing we can do *now*," said Burton; "travel as a *family*, that'll be quite a card— tell you it's a taking thing now-a-days; call ourselves the *Burton Family*." "But," urged George, "how can we play anything, so few of us, only two women and three men; don't see how we'll manage it!" "Just look here," explained Burton, "I'll figure it all out for you: two women, true enough, but you forget the *child*, she'll be a good deal to us. Bless your heart, we can play lots of things by doubling. Got plays of my own, my boy, in MSS.; they'll be worth lots to us; can cut and adapt them to suit emergencies." "You're a smart man!" cried George, admiringly; "most fellows would lose heart, but *you* take hold of your difficulties in fine shape." "Then, as for orchestra," went on Burton, smiling, "we have Snidacker here! he can play on anything! he'll be a host in himself; he can furnish music enough." "What," gasped George, "an orchestra composed of only *one!*" "That doesn't matter," answered Burton, sturdily; "remember we travel as a *family* now; can't afford more than *one* musical brother in a family small as ours. As this landlord is so kind to us, the best thing we can do now is to pack up and make for the first smart town; we can look over some plays with a short cast, and plan out the first performance as we go along; after a few days we can get something the child will work into—for instance, 'King Charles,' in 'Faint Heart Never Won Fair Lady.' A child is very pleasing before the footlights; Crissy will help to teach her."

This being settled, the small remnant of the show was soon on the road again. All had been transacted so quickly that when Crissy found herself on the train once more she had no opportunity for uninterrupted reflection, for, as they journeyed along, the little party looked over plays and MSS. together, even the child, who seemed to take an odd pleasure in finding herself a working member of the group, volunteered suggestions. Burton bent all his energies to this new task. He eschewed liquor, being the genial, painstaking soul that Crissy had first known him; his wife was equally happy. She conversed with Crissy on the ever-momentous question of "wardrobe." She found, on their first acquaintance, that the girl was remarkably ignorant of the art of sewing, so the older woman imparted knowledge to her in this indispensable adjunct to feminine learning; together they planned many interesting costumes, where gossamer materials and wall-paper flowers figured conspicuously. From this time out they would have a good deal of such planning and alteration on account of the doubling of parts. Mrs. Burton said, "You'll learn to make these changes of dress very rapidly when you double so much; every second counts then. It will be just as well for you to learn this; really, you will get on much faster in understanding professional duties than if we had remained as we first started out."

George's reasons for remaining with Burton have been slightly touched upon before; he had the additional one that in traveling westward he would also be journeying homeward. This youth was the red-headed one pointed out to Crissy on that first memorable morning as "our walking gentleman." When they made their plans together after the breakup of the company, this youth was the most sanguine of all. He talked incessantly of what they might be able to accomplish, of the good luck they *might* have; he adduced examples of what a few people had done in traveling theatricals. He told them with considerable verbosity that his abilities, such as they were, would be entirely at their disposal—for instance, he might say, without incurring the accusation of selfpraise, that he was quite a hand with the *brush*. Give him some big paper, a brush and colors, he'd turn out *posters* for them that would astonish the natives. Really there was nothing more captivating to the rural imagination than posters, your big red, blue and yellow ones, that would cover a whole fence! He then proceeded at great length to tell of companies who had made independent fortunes by the judicious use of such conspicuous advertising. Mrs. Burton responded that such talents as George's should not be wasted, that upon arriving at their destination he should go to work at once upon the preparation of these colored productions. Crissy thought that, after all, they seemed much happier together since their misfortunes than they had ever been before. Her acquaintance with George the voluble might be said to date from this period. Snidacker the musician listened to these plans with a benign smile, saying that he would do all he could for them in the musical way, also working in on general utility. Of the private sentiments leading to Mr. Snidacker's desire to remain with them, more will be said hereafter.

Fortune, for a time at least, seemed to smile upon

the little party. As one family on the bills, they made quite a startling impression of the versatility and talent sometimes to be found in a single family. In the meantime Crissy and Mrs. Burton carefully instructed the child in the characters of "King Charles" and "Eva." At the time we write of, "Uncle Tom's Cabin" was one of the "big cards" in the northern theatres; owing to the great stir being made by the abolitionists, this play generally drew well whenever presented. It was not the Uncle Tom's Cabin of the present day. It was an eminently respectable play, in comparison with the wretched travesty presented to the public own. It was a six-act play, taking a long, sometimes a *very* long, evening to play it through. The eloquent language, Mrs. Stowe's own, was to a great extent retained. The Eva of those times always created strong sympathy, especially when—as in Leoline's case—the child bore so close a resemblance in form and feature to the beautiful original. The child learned with great rapidity; she understood thoroughly the expression she should put into her lines. Crissy was charmed by so apt a pupil, looking forward with pleasure to the production of this play by their little family, though with any amount of doubling, they scarcely saw how they could put it on. In "Faint Heart" and kindred plays they managed nicely. Leoline's success as Prince Charles was very flattering. When the boy's slight form, with his wealth of golden ringlets hanging over his shoulders, clambered in at the window, he was invariably greeted with shouts of delighted applause. They had now by slow degrees journeyed considerably westward. Crissy was continually finding new cause for wonderment and laughter in the odd fancies of her friend George. He said frequently, "wait till you see Chicago! that'll be a treat I can tell you; I was *born* there." "Indeed!" said Crissy quietly, "is that the circumstance which makes that city so far ahead of all others?" George laughed good naturedly. "You can't form an idea of the splendor of my native city until you *see* it, it really is something to be proud of; the fact of having been born there." "*I* was born in a very fine town in England," said Crissy, "but I never thought of making a boast of it." "England," answered George contemptuously, "why all the cities and towns in England are *old*. What makes Chicago so wonderful is its *youth*. Just imagine it, that thirty years ago, nothing more than a few miserable log cabins and the like stood where a city is now stretching its long arms upon the lake shore." Then George went on to tell Crissy a very thrilling story, which she couldn't thoroughly understand, of how his, George's father, would have died a rich man, if some canal running through the city and projected by said father had only been accepted by the council, or by some body of men, at the proper time. But, as it turned out unfortunately that George's father expired before any of these hopes could be fulfilled, his mother kept a boarding house, assisted by his younger sister, that he and his brothers did what they could to help the old lady, hence his—George's—wandering life. Being convinced that he had dramatic talent, he was determined to keep on in this line until he learned his chosen profession. Crissy, finding him a congenial spirit in his dramatic aspirations, imparted to him in turn some of her hopes and fears. George listened sympathetically, telling her to count him her friend in everything. A few days succeeding this time, the "family" lost one of its members, receiving a severe mental shock simultaneously. Mr. Snidacker had proved as good as his word about making himself generally useful; he played touching selections between the acts for them; furnished slow or fast music for the scenes as occasion demanded, came on sometimes as heavy old man. He was so quiet and reliable, that Burton often said he didn't see how they would get on without Snidacker.

It chanced that the town they were stopping at had, for that very afternoon, a counter attraction, a "circus,"—the regular old fashioned circus, elephant and all! It is an odd thing that professionals, though they abhor circuses, considered from a caste point of view, can seldom resist going to them. At that time it was a courtesy extended to all professionals, that they were admitted free of charge to any entertainment of this nature. At dinner time, Burton and George laughingly proclaimed their intention of dropping in to take a look at this show. They went accordingly. Shortly after, Crissy was passing alone through one of the corridors of the hotel when she met Snidacker. "Little girl," he said kindly, "you'd like to go to the circus, wouldn't you?" Crissy's face beamed with pleasure, "O yes," she answered. "Then run, put on your bonnet," he said, " I'll take you there right away." "I'll have to ask Mrs. Burton, first," said Crissy, rather startled by his suddenness. "Never mind then," he said crossly, "I can't wait, it's late now!" With that he turned on his heel and was gone in an instant. Crissy felt surprised, somewhat disappointed, too, but girl-like forgot the circumstance in a short time, not even remembering to mention it to Mrs. Burton.

In this town they were making a two-nights "stand." The next afternoon Crissy was walking rapidly along the main street, holding in her hand some little purchase Mrs. Burton had sent her out for, when she came upon Snidacker again unexpectedly. He darted around a corner, and catching her by the hand, said excitedly, "Mrs. Burton sent me after you, they have changed all their plans; won't play here to-night, go by a train which leaves here in ten minutes. She told me to bring you to the train at once, so come along!" "Oh!" cried Crissy, catching her breath with surprise, "how *can* it be? She never said a word to me about it when I left the hotel!" "Come on," said the man, impatiently, "the train goes in ten minutes." "Go to the train then," said Crissy, "as soon as I get the parcel I left in this store, I'll join you." As she spoke, she motioned toward a store close by. "Hurry then!" cried Snidacker, as he made hastily in the direction of the depot. Crissy disappeared into the store to emerge in an instant breathlessly from a side door of that edifice, opening on another street, where she took to her heels for the hotel. A few moments later she found herself panting in the middle of Mrs. Burton's room; the latter, seated quietly at her sewing with Leoline near her, rose in astonishment as Crissy, hot and disheveled, tore into the apartment. "You are *not* going then!" exclaimed Crissy; "why did he tell me to go on that train? what does it all mean?" Mrs. Burton tried to calm the excited girl sufficiently to get the true state of affairs from her; the surprise of the older woman was unbounded. "It's a fortunate thing you used some judgment in this, Crissy, and came here first to make sure of the truth of his statements," said her preceptress, gravely. "I will send for Mr. Burton at once to have this looked into." The looking into only developed the unmistakable fact that Mr. Snidacker had left, and that he intended to have taken Crissy as his companion, had the girl shown that implicit confidence in what he told her, that he evidently expected she would. This turn surprised all, but no one more than Crissy. She did not realize how great her escape had been. Mrs. Burton looked after her more closely than ever from that time out; she also gave her some warnings for the future.

Many and unexpected as had been the vicissitudes attending her stage career, this last episode astonished Crissy the most. She never wrote a word of it to her mother, for she saw from the gravity of Burton and his wife that they regarded it very seriously. Thinking it all over, she concluded it would be better for a time at least not to let her mother know how very different the stage of reality was to that of their expectations. The loss of Snidacker crippled them greatly; they had to have some music, and hired it from place to place. This was precarious as well as expensive.

Even under this misfortune George's spirits, as usual, rose triumphant. "Wait till we strike the Far West," he said, "then we'll get big business and lots of cash! Tell you, the westerners are the people for fun and generosity; hard work to squeeze money from these eastern fellows, they are naturally stingy, they count every cent, *they* do; but from Chicago, westward, everything will be booming!" George's high hopes scarcely seemed likely to be realized, for this was an unfortunate time financially for the whole world of amusement in this country. The nation was occupied by agitations so intense, thoughts so momentous, that very little time was given to patronizing pleasure; money, too, was tight, *very* tight, people in the lower and middle walks of life found it as much as they could do to "make all ends meet." Amusement being a luxury, could be dispensed with; even now, the throes of that great convulsion which armed brother against brother in our civil war, began to shake the nation through every fiber; only a half interest was felt in anything which did not relate to the great topics of the day.

In spite of themselves the party could not resist being somewhat cheered by George's glowing pictures of the West; hope had carried them through so many ups and downs they surely could wait a little longer for the golden rewards. One stormy evening in December they arrived in Chicago and put up at the old Girard house. This landmark of Chicago has long since departed. A light snow was falling, which, mingled with the black mud of the streets, made walking horrible—the air was smoky and heavy. Crissy shook with cold as the raw wind from the lake struck her slight figure. Leoline with a child's frankness called out: "Oh George! your city is dreadful, I don't like it one bit!" The weary party reached this point at eleven o'clock at night; they retired to their needed rest as soon as possible; they had no intention of making a stay in the city—they wanted to push right on—but railroad travel in those days was not what it is now; they suffered exasperating delays very often in making their connections. The next morning Crissy was astir early, being anxious to take a look at George's boasted birth-place. As she stepped from the hotel the first thing which riveted her gaze was the lake. After the storm of the previous evening the morning broke sunny and clear; far away spread the blue water, reflecting sun and sky in prismatic hues. Crissy looked at it enraptured. Oddly enough, this—the crowning glory of his western home—George had said little about. She then turned her footsteps along the streets, inspecting all about her with girlish inquisitiveness. As she walked slowly along George overtook her; she was on Lake street, climbing laboriously up a long flight of rough wooden steps. What an odd place it was, to be sure, for she had scarcely gone thirty feet on the level when she had to descend again; then another flight of stairs. "Well," inquired George airily, "how do you like it?" "Like!" answered Crissy. "I really can't say, it's the strangest place I ever was in!" She turned interested looks on magnificent buildings, to her eyes marvels of architecture, standing on either side of a broad but desperately muddy thoroughfare, with always—every few steps—this business of climbing up, then down again. "You don't like the stairs," said George complacently. "That's all right, they're just raising to grade—when this street is finished it will be the finest in the world." Crissy glanced quickly at her companion to see if he was serious; he certainly was—he spoke from the depths of conviction. "Perhaps," said the girl timidly, "you may be right, I don't know much about such matters, but at *present* it's very uncomfortable and incongruous." She relapsed into silence during the balance of the walk. But not so George. He entered into elaborate explanations of all the improvements planned for the city of his love, the brilliancy of its future. Crissy finally interrupted these rhapsodies to lament that it was so very flat, not a hill in sight—it would be so much prettier if hilly. "Hills do not amount to anything," said George, contemptuously, "they're only a bother! If we want hills very badly we can *make* them after a while." Crissy laughed at this. They then repaired to the hotel where, after a hurried breakfast, they were soon on the road again. During this journey George was not as loquacious as usual owing to his intense weariness. He informed Mrs. Burton that he spent the previous night in conversing with his family about his past adventures; having only a few hours in which to do this, he had been unable to get any sleep; this solace he soon secured, however, aboard the train, though it was rough traveling those times.

They took in the small towns along their route. An unusually severe winter was closing in upon them; they began to think seriously of giving up the plan of reaching the Mississippi in time to accomplish anything that winter. Now, too, Burton's besetting sin assailed him again. This made their mode of living even more precarious than it had been, for at these times he was so little to be depended on that on several occasions his wife was obliged to don his costume and take his place before the footlights. Nothing much was said by anyone about Burton's eccentricities; they all made the best of the misfortunes caused by him. From the time that the remnant of the company merged into one family on the bills, Crissy had always appeared as Crissy Burton. When Mr. Snidecker took his sudden departure it was decided that from that time out it should be understood, wherever they went, that Crissy was Mr. and Mrs. Burton's own daughter. George was the only one outside of themselves cognizant of the truth; he would say nothing; it was thought that this might prove a protection to Crissy in the future; she, poor child, began to think that she really *ought* to write to her mother acquainting her with the true condition of affairs. Then she would steal a glance at Mrs. Burton's pale, sad face, near the pensive countenance of the little Leoline, and change her mind. Another feeling, too, moved powerfully against telling her mother all; this was *pride*. It would be such a blow to the anticipations of all at home. Her time was not lost either; she was learning more every day; she couldn't reasonably expect to gain much more than knowledge the first year. There was more to learn in this than her mother had ever dreamed of; no, she would go on leading this vagabond existence for awhile longer. She would not turn back at this early stage; she would remain at it until she could demonstrate her own capacities, for she now felt serious doubts; she began to realize that possibly she had mistaken her calling; *this* was the bitterest disappointment of all; she would make sure, though, by waiting. In a large town in Northern Illinois they came unexpectedly upon some of Burton's professional friends; meeting in a locality so far from home, they all found topics for conversation. One of these friends—a gentleman named Hendricks—was organizing a stock company to remain in this place—a smart mining town—for the balance of the winter. Our little party had so sickened of their wanderings in such inclement weather that, when Hendricks proposed they should all remain with him as salaried members of his company, they received the proposition favorably. Crissy was in her heart the most pleased of all by this change; she was heartily weary of the nomadic life they were leading, it had curtailed her opportunities for study, beside the many hardships and exposures connected with it.

It soon transpired that Mr. Hendricks was a man who expected the full worth of his money; the people he employed certainly worked very hard for what they received; he had the name—a well-de-served one—of being a man of his word, whatever he agreed to pay or do was performed to the letter, he in turn exacted the same treatment from others. This reputation enabled him to secure good talent wherever he went. In those times, so precarious in the show business, a manager with such a reputation as his was an anomaly. In order to meet every expenditure he contracted he worked hard, looking for his employés to do the same; he was stage manager and proprietor, also playing heavy business, his doing the latter was a vanity as well as an economy. He was totally unfitted in voice or figure for the part he played, his form was after the pattern generally denominated "squat," his hair and beard of a fiery redness, his eyes small and features heavy. As Macbeth, Hamlet and kindred characters he seemed so utterly absurd that Crissy wondered how he could have the courage to attempt them. In his capacity as stage manager he was extremely severe, he made Crissy perfectly aware of her own ignorance; after two weeks under his direction she realized what a tyro she was; she discovered that her preconceived notions of acting as an art must have been mistaken; her fancy that people should act naturally was entirely wrong, that to laugh, cry, declaim, walk or faint upon the stage, must be done in a manner never attempted by people in real life; then, too, her voice was weak, her figure too petite, her understanding of stage business very limited. On the whole, Mr. Hendricks played a successful season through, the sagacity and honesty which years after raised him to an elevated position among his compeers stood him well through these troublous times, enabling him to make bread, butter, and something more where many other men would have failed.

Despite her disappointments and failures, these proved pleasant weeks to Crissy; her time was filled by occupations of such regularity, what with rehearsals in the forenoon, the mending of wardrobe and packing champagne baskets in the afternoon, the playing at night, and no matter how weary — the conning over her lines for next rehearsal just before she retired for the night — her time was completely filled. Then, too, it was agreeable to know that when the pangs of hunger recurred with that annoying regularity which is their characteristic, there would be something to assuage them; frequent suffering from hunger had been a concomitant of their traveling experiences.

Crissy's mind being after the true feminine pattern, "took notes" continually; she found the persons she met who seemed most successful in dramatic art — most thoroughly qualified for it — had been literally "born" into it; their parents — in some cases even grandparents — having been in the profession all their lives; of course she saw a few brilliant exceptions to this rule, but very few. Mr. Hendricks' wife, a young woman with a beautiful face and figure, was the daughter of an actress — now dead — who had been celebrated in her day.

Mrs. Hendricks was attracted by Crissy's youth and unsophisticated manners; she entered into conversation with the girl, giving her sketches of her own early history. From these Crissy learned that this lady began her professional career at the tender age of six months, being frequently carried upon the stage in cases where a real live baby was indispensable; from the time she could walk and talk she appeared in children's parts, the stage had really been her study from infancy. At the end of the winter engagement Crissy said good-bye to this attractive little lady; she never met her again, but heard of her many years afterward as a talented and successful writer of plays. Crissy thought that people like George and herself, joining the great caravan of dramatic art, seemed like the hangers-on following some big army,—the army trained and equipped for fighting, did all the work, whilst the rabble rushed in to share the spoils; more and more the conviction was forced upon her of her disqualification for this sort of employment. Then, too, the women who proved successful at this had to have what might be called, "a choice assortment of genius;" they had to do almost as much acting off the stage as on it,—they must flatter, wheedle and flirt. To Crissy's ingenuous disposition all this was horrible, particularly the latter; but even Mrs. Burton—who, in Crissy's estimation, stood nearly as high as the dear mother at home—often resorted to these expedients to smooth the hard path she trod. Her smiles, her gentle words, had taken the edge from many a landlord's righteous wrath, had gained the good will of many an impressible newspaper man. They didn't call them *reporters* those days. Flirtation, this lady explained to Crissy, was the harmless but glittering little sword with which she cut her way to favors and leniency; undoubtedly this was the case, but Crissy didn't like it, feeling that if this was a portion of the training for public life she'd sooner be out of it. The young girl was heartily sorry when the time came for the company to break up. They were all good people—most of them had been very kind to her, she had grown to look with pleasure to the meetings at rehearsal, the short conversations at the wings—in the companies of those times they had not the strict discipline which now enforces silence behind the scenes. It was almost equal to leaving home a second time when she bade these kind souls good-bye. They started once more under cheerful auspices. Burton had behaved very well; their joint earnings had paid the living expenses and left them a handsome surplus to make their way with; the faithful George accompanied them, saying that it had been the dream of his life to see the Mississippi; he said to Crissy, confidentially, that, "next to Chicago," he reckoned the "Father of Waters" was the finest sight in the United States! Hearing so much of this great stream, the girl was impatient to see it.

When they reached Burlington at sunrise one morning they had their first look at it. Crissy was disappointed. It wasn't half so fine as she expected. "Oh!" said George, "you can't tell by *this;* this is only a little patch of it!" They went down the river about thirty-five or forty miles to a flourishing town on the Iowa shore. Burton had heard that this town contained a nice little theatre and amusement-loving population. As they progressed down river Crissy confessed that she had been mistaken in her first impression, for at their final destination the river was grand and beautiful. Here, then, was to be their stopping place for a time. It was the month of May; the delicate verdure of the early season beautified the wooded shores on the river; the line of beach glistened with white pebbles and bits of sparkling shell; along some portions of the shore great trees were standing, as one might say, knee-deep in the water, for it was the time of Spring freshets. Life and activity blew in the fresh winds about them as mother earth sent forth her call to wake the sleeping flowers. Crissy shared Leoline's delight in the panorama of gorgeous colors unrolled before them; hand in hand they wandered along the river bank to gaze on everything with unsurfeited pleasure. No whisper of misfortune, crime and death was in the balmy breeze, no hint of wretchedness to come; the future locked up its secrets with jealous care, as the little party of friends went on to meet their destiny.

Burton began his operations immediately. He rented the theatre, which proved even better than he had been told. He got a few good professionals together; these, with Crissy, George and his own family, made an excellent stock company. Then he wrote to different parties to make arrangements for "stars" to come to him every week or so. This was the favorite method in the middle of this century for supplying the public with variety. It was pretty hard on those who "starred" it; in every place an entirely different support to the star, often the support was indifferent indeed.

The prospects for patronage seemed to justify Burton in these undertakings. The first few days in this town they put up at the best house, but Mrs. Burton's good sense soon convinced her husband that it would be better to be careful of their means and go to a private boarding house.

They opened to crowded audiences, though their first attraction had not yet joined them. George expressed his satisfaction over their success with his usual volubility. He reminded them of what he had said about the open-handed generosity of the Westerners. The stars came along with reasonable punctuality. During these weeks Crissy came into personal contact with some of the most famous dramatic talent of the day. Charlotte Cushman was a warm personal friend of Mrs. Burton's; she engaged to play with them some weeks later in the season, but by reason of illness was obliged to cancel her dates.

Crissy was most deeply interested, however, in a certain young woman of great beauty and promise. This lady owned a voice of rare sweetness and power; crowds flocked to listen to her singing. The way in which she rendered Irish melodies was something never to be forgotten. Her acting at that time was decidedly faulty. This was from youth and inexperience, as she could not have been much over twenty years of age. Her commanding presence—she was tall, with a faultless figure—her beautiful, expressive countenance, overbalanced these deficiencies. The two weeks she spent with Burton's company was a season of continuous ovation to her charms. She showed a decided partiality for Crissy's society; she said that Crissy made her think of a wild flower placed amidst half faded, fully overgrown exotics. She would stand behind the scenes with her beautiful white arms twined around Crissy's little figure, listening with pleasure to the girl's artless talk. Crissy in turn was attracted by this superabundance of beautiful animal life, the nightingale voice, the mesmeric kindness of the lovely woman. Ten years later she learned that this living embodiment of grace and genius died a raving maniac in one of the asylums of her native state.

The late summer was upon them, and business getting very slack. At that hot season of the year most people who could manage it spent a few weeks farther north; the lively town was comparatively empty now, but a greater trouble than the slackening business came to them. Burton who had for a little time been "tippling" went on one of his wildest sprees. He neglected things entirely, defying control of any sort. George essayed reason with him, even pleadings, but uselessly. The demon *drink*, whose victims, once millions, can now scarcely be counted—they are too numerous for that—held sole sway over an intellect, which, had it not been for this vile habit, would have made its possessor a "light in the land."

The lease of the little theatre had to be closed prematurely, with the lessees something in arrear; worse yet, they found a board bill increasing on them; they knew not which way to turn. George searched the town for work of some kind, no matter what; to earn their bread he would do anything within his power. Just as things had reached the darkest point Burton regained his senses again, to find his family reduced to a shocking predicament by his folly. For a few days succeeding Burton was very ill, as men generally are after excesses.

The first day that, pale and shaking, he crept from his bed and regained his feet once more, George rushed in excitedly; he had been absent a couple of days in his hunt for work. "It's all right," he shouted, "lots of work to be had outside of this in the harvest fields; men scarce; wages high; you and I," this to Burton, "will go to work at once and save the others from starvation." The kind-hearted fellow danced around for joy. The landlady, who was a widow, pushed a fat, puckered and sour face in the doorway, and hearing what was going on, reminded them of their indebtedness to her.

"Now, my good woman," said George, persuasively, "what we already owe we haven't a cent to pay, but we'll go to work at once and pay for these from this time," pointing to Mrs. Burton and the girls. "We will keep you paid for their board right along; just as soon as we get on our feet again we'll pay you what is due."

The woman looked at him with flashing eyes, then making a hasty stride to the middle of the room said, "No you don't, mister! you'll not cheat me out of my board bill that way; you think you can skip and leave me in the lurch, but there," (pointing toward the two chambers occupied by Burton's family) "are your trunks and baskets. You'll give me them things for security; I'll keep 'em too till the back board is paid."

"Impossible!" cried George, aghast, "why we wouldn't even have a change of linen! besides they would be comparatively worthless to you."

"Look here!" said Burton to the woman, "you would keep from us the tools with which we work in our profession; what could we do without any wardrobe? As for a lot of muslin trash, covered with gold lace and spangles, being of use to *you*, that's sheer nonsense!" "Yes," answered the woman with a cunning leer, "that's true enough, but it's of great use to *you; you'll* need it; you'll raise heaven and earth to get it, and manage to raise what's owing me." "You talk like a fool!" said Burton, impatiently. "If I know anything of law you couldn't take such security anyhow, as nothing belonging to me individually is there; the *man* is the party held responsible in these cases." This was true, for it happened in the recent confusion that Burton's wardrobe, and even manuscripts and plays, had been left in the property room of the theatre. "I don't care," said the woman doggedly, "you shall go yourselves; I'll not feed you a day or an hour longer, but your belongings don't leave this house if I know myself. *You* calling me a fool, too!" with a blazing glance at Burton and a shrill raising of her voice; "you, a drunken sot! bringing your fine lady wife and stuck-up girls to steal a poor widow's bread!" George trembled with rage when he heard this. Burton said, angrily, "Put on your bonnet, Lizzie, we'll go down the street to Lawyer Haley's office and consult him at once on this matter; you stay *there*," looking at Crissy, and waving his hand toward the door of the chambers occupied by them. "Come with us, George, and help unravel this tangle." Just then a childish voice piped out, "Let me go, too, papa!" Leoline had been noticing all that passed, and felt afraid of this cross, fat woman. "Come along, then," said Burton, hurriedly. Crissy, with her eyes full of tears, retired to the chamber, where she sat upon the broad old-fashioned windowsill and watched the rest walking down the street in anxious consultation. What would her mother think could she look in upon her now? This episode seemed to Crissy even worse than the horse-thief one; always this way just as things began to look bright to them — this awful drunkenness laid all waste. Her melancholy reflections were interrupted by the harsh voice of the landlady at her door. "Miss Burton," she said, "there's some one at the front door wanting to see you in a hurry." Crissy sprang to her feet and ran from the room unsuspectingly; she opened the front door, no one was there; she heard a clicking sound, a lock turning; she looked around—there was the landlady locking the chamber door; she placed the key in her pocket and said with a disagreeable smile, "Now I've fixed you!" "What do you mean?" asked Crissy, bewildered. "I mean," said the woman, "that I've got your trunks and all for keeps; possession is nine points of the law; I rather think I'll hold possession." "Oh!" cried Crissy, wringing her hands as the truth flashed on her, "what shall I do!" "Go," said the woman, "and tell that precious father of yours that I've got the better of him!" She had no more than spoken when

Crissy was on the street, bareheaded, running to the lawyer's office. She ran in and told her story; they all regarded her for a few minutes in silent consternation; then Burton, being in reality the one most to blame, upbraided the girl sharply; she wept. "Never mind, Crissy!" said George, "it's not right to blame you; none of us thought to tell you to be sure not to leave that room on any account." "That's true," said Mrs. Burton, "we should have explained it to her before leaving her alone there." The lawyer was listening attentively, but with a contracted brow." "See here!" he said to them, "there's no time to be lost. If none of your property," addressing Burton, "is there, we must take an affidavit from your daughter to that effect—I don't know that your wife's testimony could count. Come here," continued the lawyer, looking at Crissy. She crossed the room and stood in front of a kind of railing with a desk inside of it. "Put your hand—the left one —on the book." Crissy, not knowing in the least what it all meant, but following the lawyer's eyes, which rested on a small black book, placed her hand upon it as directed. "Now raise your right hand." Crissy did so. "That's all straight," continued the lawyer briskly. "Now we'll get out a search warrant at once and replevin the goods, if we are in time. You may be sure that woman is not idle; I know her well; she's a hard one. If whilst we are fooling here she gets the things out

of the house and hidden, we can't help ourselves."
What the lawyer apprehended came to pass. By
the time the search warrant was out and an officer
procured to serve it—law in some cases seems
specially adapted to frustrate justice—the landlady had removed every vestige of the property
belonging to the poor players. A thorough inves-
tigation of every corner of the house failed to
reveal even a shred of it. The family had repaired
with the officer to the landlady's house; they all
stood in the parlor anxiously awaiting the result of
the search. When informed of its uselessness,
despair was stamped on every face; the landlady
contemplated them with a sardonic smile.

Crissy was desperate. "It is all my fault!" she
cried; then running to the landlady she caught
that person's big, hard, right hand in both her
own and said: "Oh, let me work it out; take me
into your kitchen to wash dishes, scrub, do anything until the amount is paid; only let them have
their clothing."

The woman gave a derisive laugh. "*You*," she
answered, "a little fine lady in the kitchen, much
good you'd be. No, no, you'll never get them till
you pay, so be off!"

The little group turned into the street without
the faintest notion where they would go. "Let's
go to the theatre," said George,—"the offices are
open; if not, I'll get the keys; we can talk it over
there."

Having nowhere else to go they took his advice; they walked sadly enough to the broad flight of stairs leading to the vestibule which opened the way to the disciples of Thespia. On either side, at the head of these stairs, stood the offices, large, high ceilinged rooms with windows facing the main street. They sat down wondering where and how they could live.

"Tell you what," said Burton, "you and the girls must stay right *here*, Lizzie; we'll all go up into the property room and look around there for furniture; we can get benches and cushions to make beds for you and the children."

"That's grand!" said George gayly, "we can find lots of things for housekeeping; here's a stove, too, to cook the meals on;" he pointed to one of those long-shaped stoves adapted to the burning of extra large sticks of wood; near it was a wood box with a few sticks left in it, "lucky it's warm weather, we'll fix things up firstrate for you; we must leave here the first peep of day to-morrow morning to start work for our farmers."

They found many things in the property room for their wants; even some corn meal and a few potatoes. It happened in a play recently performed by them that an Irishman—by one of those remarkable vicissitudes of fortune common on the stage—became a Rajah somewhere in India, and when asked what he would have for dinner he demanded "praties," and the real article had to be produced to satisfy him. They managed quite a supper for all by making some corn meal mush and boiling the "praties." With the last small coin he owned, George purchased a loaf of bread and some salt. The poor things had quite a pleasant meal set out in the dishes with which Claude Melnotte's mother had her simple supper table laid when she was expecting that hero home. Leoline enjoyed the novelty when her mother tucked her into the improvised bed formed of theatre benches and crimson cushions; she said it was ever so much nicer than living with that cross woman.

The next morning, as day was breaking, Crissy woke from slumbers which had been sound despite her strange surroundings; she remembered at once that the men would be starting for their new occupation. She dressed rapidly and noiselessly, not to disturb the sleep of the weary woman and child. Stealing softly from the room she endeavored, from the scraps of the evening's supper, to prepare a meal. The corn meal mush slightly warmed over, with a few cold potatoes, made an indifferent repast, but George, gay as a lark, assisted Crissy with the breakfast, giving at the same time a description of how he and Burton had slept in the auditorium of the theatre, and how, upon the stage lighted by the moon shining through an open doorway in the rear, they saw the rats come out to give a very private and select performance.

"I assure you," he said, "that they made quite a large company; if I had not been so sleepy I should have enjoyed watching them immensely."

The men soon departed, but not before Burton had tip-toed into the room where his wife and child lay sleeping, there, finding his wife awake, he kissed her tenderly and bade her be of good cheer, telling her that as soon as they could earn and get some money paid them, he would bring it with all speed to her. Then with moistened eyelids he strode rapidly away. This man, when sober, was the gentlest, kindest soul who ever breathed; this sweetness of nature, which showed so strongly in his periods of sobriety, was the invisible chain which held the patient woman true to him through shame and starvation in the terrible years of their wedded life.

George gave Crissy a friendly good-bye shake of the hand, looking meantime into her eyes a very long and earnest look which the young girl scarcely heeded, certainly did not understand.

Shortly after the departure of Burton and George, Mrs. Burton joined Crissy in the room where they had breakfasted; the child was still sleeping. Upon the table, where many a ticket seller and treasurer had beguiled the tedium of the evening performances by games of cards, lay the remnants of the breakfast, consisting of a handful of raw corn meal and the "heel" of the loaf of bread; the bread would be about two slices. The woman and girl looked each other squarely in the eyes; from the two pairs of eyes looked the same thought; that thought was the *child!* "Give her a part of the bread for her breakfast," said Crissy, "the rest will do for dinner time, when she hungers again." Crissy looked at Mrs. Burton for a suggestion. Mrs. Burton sat down with her hands folded in her lap, thinking deeply; Crissy regarded her with silent attention. People in sorrow and perplexity do very little talking; anticipation and happiness are always loquacious.

After what appeared to Crissy a very long time Mrs. Burton said, in a voice which had a tremor in it, "There is nothing I can do just now; the burden must fall on *you;* I am so ill and weak this morning that it is hard to walk even a few steps, yet something *must* be done, or we will starve before help comes; to *beg* is terrible! but it cannot be a shame to beg for *work;* you are so young and helpless looking that they will be more inclined to assist you then they would me; if we could get some sewing to do, we could, between the two of us, at least earn our bread until the men get back."

"I will do it," said Crissy, sturdily; "just tell me how to go about it; let me start at once!"

Mrs. Burton smiled sadly at her eagerness. "It will be best," she said, "to leave the business portion of the town, and, walking along the residence streets, go from door to door, asking them to give you work to do, stating to them plainly and truthfully the circumstances; telling them, if need be, that we cannot earn our bread by our profession just now, as our wardrobes have been taken from us. Tell them that we can do almost any kind of hand sewing, that we will be very thankful to get work."

At the period we write of, the sewing machine was a comparatively new invention, very few of them being in general use in the Far West.

Crissy was all anxiety to start at once; but what should she put on her head? The broad brimmed hat she was in the habit of wearing was locked up with all the rest by that hateful woman. She had to don the matronly little bonnet worn by Mrs. Burton. This was of course more respectable than going bareheaded, but was useless in warding off the rays of a burning sun from her face. It could not be helped; so Crissy, with a brave assumption of cheerfulness, trudged off.

Crissy having had no experience in this sort of rôle, started out with a stock of hope in her active little brain. She walked quickly up the main streets to those outlying ones where well-built houses, surrounded by trees and gardens, stood invitingly. She trembled and blushed at the first door where she made her humble application. A stylishly dressed young female opened it. She regarded Crissy with inquiring eyes, the expression of which changed to strong disfavor when she

knew the nature of her business. She said with
great decision that they did not require to give *out*
any sewing, as they had *reliable* and *respectable* persons employed upon it in the house. Crissy
turned away, more dismayed by the tone and look
than the blunt refusal. She called at fully thirty
houses or more during the blazing forenoon with
the same discouraging result. Then, being quite
worn out by the heat, lack of food and drink, she
sat under the shade of a tree to cogitate. Crissy,
drawing upon the memories contained in her life
of fourteen years, found staring her in the face
one indisputable fact,—this fact being that *rum* was
the cause of all the misery she had known in her
own experience, as well as that of those around
her.

She was too young as yet to reason out that as
every sickness in nature has its palliative and cura-
tive medicine, so must this awful vice have somewhere in the wide universe something to counter-
act it. If you had asked her, at that immature
age, what *she* would do about it, had she the
power, she would have answered instantly, "Abol-
ish every form of intoxicating fluid; put it where
men can't get it; *that* is the only cure." Then
when you told her, gravely, that it was an impossibility, because it would destroy the "revenues of
her country," how astonished she would have been.
How much more astonished when you supplemented this statement on "revenue" with the old famil-

iar twaddle about the redeeming power of "home influence." Think of Crissy swallowing such pap as that after her own experiences.

This idea of "home influence," as a saviour from the liquor habit, has been refuted over and over again. How many thousands of true-hearted men and women have clung to this faint hope, this very straw, only to see those they loved best pass to their dishonored graves victims to the last of this frightful practice. One of the most earnest men of our age, who has examined this subject thoroughly, tells us that "nine-tenths of our poverty, squalor, vice, and crime, spring from this poisonous tap-root." Think of it,—nine-tenths; and yet, what efforts have we made, or are we making, against this devastating sin? The rum-shops stand in close array about us, tempting our poor fallen creatures at every hand; we try by heavy licenses to control the increasing sale of intoxicants. It has been demonstrated how little that course avails.

The struggle waged against intemperance in our times has many pathetic features. When women, rendered desperate by their increasing agonies, rushed upon this hydra-headed monster, endeavoring by force to kill it, an unthinking multitude stood by and laughed, as despairingly these women tore open the hoards of the rum-sellers and threw the fiery liquids in the dust. Such futile attempts may have possessed a certain grotesqueness, but they are dignified as the expression of a righteous, albeit impotent, wrath.

Alcohol is the torch which lights treason and anarchy to their deadly work. With that removed, you would need no armed detectives; no troops. Reason, unclouded by the fumes of liquor, would listen to reason. If the labor question is to be the great question of the day, as many say it is, it will be met far better when sobriety is the rule not the exception. Talk of agitators! there is no agitator whose influence can equal that of whisky.

Crissy found that chewing the bitter cud of reflection was not likely to help her toward getting food; she rose wearily, very dejectedly now, to essay the task again. At the different houses she had plaintively stated her case thus: She wanted work; she needed work because those she loved were suffering for food. She had not told the story of how they happened to be in this predicament, for this would involve the mention of their profession. Crissy felt some lately-born instinct within her which kept her from telling *all* unless positively necessary. The day was advancing; by this time Leoline would have eaten the last mouthful of that precious piece of bread,—where would the next come from? Strengthened by this anxious thought, Crissy went on.

At the first door a middle-aged matron appeared; a number of giggling young women, eager to hear what was going on, pressed behind her. Crissy began to make her application for work and state her case; the middle-aged lady listened with interest. Crissy, feeling encouraged thereby, stated the whole case. She was painfully conscious that the faces in the rear began to look scandalized; the middle-aged hardened visibly, and said it was a very *peculiar* story; she *might* call at the theatre next day, look into it and see what she could do. As the door was closing Crissy could hear one of the young women say scornfully, "That play-acting girl!" Crissy tried not to cry, but the tears rolled down her hot cheeks. She thought, what am I now? a mere vagrant! a vagabond on the face of the earth! Ah, what would her *mother* think of this, could she see her now? Nothing could have induced her to go on after this rebuff save the thought of the feeble woman and little child; she felt that to lie down in a remote corner of some unnoticed place and starve to death would be easier than to beg work from these hard-hearted ones. She had sometimes before this suffered hunger in her own home, but she had not been exposed to sneers or insults. Go on she must; her story in most cases met an incredulity masked by a veil of cold politeness; in other cases with open insult, particularly when she spoke to men more particularly when these were old men.

If Crissy had realized the import of the glances these old men cast upon her she would have thrown herself into the river sooner than run the gauntlet of such dreadful insults! Her innocence was the thick wall which stood between her and this knowledge. The stage was unjustly regarded as a degrading institution. At that time there was scarcely a pulpit in the land which did not thunder forth denunciations against it; respectability pulled its cloak very closely around it when anything connected with the drop curtain and footlights passed near. We think a more liberal, certainly a more Christian spirit, prevails now.

The blazing sun, which had nearly blistered poor Crissy's face, was traveling quickly to its rest. She had accomplished almost nothing. At her last stopping place a sallow-faced young matron, with an infant in her arms, had listened rather kindly to her. After a long spell of thinking, this matron had placed her baby in its crib and brought to Crissy a piece of white work she would like done; also a tiny package containing perhaps a quarter pound of tea. By the way, this work was a night gown, woman's size, to be embroidered around the collar, sleeves, and down the front after being made. Some days later the matron paid Mrs. Burton the munificent sum of fifty cents for this piece of work—and the tea aforesaid.

Crissy accepted this help very gratefully, though she felt some doubts as to the tea satisfying those places which needed filling, she was too afraid of degenerating into utter beggary by saying how much sooner she would have bread than tea. Then she trudged forth once more; as she looked about her, she thought very sadly that the town and river never seemed so pretty before, the town with its white streets. Upon these nicely graded streets a very white stone finely crushed was spread, making a beautiful contrast to the green of trees and lawns, which sloped gently down to the levee, and beyond this lay the broad river, blue and silent, holding in its translucent depths the mirrored shores.

Crissy trembled with fatigue and faintness as she gazed. "Ah!" she groaned wearily, "how *can* things be so lovely in this world of sin and trouble!" She made her way to the main streets; her thought was always no food, no food. How could she go to those waiting ones without it? As she was passing a large church its broad stone steps invited her wearied frame to take a few moments rest. She sat down despondently; she was too tired to even think. How, after a melancholy interval, the idea came to her, she never quite knew, perhaps it was from a longing for her mother. She remembered in a hazy, dim way, that no one had called at the postoffice lately. She had failed to procure food, perhaps she could get letters.

She dragged her tired limbs to the postoffice. A supercilious young man at the little window looked at her impudently, and hardly troubling himself to search, said carelessly that there was nothing. Crissy turned away silently; there was such a plaintive limpness in her young figure, such wretchedness in her burned, tear-stained face, that the young man, after another look at her, seemed to receive a nervous shock, which caused him to search again, with the result that he ran out, just as she stepped from the door, with a letter in his hand. Crissy looked and saw joyfully that it was her mother's handwriting; she had not heard from her mother for a number of weeks. She sat down on a step in the street; then, heedless of inquisitive glances, opened it. Something dark was carefully folded into the letter. Crissy drew it out;—bank bills! Here then was food for the starving ones! Crissy was astonished beyond measure. Why should her mother think of sending her money? She would read later on and see; but now—to the nearest baker's. With help in her very hands Crissy's despair was gone, and her healthy young appetite revived.

It did not take her long to obtain enough to make a hearty supper for three. Just as the sun was sinking she turned her steps, quickened now by the joy she was bringing, up the stairs of the theatre. A childish voice was calling "Crissy" the minute she had mounted the first three stairs. "Dear, dear Crissy!" cried the child, excitedly, "have you come at last? The day was so dull without you; poor mamma was so sick, and I am so *awfully hungry*, only I didn't tell mamma *that!*"

Crissy laughed, showing her the bundles. They entered the room together. Mrs. Burton sat in one of the big office chairs quite colorless from her long fasting. It was no wonder; she had not tasted food for twenty-four hours. Crissy was too wise to do any talking till, with Leoline's assistance, the supper was spread and a strong cup of tea made from that precious little packet. Then she and Leoline went to the nearest milkman for a few pennies' worth of milk, and the feast was ready. How gladly the child, how thankfully the woman and girl, partook of this simple repast we need not tell; very little was said, but sometimes Mrs. Burton would look across the small table at Crissy with glistening and grateful eyes.

When the meal was finished Leoline neatly cleared away the remnants and washed the dishes, declaring that Crissy was too "awfully tired" to do anything but rest. Then Crissy read her letter, where the meaning of the bank bills was fully explained. By the time she received that letter her father, mother, and the rest of the family would be living in Chicago. The father had been offered a lucrative position in the growing metropolis. His wife urged him to accept it, as it would take them nearer to that West where Crissy was. The mother, after four pages of home details so interesting to a young girl, added a postscript, in which she said that in a few months more it would be a year since Crissy left home; that they all yearned to see her; that the enclosed bank bills were to pay Crissy's expenses home as soon as Mrs. Burton thought it would be a convenient time to let her come and visit for a few weeks. Furthermore, that the father was behaving admirably just now, and they all felt very happy. Crissy held the letter in her hand with a conflict of feelings. So strange that her mother should think of sending her money for this purpose. Could her mother have any suspicion of the trials surrounding her? She had been so careful never to hint a word concerning them.

Oh! Crissy! Crissy! you did not know a mother's love, her intuitions. Your studied descriptions of your journeyings, your experiences, couldn't deceive that tender, watchful intelligence. She knew that something must be wrong, and tried with a woman's delicate care to get at the root of it without seeming to question. Crissy didn't puzzle over it very long,—it was delightful anyhow that her own dear mother had been that ministering angel who lifted her from the depths.

It may seem strange that when Crissy first received this unhoped assistance she did not fall on her knees immediately in thankfulness to God. It must be remembered that she was very hungry. It is likely that when the children of Israel found the manna they fell to eating first and praising afterwards.

When Leoline was sound asleep the woman and girl sat together as Crissy, in low tones, recounted the incidents of the day. To Crissy, looking back upon it, it appeared the longest day she could ever remember, so much of varied feeling was crowded into it. Mrs. Burton listened with compressed lips and flashing eyes as the girl frankly told her the many insulting remarks addressed to her because of her profession.

"It is so!" said the older woman, sadly; "every ruffian feels himself licensed to insult an actress, no matter how good she may be; how careful in her actions, she is made the target of low innuendo. From the minister of God down to the layman she is held up as an object of derision;— it is a shameful fact." She sighed as she spoke. The next morning, at five o'clock, when the child lay wrapped in slumber, the two women sat sewing on the long white seams of the nightgown. Mrs. Burton said, with justice, that Crissy's mother, having sent that money for a certain purpose, it was their duty to try and hold it for that purpose, replacing as soon as they could the amount taken from it; for though it could undoubtedly be considered in the light of a divine providence, they, on their parts, must not take too full advantage of that providence. Crissy coincided with this. She was far too active in mind and body to want to lean too heavily on providence or anything else.

When the child, awakening, saw the women busily employed, nothing would do but she must get the breakfast; so, with a large piece of bagging in lieu of an apron tied around her, she went about it with much clatter and laughing. Crissy, however, built the fire, saying that was too much for Leoline's strength. As the long summer day was wearing to late afternoon, and the slanting rays of the hot sun glanced scorchingly through the big uncurtained windows of the offices, the women rested a little from the weary sewing.

At this period came a verification of the saying that God helps those who help themselves. Over from a dry-goods store, directly across the street from them, stepped a kindly-faced young man with a large bundle in his arms. He tapped gently at the office door. Crissy admitted him. He hoped he was not guilty of an intrusion, but he understood that they wished to secure some sewing. He had some netting there he would like them to make up. In the Mississippi river towns they frequently canopied their beds with fine netting, as the mosquito of that famous stream is renowned for the fierceness of its sting. He gravely unfolded the work, explaining how the pieces, already carefully cut, should be joined; then he named the sum he was willing to pay for it, which sum appeared to the ladies startling in its liberality. Crissy listened with the ready belief of youth; the older woman comprehended at once that the work was really a delicately veiled gift. When the youth departed little Leoline ran to the window to watch him as he crossed the street, meantime pronouncing him "a darling."

In a few minutes came another tap at the door. There stood a little, faded, sunken-eyed woman, who looked so brown and shriveled that she was exactly like an overdry bean pod; she proceeded to shake each of them warmly by the hand and to tell them, in a feeble voice, with a strong nasal twang to it, that she was proprietress of a shirt manufactory a couple of doors from them; that she understood they wanted work; that she ran a sewing machine. She said this with a tinge of pride, a sewing machine was quite a possession then, when they were high-priced and scarce,— that she could give them plenty of fine button-holes to make and gussets to set.

It need scarcely be told that they accepted her offer very gratefully. As soon as she left the woman and girl looked at each other with a world of meaning in the look. They realized that Crissy's day of hopeless applications, her wretched trudgings from door to door, had brought forth fruit at last; that the longed-for work should come from the business part of the town, from people at their very doors, seemed to them surprising.

They should not have been surprised. We never find our blessings, any more than our sorrows, in the spots where we look for them. Short-sighted humanity is always searching in the wrong places for what it wants. Thus ended the second day of their housekeeping in the office rooms of the theatre.

On the third morning Mrs. Burton laid out an organized — as she called it — plan of work. This was, two hours' sewing before breakfast; then Crissy and Leoline went out and purchased the day's provisions; then breakfast, then work again until one o'clock; then the light repast which served for dinner; then work until sundown. As they sewed the child busied herself with the cares of their very light housekeeping; she often amused herself investigating every portion of the auditorium, the property-rooms, and those loft-like places where the scene painters used to do their work. Many a fantastic drama did the child dream and play out by herself upon the forsaken stage; many an airy dance she executed to the music of her own humming voice.

The woman and girl often sat at the back of the stage as the child played; they sat with their sewing at a door, which, opening at the rear of the stage and third story of the building, was closed across its lower part by wooden bars to prevent any one from falling out, for this door had no stairway on the outside. From it they looked down upon the broad river to where the other shore, a mass of verdure, gazed at itself in the rippling water; they frequently sat here with their work to enjoy the refreshing coolness of what breeze happened to be stirring, for the weather was intensely warm. Many a time at sunset the girl would lean against the bars of this door, and looking pensively across the water, almost fancy she could see her mother — a graceful figure, with soft, dark eyes and blackly-falling hair — step gently over the watery chasm to come to her. The child played out her day dreams on the empty stage; the girl brought her's out in the sunset light and kept her courage up by the pleasing fancies her affections evoked.

The days wore on to nearly a week of their strange housekeeping, yet not a word or sign from the men who had gone to the harvest fields to earn them sustenance. Mrs. Burton remarked that if they had been content on their parts to remain supinely waiting for that assistance, they would have had a long wait of it!

In the meantime they received ample help in the way of employment. For a wonder, no one appeared to remonstrate with them on the forcible possession they had taken of their odd lodgings; they had suffered some natural forebodings on this score. Perhaps the owners of the property, hearing of their forlorn condition, had concluded not to interfere with them.

"Well," said Mrs. Burton, as they sat diligently sewing on the morning of the sixth day, "I hope we will soon hear something of Mr. Burton and George. Now that we have, for the present at least, solved the enigma of how to earn our bread, I begin to feel some anxiety on their account."

"You needn't, mamma," said Leoline, confidently; "they are all right; it's easy for a man to come out all right." Mrs. Burton smiled at the child's implicit faith in manhood.

The afternoon of that day brought them a great surprise. A dray stopped in front of the theatre; a stout drayman alighting from it, began carrying heavy packages up the stairs. Mrs. Burton stepped into the corridor in surprise to see what it meant; the man, tipping his cap to her, produced a card, upon which her own name was written in a large, clear hand, underneath, in smaller writing, a few lines to the effect that, hearing of the sad necessities of herself and family, some parties unknown took the liberty of sending these necessary provisions to them.

The man carried all into the apartment which served as kitchen and dining room, then silently departed. The women felt quite overcome by this unexpected kindness. Leoline examined the packages with joy, especially when she came to a very large one of white sugar. "We are in no danger of starving *now*," exclaimed Mrs. Burton; "probably when our gentlemen return we can surprise them with our abundance."

They never found out who the kind donors were. It is possible that those donors had a pretty comfortable feeling about the region of their hearts that evening. On that night, after the sun had been in bed for a long time, the woman, girl and child sat talking together by the white moonlight streaming in through the large windows. The night was almost too warm for sleep, even to them, tired as they felt. Suddenly they heard heavy footsteps on the stairs.

"My darling papa," cried the child,— and she was out of the door in an instant. She had recognized her father's steps.

In they came, the child joyously holding a hand of each; the men looking very brown indeed from the sun's hot kisses, but they looked well despite their laborious and unaccustomed work. They did what people generally do when excited and happy. They all tried to talk at once. At last Burton smilingly declared that one at a time must take the stand,— he himself would have first say. Then he recounted how they tried to get the farmer to pay for the first day's work, and let them take the money to their folks, solemnly promising to return the next morning. How the farmer wouldn't "hear to it," saying that he had a "pesky" hard time to get any hands into his fields; that it was one thing to *say* they'd come back, another thing to *do* it.

"Yes," broke in George, "he was bound to make *sure* of us, for he locked us into our bed room every night, saying he'd be "goll durned" if he'd trust us out of his sight!"

"To make a long story short," continued Burton, "he wouldn't pay us a cent till we'd worked six days for him. 'Tis an actual fact that he locked us in every night. I'm quite sure that he never expects to see us again. If we hadn't taken to our heels and run for it the length of several fields right after supper to-night, we wouldn't be here now."

They all laughed over this account, which is not exaggerated, for help was very scarce indeed; the work of the farm being done to such a great extent by hand in those days. It is difficult now to realize such a state of affairs.

The men proudly handed over their earnings to Mrs. Burton. George, kind simple soul, feeling as much pleased to have earned it for them, as if they had been his very own. When she represented to him that they had no right to it, he wouldn't listen to her. He said it was the result of his toil for the woman and child,—and that she must say no more.

"There's one thing," said George, "though we might be called prisoners, and worked from sun-up till sun-down, we feasted like lords in that farmhouse. Talk of a land flowing with milk and honey! Tell you what," he continued unctuously, " I wish I could put some of those big chunks of honey in my pocket for you, Leo! Here's all I could bring!" At this he emptied from his pockets a lot of harvest apples. The child received them with delight.

The women gave their story now, dwelling on the many kindnesses they had received, dropping from the narrative the whole extent of their sufferings that first day. George suspected there was something held back. He looked at Crissy with a suspicious tenderness in his eyes.

Burton and his young friend soon r tired to their old sleeping apartment in the auditorium. They would have the next day—Sunday—to talk things over, returning to their farmer toward evening, to be on hand for next morning's sunrise work.

At breakfast the following morning, where plenty reigned, though elegance was decidedly lacking, Burton told his wife that he was on the track of a way out of their difficulties. He had made an acquaintance in the country who would likely serve them a good turn. He wouldn't say much about it yet, but she should see. For the present they must all keep on working to try to get enough together to redeem their wardrobes. Mrs. Burton knew well her husband's extraordinary facility for getting out of the apparently hopeless positions his excesses plunged him in. The Yankee faculty, called "gumption," he employed for this purpose was remarkable in its results. If he had been a strictly temperate man, he would have been astonishingly successful in all he undertook. The Sunday passed too quickly.

When the men prepared to leave, Leoline wept and clung to her father. This child loved her father passionately. She knew he was the cause of their many sufferings, yet she felt for him a peculiar tenderness. Much as she adored her mother, she loved her besotted father still more.

Another week passed uneventfully. Their greatest trial was the lack of wearing apparel. They had to put Leoline to bed till her clothing could be washed and dried. The poor child, covered by a light quilt—sold to them by the kindly-faced young dry goods man, at a price which was a mere pretence of selling—would sit in her bed of theatre benches, conning over old play books to amuse herself. None of them minded these trials very much; there was hope ahead.

When the men returned the ensuing Saturday night, George brought Leoline a bunch of flowers as big as his head. The central blossom of this great bouquet was a sunflower. It appeared that the farmer felt such delight at their totally unexpected return to him, that he inquired more closely into particulars about their "folks." Ascertaining that a child was one of the group, he sent her "this han'ful of hum grown posies." Burton also carried, as an offering to the loves and graces, a dish of that delicious honey.

On Sunday morning Burton produced his "plans," fully matured, for the admiring inspection of the rest. He had formed the acquaintance of the captain of a steamboat, a stern wheeler; "never saw her yet"—observed Burton parenthetically,—"but understand she's a great big thing, slow and sure; that will be all the better, we won't want anything fast for our purpose."

His wife looked amazed. "What under the sun," she exclaimed, "would we have to do with a steamer?"

Then Burton went on explaining how they intended to turn her — meaning, of course, the steamer—into a floating theatre; go up the Mississippi, stopping at all the small towns on the way. The novelty of the thing would draw crowds. There would be no hall rent to pay. No knocking about. Would be living on the boat all the time. Could get together a fair sized company in a few days. Play Uncle Tom's Cabin in those northern towns; it was sure to be received enthusiastically. All that was needed was the wardrobe. Captain Glockner could put his hands upon an engineer and pilot who would be delighted to have the chance of going out with a theatrical company. As for salaries, all who went would arrange that that should be according to business. If successful, as it surely would be, the captain, on account of furnishing the boat, the crew, and manning her, should have half the profits over and above the expenses. So far as Burton could see, it was a fine idea; anyhow it would run them out of this rat-hole of a place. As for people to act, no trouble about *that*, the town was full of stage-struck young men, and women, too! Captain Glockner knew one young woman who was bound to run away from home and go on the stage. She'd go anyhow, so she might as well go with them. One more woman would fill the cast for Uncle Tom's Cabin.

They listened to this rapid summary of the "plan" with deep interest. Crissy felt something of a shock over the young woman who was *bound* to run away from home. Crissy, feeling herself unable to do anything against her mother's wish, could not quite understand how any other girl would defy the parental authority. To be sure, Crissy's father, when sober, had interposed objections to her stage career; but when a man fails in the fatherly duty of providing food and raiment for his young—when he fails by his own fault—his authority, to a great extent, must become null. Crissy, drawing upon the deeps of her ample imagination, did what the female mind does with such facility—personified the idea. The girl stood before her at once; enthusiastic, yet modest; eager, yet diffident—then Crissy's heart yearned toward this creature of her young fancy.

Burton was still talking over details as Crissy thought all this. The child was charmed by the thought of living on a boat. "Shall we always have our breakfast and everything on it, papa?" she asked.

"Yes, darling," her father answered, "so long as we are able to earn the breakfast. In a few days more we will have saved money enough to get our baggage back, then Ho! for the river and a free life."

Mrs. Burton did not secretly like the plan any too well; she had a notion, not ill founded, that river men generally were a rough lot. She knew that there would be breakers ahead, but she did not like to openly object, as she on her part had nothing more feasible to propose. She also knew that her health was quite inadequate to bear the protracted strain of the kind of life they were living. She set her fine executive abilities to work, therefore, in aiding and shaping her husband's plans—she, like Crissy, was anxious over the girl "bound to run away." When alone with her husband, she questioned him. "See here, Lizzie," he said, "as far as I can hear the girl's character is all right; she is very handsome, perhaps talented. We are not in a position to be over squeamish anyhow. You *know* we can't stage "Uncle Tom" without another woman. It isn't every girl has snap enough to run away from home; we'd better take what we can get."

Mrs. Burton assented rather reluctantly. Burton then, considerably to his wife's astonishment, revealed the fact that the carpenters were at work already upon this boat, building a stage, turning the largest portion of her into an audience room with quite a seating capacity, arranging dressing rooms back of the stage, etc.

"All rough, of course," said Burton, "but good

enough for the class of amusement seekers we're likely to entertain." He said the boat was in a sheltered position a few miles down the river, where she would be free from observation; for business reasons "they didn't want to give the thing away." If Burton suspected the captain had any other motives for keeping the boat in this sequestered spot, he did not mention them to his wife.

Some time during that Sunday, George noticed Leoline running about the room hugging her big bouquet with the ardor little girls display toward anything they love. "Ah! Leo," he said, "some day when you're a famous actress they will pelt you with roses. Then you'll have more flowers than you'll know what to do with."

A sudden sedateness fell upon the child; she stood still before him, with a world of meaning in her lovely face. "George," she said, gravely, "often there," pointing to the baize-covered doors which led to the auditorium, "I play upon the stage—queer little plays, you know, that are made out of my own head—I dance pretty dances that I make up as I go along. I clap my hands at the good points, having to be audience as well as performer. I *love* it, George, and yet—" she paused for a long spell and looked dreamily beyond him, "and yet, I seem to *know* that I'll never be a famous actress—never an actress at all perhaps."

George looked at her in perplexity. "Why Leo,"

he said gently, "you're an actress already. You have acted, and you're going to act, you're going to be the sweetest little Eva on the stage."

The child nestled her head with its crown of golden ringlets against his shoulder; she looked very pensive. George was aware of an indescribably troubled sensation.

The men concluded to let their farmer have a couple more days. George said the old fellow had been pretty good to them despite the locking up. It was a shame to leave him with the unbound sheaves upon his fields, anyhow, by the end of that week, they would be rehearsing aboard the boat and steaming off to regions as yet unexplored by them.

All now was anticipation and hope; the women still sewed, however. The child trotted over every part of the theatre, bidding affectionate good bye to those dark corners where she had played so often. She presented to an imaginary audience a farewell play and dance, interspersed with choice vocal selections rendered by herself. On Thursday evening the men returned. George laughingly told Crissy, that the trouble with their new venture was, that more young fellows wanted to join than they could take; that lots of the boys importuned him with representations of how they could musicate, dance and sing; that the plan with the young woman *bound* to run away was settled. That the next evening, about ten o'clock, he and another young fellow would stand under a window of her residence, from which she would throw to their keeping a large bundle of clothes. They found this the only way to manage it, as the girl said she couldn't go without her clothing. She would leave the house unobserved the day succeeding and join them. The wardrobe, rescued from the clutches of that woman, should be sent to the boat at once. On Saturday afternoon a wagon would be provided to pick up the different parties going; they would drive out of town a few miles to where the boat was fastened, then up steam and away.

The morning of that Saturday Burton secured a buggy to drive his wife over to the boat, as the wagon would be a rough conveyance for her; Crissy and Leoline would follow in the afternoon with the rest. George was aboard already, superintending everything in his usual helpful manner. There is one period of a woman's life which appears to stand distinctly in the foreground of her mental vision — that day, or time, when the light-hearted exuberance of her girlhood took flight forever, leaving her the woman's intellect unadorned by that unquestioning happiness which had been its companion. With some minds this change is gradual, with others it seems to be a sudden unaccountable leap from heedless gayety to realms of seriousness.

This day had come to Crissy; she never forgot the drive of that afternoon, through roads which bordered scented clover fields, or skirted stretches of woodland; where the bobolinks and thrushes warbled to them, or wound through fragrant meadows where wild flowers bloomed in bright profusion. What a day it was! how full of light, of color, of unthinking joy! Leoline and Crissy, after their long incarceration in the dusty town, felt it a transformation scene. The fresh breeze from the river, the insect life in its hum of summer work, the murmur of grass and trees under the balmy wind, all these made an unforgotten day. Crissy almost wished this drive might never end, with its unexpected delights, its jocund surprises! The young men, seeing the pleasure of the girl and child, sprang from the wagon to gather blossoms for them; tendering these tributes with a rustic manner through which shone their kind-heartedness like a diamond in some dusky corner.

The maiden who ran away joined them a couple of miles out. She was a tall, finely-formed girl, with a profusion of dark hair, and bold, dark eyes. She showed none of the shrinking modesty Crissy had expected; she settled herself in the most comfortable place she could find in the wagon, and looked composedly about her. She had little or nothing to say; whether this was from natural reticence, or the fact that not having much to say, she didn't care to say it, couldn't be determined. Leoline looked at her much as she might have looked at some animal she was afraid of, and nestled more closely to Crissy's side.

At sundown the drive was ended. In a bay-like place upon the river, which they had been following for some time, they came suddenly upon the boat. A big thing, sure enough; there she was, a queer looking monster, with two large smoke stacks, and an immense stern wheel, which filled Leoline with surprise; her lower guards unprotected by railings — which was the case with most of the river boats used, as she had been, for transporting merchandise — gave her a rough, unfinished look. It had to be confessed that she was not "a thing of beauty." There was Mrs. Burton waving her hand to them from the upper guards, and calling to them to hurry aboard, for supper was all ready. There was George with a pencil behind his ear, a carpenter's apron on, a hammer in his hand, smiling down on them. They unpacked themselves from the wagon — by the way, quite a number of the young men took turns walking, the load being over large — then over the gang plank they ran, eager to inspect their new lodgings; no time for this right away, for they were hurried up a queer, narrow stairway to a cozy cabin which had a carpeted floor and a long table in its centre, on which the supper stood invitingly. That they did justice to that supper goes without telling. As the repast progressed they began to get acquainted with each other. Crissy was surprised to find they had five musical young men who could play on most anything, could sing songs both comic and sentimental. These young men confessed to being amateurs, but what of that—they could learn! None of them had the slightest idea how to act; had never had the chance before; but never mind that, they'd soon learn! Crissy heard that all of the company had not collected yet, the rest would arrive during the evening. The captain, a dark, morose man, sat at one end of the table, Burton occupied the other. The captain spent his time, as the others conversed, in looking gloomily into his tea cup with a preoccupied expression. The supper concluded, Mrs. Burton drew Crissy and the child into the little state room fitted up as their sleeping apartment, showing them the conveniences she had contrived for them; then into the dressing room arranged for the ladies; in this stood the trunks containing the lately recovered wardrobes. As this was going on, the young lady recently added to their circle sat on a cushioned seat in the cabin — which did triple duty as dining room, green room and parlor—smiling affably, though silently, on those around, and looking very handsome. Burton, seated at one end of the table, had a lot of the young men about him, looking at play books and talking volubly. Crissy returning to the cabin sat in a corner looking on with interest; her position commanding a view of the double doors which opened at one end of the cabin directly back of the stage. This arrangement was a necessary convenience; for the characters in the plays, using this cabin as a green room, could slip quickly into their positions at the side entrances of the stage through these doors. Crissy's gaze following a sudden, banging sound, she saw these doors thrown open to admit the person of a young man. This young man held an open play book in his right hand raised to the level of his eyes. He came through the door with a dramatic stride; he was not a handsome young man — not at all — his face was of the "platter" pattern, he wore a brown mustache and a long tailed green coat unbuttoned its length of front. The young man entered after this fashion to produce an impression; he certainly produced one on Crissy, for she could not restrain her laughter. Burton, hearing her merriment, looked up to ascertain its cause; an involuntary smile crossed his countenance as his eyes encountered the strange figure. He rose to welcome him, introducing him all 'round as his young friend, Mr. Durand, who had kindly consented to undertake the "juveniles."

Crissy, with the smiles still playing hide and seek with her dimples, rose dutifully to shake hands with the new comer, who looked down upon her with a haughtily benignant smile as if to say, "go to, thou naughty child." Mr. Durand joined the group at the table with an interested yet "touch-me-not" air, which was highly edifying.

Mrs. Burton, entering the cabin shortly after, stood transfixed at sight of this personage in his green coat and egotistical condescension; catching Crissy's merry glance the older woman was constrained to sudden laughter. In the guise of absurdity, the tragic element of their future stepped in. There is an extraordinary vibration in the first touching of two lives destined to act upon each other for a lifetime, even if that action should be principally through remembrance. This vibration has been experienced by almost every man and woman, at least once, through their allotted time. It is often erroneously termed "love at first sight." We say erroneously, for the singular interest of such first sensations does not reach love at all. Why it should be mistaken for this serious passion, it is hard to tell; that it is frequently the prelude to this passion cannot be denied. Crissy experienced this vibration, knowing not its elements of danger; repelled, yet strongly attracted by Durand, she found herself observing him more than she was wont to observe young men. Another thing, Crissy felt that she had committed a solecism. Crissy knew very well that young persons don't like to be laughed at, yet she had been betrayed into this rudeness. Her disposition being generous, she was more than ready to render the *amende honorable;* she proceeded to do this after the manner of girls. When Durand's eyes wandered in her direction she met their gaze with frank kindness; when, later in the evening, he asked her idea as to the reading of certain passages in St. Clair—he had been cast for this—she modestly and quietly gave her opinion.

So much had to be arranged, that all sat up till late that night. Burton ended the evening by calling upon them for a rehearsal the next forenoon. Though they never even *thought* of giving a *performance* on Sunday, they found it would require much rehearsing to get these raw recruits into anything like playing shape. Crissy wondered that the boat did not start; she supposed they would be off as soon as all the company came aboard; it was midnight now, and not a sound of preparation from the steamer.

Early in the evening little Leoline had fallen asleep in the upper berth destined for the use of herself and Crissy. When Crissy essayed to get into it, she found the task more difficult than it appeared; how queer it was to be sleeping in a berth. However the mattress was soft, the linen delightfully clean, and Crissy was soon in the land of dreams. She woke at two o'clock in the morning with a frightened feeling, she could not recall at first just where she was. Putting out her hand, it struck the boarding of the partition; she had a drowsy sense of being shut into a box; then she became aware of a trembling movement in all surrounding her, a pulsation like the beating of a tremendous heart, under, above, all about her. The boat was under steam, and passing swiftly, in the blackness of that early morning hour, the town where Crissy had suffered so much.

The sun had scarcely risen when Crissy became thoroughly awakened; she turned her gaze upon her little companion, the child was lying quite motionless but with wide open eyes. "Dear Crissy," she whispered, "I have been awake a long time, but I didn't want to disturb you or mamma."

Crissy kissed her smilingly, the child whispered again, "Do you think we could get up ever so softly and dress without waking mamma, it must be beautiful on the deck."

Crissy said she would try; letting herself out of the berth by the process of backing out, where, with her arms on the edge of her couch and her legs dangling in the air, she hung for an instant scarcely daring to let herself go. The child peeped laughingly over the edge. At last Crissy let go and reached the floor with realistic solidity. She assisted Leoline from the high perch, and they soon made their way to the deck.

They were steaming along at what they thought a good rate of speed, though Crissy heard after that this boat was far from renowned for her swiftness.

All was beautiful indeed; the river gurgled lovingly along the rocky shore or wandered inland to little creeks and bays. In some places great trees dipped their branches in the water, while from them rose the morning hymn of feathered songsters. Inland in little pools they saw the water lilies looking at themselves in the transparent depths; from the blue sky tinged with its morning blush, from the dreamily murmuring water, from the depths of foliage on either side of the grand stream, came a voice of gladness bidding the earth be blessed. The girl and child contemplated everything with unspoken rapture, they joined unconsciously in the great pæan of this morning hour.

As they stood leaning against the guards, Durand sauntered up to them,—the revealing light of the early hour made the plainness of his countenance more pronounced. He had divested himself of that ridiculous green coat, disclosing a fine figure, above the medium height. His movements were full of natural grace; he greeted them in a way carelessly pleasant, then looked unconcernedly about him. The child glanced at him with an expression which intimated plainly that he was an interloper; for her the charm of the morning was broken. He talked with Crissy about the play and coming rehearsal; the girl lingered, held by some undefinable attraction. The conversation was finally interrupted by the call to breakfast.

The rehearsal proved a trying thing to Burton, who was stage manager and drilled them all; the rehearsal might be said to be the crucial test of their abilities. On the whole they did better than could have been expected, with one exception,—

that exception was the damsel of the luminous black eyes. It was just impossible to make Clara read her lines understandingly. When Burton endeavored to explain the stage business to her, she looked bewildered and said it wasn't in the book. If she had been confused or anxious he could have helped to make something of her, but she was only stolidly dull. Clad in her "panoply of beauty" she trod the boards like a queen, and might have got on famously if it was not necessary to open her mouth. At the close of rehearsal Crissy heard Burton mutter to himself, "handsome fool!"

This girl was a puzzle to Crissy from the first. Though so attractive in form and feature, her attractions appeared to be ignored by the young men of the company; her taciturnity was seldom intruded upon. These young men being Clara's townspeople may have had their own notions about her; at all events they gave her, in sailor parlance, "a wide berth." To Crissy, who was nothing like as handsome as the other girl, they displayed every kindness and attention. Crissy found it impossible to form a friendship with Clara, they had not an idea in common; she had moreover an undefined suspicion that Clara considered her a mere baby. Crissy asked George one day what he thought of Clara. George replied emphatically that he didn't think of her at all; that she wasn't *worth* thinking about; she was nothing but a handsome creature without a particle of soul; as for acting, she'd never learn *that*, if she was at it for a hundred years!

Uncle Tom's Cabin was produced in fair shape, considering the large amateur element pervading it. The boat performances proved, as Burton predicted, quite taking. Leoline's Eva was received with liveliest commendation. Crissy as Topsy was equally successful. They usually arrived in a town on one or the other side of the river in the morning, then they sent some of the young folks out to bill the town, Burton and the captain going ashore to purchase supplies. They had an excellent male cook, a young man devoted to the captain; their pilot was a good one, well acquainted with the river. He had a weakness though—he sometimes looked too deeply into the flowing bowl. Immediately after the night performance, they would up steam and off toward the next stopping place.

A number of weeks slipped by; with these weeks came changes imperceptible at first. Durand proved equal to the call upon his histrionic abilities, being by far their best actor next to the professionals. He also slowly, no one could have told how, gained a sort of ascendancy over the humanity around him; not that they grew to know him any more—none of them ever did that—perhaps it was that he knew *them* better. He had a magnetism about him none could resist, and yet they did not like him; they knew instinctively that he was not of them. His language, his general carriage, was that of a highly educated man. In this motley gathering of partially educated persons from different walks in life, he stood a startling exception; among these rather indifferently clad and rather uncouth young men, he walked carelessly in neat apparel, every shred of which seemed adapted to his lithe, graceful figure. He was never short of money. This alone was a distinctive characteristic where the rest suffered from an incessant lack of the "needful." There was not a man among them who would have put a hand upon his shoulder and talked confidentially with him, yet not one of them would refuse to do anything he asked them. Not that they did things because they liked to do for him, but because they felt impelled to do them. This man was gaining over Crissy the unexplainable influence he had over all the rest. He didn't mean to do it or care to do it; love was the remotest thing in the world from his thoughts just then.

The girl was a phenomenon to him. Virtue in *any* girl, particularly an actress—you see he shared the popular impression—was amazing to him. He would gaze with an ever-increasing perplexity upon this girl, whose soul, innocent as a young child's, looked gravely at him from her large eyes, he had a singularly abashed feeling when with her, if there was any good in him it asserted itself through this abashment. His thoughts, when she stood near him, lost their wicked retrospect, turning hungrily to the simplicity of her gentle fancies; he liked to talk with her, but he didn't like that any should observe him doing so. The consequence was, that when Crissy was with others he scarcely noticed her, but often, very often, after a few weeks, as she sat alone upon the deck or near the guards, he would suddenly stand beside her; it always seemed sudden to Crissy, for she seldom saw or heard him coming. It was a number of weeks ere Crissy observed the fact that he sought her society when no one else was near; when at last she noticed it, it came upon her with a sense of shock.

Crissy, always as transparent as the day, showed plainly that she was not her old playful, happy self. She took long spells of musing; she was much more pensive now than in their greatest hardships.

One day George came to Mrs. Burton with a troubled face; for weeks he had felt that Crissy was drifting away from him,—the poor fellow was growing desperate. Mrs. Burton who was getting exceedingly anxious herself, knew what was coming. She, in fact every one, except Crissy, knew how dearly George loved the girl; his honest nature could not conceal such a tenderness as this.

"What is it?" asked George, "what has come over Crissy? She's not the girl she used to be; she was always so gay—now she mopes around and hardly speaks a word."

"I can't tell exactly," Mrs. Burton replied. "I know how you feel, George. I am worried, too. I'll try to find out why she is so unlike herself." With this George had to be content.

Mrs. Burton had her private suspicions as to the real cause of this change. She felt—she didn't reason it out—but felt—that Durand was a man to be dreaded. She was well aware of the influence he exerted on all who approached him, but what could she do? The girl was evidently falling under his spell, but nothing had been confessed to her; there was really nothing tangible to work upon. Knowing the natural bent of youth, she feared that warning Crissy against this man would precipitate a passion on the girl's part. One thing she was convinced of, that if Crissy loved him already, she—Crissy—didn't know it herself. She could do just one thing in the present position of affairs, and only one,—make a barrier of herself between Durand and Crissy; keep him beside her on the pretext of an innocent flirtation, distract his attention from the girl. His vanity—she was sure he had plenty of it—would soon bring this about. She knew well that Crissy had a proud little heart which would resent any slight to her affections. This girl—who was not too proud to beg for work upon the streets, to face opprobrium, danger or trouble of any kind to help another—had a spirit which would make her sternly crush an unreciprocated love, and turn with scorn from any one who made light of her feelings. Mrs. Burton did not know how often Durand had contrived to spend hours alone with Crissy. The girl somehow couldn't tell her this. There wasn't much to tell. Two people sitting or standing near each other, exchanging utterly commonplace remarks, or looking dreamily at the river for half an hour at a time without a word.

Mrs. Burton opened her batteries at once, yet under cover; she knew how important it was that the enemy should not suspect her designs. The wisest, the most skillful player at any game is liable to serious mistakes; a false move at the start may do so much. One should remember that the bystanders who watch the game may have a mistaken conception as to the meaning of our play. Mrs. Burton could not take Burton into her confidence in this matter. She knew he would be so angry at the thought of any one trifling with Crissy, that it might lead to open recriminations between Durand and himself. Besides there was a chance, a mere chance, that she was mistaken in her hypothesis; if so, how ludicrous the situation with Burton flamingly angry against an innocent party.

She began operations immediately; she was surprised to find how readily Durand fell into the position assigned him. He sat near her as she sewed, and read aloud to her. If she and Leoline took a little walk ashore, he was with them. Did she want some trifling errand performed, Durand was near to do it. He talked to her with a deferential tenderness as if she had been his mother. She didn't know — how could she, not being able to look inside the man? — what a wily adversary she had. From the instant she began to keep him at her side, Durand knew what she was-about. He was inwardly amused. This was no new game to him; he would humor her, but henceforth he would be more circumspect with little Crissy. She was a sweet girl; but pshaw! what did he care for girls or women? He had had a surfeit of what people called love.

For a week succeeding, Crissy never saw him alone. As it was falling dusk one evening, she walked from her lonely place on deck to answer the summons to supper; unexpectedly to both, they came face to face. Crissy, never an adept at concealing her emotions, was at such disadvantage now, that before she could control herself her eyes sought his with a world of silent reproach and sorrow in them; heavy tears gathered in them; without a word she passed him and entered the cabin. Durand stood stock still, more shaken by this look than he had ever been by any of the griefs or hysterics of his erst time mistresses. Then she *did* miss him; she liked him. He had no feeling of conquest or pride in this knowledge; a scorn of himself — knowing himself as he did — came over him; that this pure girl should love a libertine like him! It was a pity that Crissy had given him this peep into her heart; it was such an honest heart that it attracted him by the law of opposites.

He paid Mrs. Burton more assiduous attention than ever that evening; waiting at the sides as she came off the stage to compliment her acting and appearance, following her about with humble obedience to her every look and smile. Even George, usually obtuse in such matters, noticed wonderingly the growing friendship between the two. There was another who watched it with gloomy eyes.

For a few days succeeding, Durand vacillated between the desire, ever growing stronger, to see more of Crissy, and the intention, ever growing weaker, to leave the girl alone. The devil, noting that it was seeding time for him, did his best to get his work in; it is true that the soil was in fine condition for such seeding. Then Durand took a fatal step; having reasoned the thing out, as he thought, he made a compromise. He would see Crissy as often as he could unobserved, but he would never make love to her. The poor child was evidently hurt by his neglect; he was foolish after all in taking for granted that she loved him. Then he analyzed the look she had given him, and being anxious for the time being, to convince himself that she didn't love him, called himself a conceited ass for having for a moment imagined such a thing.

All drifted back to the former channel. Durand danced attendance upon Mrs. Burton before that little world the old boat encircled; in stray sequestered hours he sought his innocent young friend; she unquestioningly took back the happiness that had been slipping from her. As these things progressed, the child, who from the first had taken an unconquerable, unshaken dislike to Durand, clung more closely to George and her father. Not that Burton or George could be said to be neglected by Mrs. Burton or Crissy. They were together most of the time, but we all know what it is to have a friend beside you; yet the distance of a continent between, an unexplainable line of division exists, the harder to cross because impalpable. George, secretly chafing, wondered that with all Mrs. Burton's promises to help him, he got no nearer to Crissy.

An incident occurred now which challenged the general attention. Clara had pursued the "even tenor" of her way — which was an aggravatingly stupid one — without any improvement in her Thespian efforts; without evincing the slightest desire toward even ordinary progress. All had settled to the firm conviction that she was to the company what a mantel shelf figure is to the drawing room.

One afternoon — they were well up river and stopping at quite a large town — Crissy coming into the cabin after a long walk with Leoline, Mrs. Burton and Durand — the two last had lagged considerably behind — found a couple of figures seated in the cabin. A small table stood between the two on which was a bottle conspicuously labeled French brandy. One figure, totally strange to Crissy, was that of a heavily bearded, florid gentleman, the other, Clara. There was a deep flush on Clara's statuesque face, a wild light in her eyes, her laughter was loud and strident, as she clinked her half-filled glass against the gentleman's. Crissy stood almost petrified with astonishment. Clara, looking up, saw the girl, and gurgling out a curse word, strangely linked with one of welcome, invited her to partake. Crissy fled. An hour later she saw Burton talking earnestly with his wife; his brow was heavily clouded, he muttered something about scandalous proceedings. Clara did not appear in that evening's performance; some hasty doubling was done to make up for her. She left the boat late that afternoon with the bearded gentleman, and they never saw or heard of her again.

This event made a profound impression on Crissy. She had wandered for nearly a year with these unlucky players. She had become acquainted with many women in the profession, but never yet a *bad* one. Here was this girl Clara, not a professional, coming into their midst ostensibly to learn to be an actress, yet in one hour Crissy saw more depravity in this girl than in any female of her year's experience.

A light broke on her; it was through such as these that the profession became a word of reproach.

As they journeyed onward one thing had puzzled Crissy exceedingly, the fact of passing some large and thriving towns without stopping to play thereat. One morning as they steamed past one of these, she ventured — being on the hurricane deck — to step into the pilot's house and inquire of that officer what they passed for. "Why, Miss," he answered trying to modulate his rough voice, "you see we *has* to do it or we'd be *tied up!*" Crissy couldn't imagine what he meant, but didn't like to question him more.

The afternoon of this same day they stopped at a wild, lonely spot upon the river bank to load on wood, a large lot of which stood neatly piled up close to the river for the use of steamers. Such delays as these gave opportunities for charming strolls along the wooded shore. Crissy and Leoline never tired of the sweet wild flowers, the tinted pebbles and shells about the river's edge. So off they started, Mrs. Burton and Durand following slowly behind. After quite a ramble they found, on their return, that a large portion of the wood had been loaded on. As Crissy passed near Captain Glockner she heard him say to Burton, in a low tone, accompanied by a peculiar smile, "I'll leave my card on the balance of the wood-pile, and much good may it do to them!" Just then Crissy heard the sound of stifled laughter, and, turning, found that it emanated from the boys who had been putting on the wood; they all seemed looking in a particular direction. Crissy looked, too; certainly an odd figure met her gaze—an old man, very tall, rather stooped and out of all proportion—lank. He had on a calico shirt of a gorgeous pattern, his pants, very much patched, in colors mostly far from the original, appeared to be held in place by a pair of suspenders made of the material called bed-ticking; the old straw hat he wore was simply immense; underneath its brim looked forth a pair of sharp, inquisitive gray eyes; a mat of snow white hair and beard made a strong contrast to his deeply sun-browned face. The old man waved his hand in a friendly way as he approached. Burton stepped forward to meet him. Crissy, at a meaning glance from Leoline, lingered near enough to hear the conversation that followed.

"Wal, I swan!" said the old man, as he grasped Burton's hand, shaking it warmly; "I'm right glad to see ye, stranger; had a durned long walk to git here. I hearn tell so much about this here boat that I 'lowed I'd feel more satisfider ef I could see her; and there she is!" he exclaimed, shading his eyes with his hand to take a better look at the boat. "Wal, by gosh, she's a fine un! Rakes in the tin right lively I reckon?" This with an inquiring look at Burton. The latter, with ill-concealed amusement in his tone, answered that they had been doing a pretty fair business so far.

The old man surveyed the boat again with thoughtful admiration. "I'm in this here line myself," he said. "Got Uncle Tom's Cabin on the road in a tent; we're a takin' in about all the small towns and villages on the root. My darter's a right peart gal; the notion o' doin' the thing was hern. She sez to me, 'Dad, there's money in it ef you'll jest hump yerself and git the show a movin'.'"

Burton asked how it was paying him.

"Wal, stranger," answered the old man, "we hev our ups and downs; sometimes biz is lively and baked beans is plenty; sometimes we strike a place where the poor ornery critters is so low down that they hain't no stummick for moral plays; but the wust trouble we've had so fur is with the goats."

"The goats!" exclaimed Burton.

"Yes," said the old man; "them pesky goats is allus into something or nuther. Ye see, the idea was my gal's; she sez to me, 'Dad, we must hev some *live* critters in the play to make it more takin' like'; she 'lowed that it ort ter be dorgs, but it takes sech a heap tu feed them big dorgs. So we calkilated that goats would do jest as well. My darter sez, 'All we hev to do, dad, is just turn 'em out to pastur and hev no expense whatsomever.' So the first night arter the play we turned 'em out for a few hours to pastur, and ef ye'll believe me, stranger, they pastured on a whole clothes line full of clothes. When we went to look arter the critters there they was, a chawin' on the last of the linen! Yu bet we had tu dust out of that pretty lively. The durned things hev been into mischeef on an' off ever since."

Burton laughed, and asked the old man if he'd like to take a look over the boat. The stranger assented gladly. Leoline and Crissy followed them aboard with smiling eyes; the old man expressed warm admiration for the interior arrangements of the boat, so different, he averred, from traveling in a tent; no wading through mud after the rain storms, no loading into wagons and unloading again. As he talked thus, a female voice suddenly interposed, "Now, dad, you jest shet up your head and tote back with me!"

The peart girl alluded to was at his elbow, a large, strongly-built woman, with a freckled, good-natured face. Despite her admonition to her "dad," the girl cast a look of intense interest about her. Crissy, interpreting the look, said she would be pleased to show her about the boat. A number of the company clustered near the old man, listening to his amusing descriptions of tent life; the warning whistle soon sounded, however, to show that the boat was about to start, and the strangers bade them a hasty adieu.

At a number of their stopping places Burton and his family were treated with great kindness by some of the more prominent residents of the places. In many cases he and the family had been

invited to such pleasant socialities as taking dinner
or tea with these kind-hearted people. As the
greatest attention was bestowed upon the Topsy
and Eva of the play, Mrs. Burton frequently
excused herself and husband, allowing the girl and
child to sometimes enjoy themselves for an afternoon this way. Crissy never forgot one of these
delightful afternoons, when a genial, stout, old
farmer, called by the people around him "Judge"
—though whether he was a judge or not Crissy
never found out—came to the boat in a comfortable light buggy, and helping the girls into it
drove them a number of miles out of town "to
visit with his folks to the farm." The ride was in
itself a delight beyond compare, the road sometimes winding in between great oaks and partially
cleared woodland where wild birds called and
whistled continually, then coming suddenly out
upon some high bluff overhanging the river whose
broad bosom was dotted here by many islands;
then when they reached the large farm house, with
its strip of smooth grass down to the road side, its
garden blazing with old-fashioned flowers, its well
sweep, the stacks standing near it, and the many
sounds from poultry, pigeons, cattle and horses,
the girls beamed with pleasure. Out and out
country life was something new to them. Then out
ran a dear old white-headed lady to meet them,
and two young girls, and a black-eyed young man,
the very image of the old judge grown young

again, and they all seemed so glad to see them and hoped that they didn't feel the drive too long —the very idea of such an ecstatic drive being too long—and hoped they had good appetites, for dinner was all ready. Then the old lady said, "Was this the little Eva they had all cried over the night before? She would have to kiss them all 'round now to make up for those tears;—and here was Topsy, too! Dear me! to think of her blacking her face and arms and acting it all out like that!"

Then the young girls took them to a little room with a white curtained window, where they could wash the dust from their faces and hands. This room was full of jugs and bowls and glasses, filled with the most beautiful wild flowers and ferns. The child and Crissy ran from one bowl to another smelling and admiring them till the girls said they "must really come and eat their dinner now, for mother was calling them."

What a dinner that was, with the genial old judge asking a blessing upon its abundance, and the young man helping them so liberally with those big brown hands of his, with the white headed mother smiling over everything! There was such an atmosphere of kindness in all they said and did, that Crissy felt as if through some mistake she was getting a short vacation in Heaven ahead of time. After dinner the girls took them through the orchard; such an orchard it was too!

with the apples turning bright red cheeks toward them as if to say, "Eat me; you know you can't resist me!" with the crooked old apple trees spreading out such loving wealth of branches over the kind earth beneath them; and then the big barn; was there ever such a delightful place as that! with its sweet smelling hay, its nice stalls for the horses, and a large swing, where the girls insisted on swinging Crissy and Leoline. Then the fun of searching in queer nooks and corners with the girls for eggs which some refractory hens *would* hide away instead of putting them in the orthodox places prepared for them! But lovely pleasures end too quickly. It was time to go back to the dingy old boat; the tiresome routine of evening work. Then the family clustered around them for good-bye. They kissed and praised Leoline, they twined her golden ringlets 'round their fingers and thought her the most talented child on earth; then the old lady took her in her arms and wished her all happiness in her journeyings; then they loaded them down with fruit and flowers, and watched them out of sight, waving their handkerchiefs as the last turn of the road hid the departing ones from view.

With the exception of that private source of anxiety understood between Mrs. Burton and George, things had gone well so far. As might have been anticipated with a man of Burton's proclivities the turning point was not far off. Burton could not stand prosperity; when that sun shone at all brightly on him the snow of his resolutions melted very fast. When difficulty made close attention and strenuous effort necessary, he would put his whole mind and body to the task, abstaining from liquor entirely for the time being. When Burton began to drink again the pilot was not slow to follow his example. "Any excuse is better than none." The pilot was getting rather oppressed by his sense of moral rectitude in having kept sober so long; the captain, too, had a leaning in the same direction, only he did his drinking, as he did everything else, in a gloomy and self-contained manner.

Durand noticed these things with a scornful lifting of his eyebrows, a sneer of his full lips. Drink had no fascination for him; he counted his vices as being of a more genteel description.

This man was traveling with these theatricals under an assumed name—all actors, he said to himself, have a *nom de plume*, why not he? The study of the people around him roused all the cynic in his nature. From the stately Clara, whose debased inwardness he had fathomed the first instant he saw and talked with her—how soon depravity recognizes its companions—to the drunken talent who, as he essayed to instruct and control them, was himself controlled by the more potent power of alcohol, down to the good-natured cook, Durand had learned them all. In one thing, even with his capacity for understanding wickedness, he deceived himself. He thought Mrs. Burton not as good as she really was. He could not understand why she placed herself in such a position toward him to save her own child from his society. It would seem that most mothers in such a case would appeal to the duty and good sense of the girl herself; it was not because Crissy was not a thoroughly *good* girl; she was innocent as an angel in sexual matters—of that he felt convinced.

An accident revealed to him the fact that Crissy was not Mrs. Burton's own daughter. He had often noticed with surprise that Crissy bore no resemblance whatever to the rest of her family; even her voice, with the sweet fullness of those English tones derived from her own father and mother, sounded different from the elongated yet slightly nasal utterance of Burton and his wife. The delicate shyness of Crissy's manner was altogether unlike anything he ever met before among professionals. George was the only one who knew that Crissy was not Burton's child. George, for motives of his own, was the last one in the world to impart this information to Durand.

One day as little Leoline sat on the deck beside her mother, looking at the people thronging near the gangway of the steamer—long before the evening performance many would come down to have a look at the "show boat," as they called it—Leoline caught her mother by the arm and said, in a shrill voice of childish excitement, "Look there, mamma, at that girl; she's got a bonnet on just like the one Crissy wore when she *first came to us!*"

"Hush, child," said Mrs. Burton, as turning her head she saw Durand regarding her steadfastly. It was too late however; all flashed on him at once. This was the explanation of Crissy's dissimilarity to the others. An intention, which up to this time had stirred but faintly in him, began to shape itself. Now he understood better Mrs. Burton's attitude toward himself; he saw that she was really afraid to say anything to the girl. There had been nothing in his actions she could have spoken about; he was quite sure she did not know how often he saw the girl alone.

Durand had spent his life up to this time on the agreeable principle — as he thought — of never denying himself anything he desired. The son of a rich man, brought up by an indulgent mother — that is, indulgent in most things — he had gone through school and college in a manner which, considering his unbridled license in some respects, reflected credit on his ingenuity for escaping consequences. Durand's mother, a lady of education and worldly refinement, married at an early age a man who was coarse, uneducated — self made, they termed him — but enormously rich. A few years of married life proved to her the impossibility of ever assimilating with such a man; she was a proud woman — proud of her family, her culture, her distinction as a social leader; but though she wrapped her mantle of pride very closely about her, she found it cold covering. In the meantime a son was born to her; on him she lavished the pent up ardor of her soul,—cold and stern to all the world beside, to this boy she was the very fire of love. But the woman was worldly wise; the evils which later cropped out in the boy lay at the root of her own being. He was denied nothing which did not militate against the tenets of that world—that exclusive world of the upper ten which was her only deity—to which in the privacy of the secret closet of her thoughts she yielded up her orisons. She made him understand that she did not object to a little wildness in his youth; it was, in fact, quite the proper thing in society for a young man to "sow his wild oats." But one thing she and society would never forgive in him—that thing was a mesalliance.

Fancy what life is to a man who has no necessity for exertion, mental or otherwise; who is brought up to lean upon his fathers fortune; who has no higher aim before him than to shine in a society formed, for the most part, by a combination of moneyed people,—a combination made for display of wealth suddenly acquired, whose possessors do not realize the tremendous powers for regeneration, or the following of all the nobler instincts which it places within their reach. We speak of the society of some of our western cities as it was thirty-six years ago. In the present instance, witness one of the results of that training. Durand had lived a great deal in the short space of his life; he had lived fast, he felt old already. A certain splendid butterfly — one of the most beautiful and erratic women then on the stage — had lured him to the banks of the Mississippi. It had been a long chase, ending on Durand's part with deep disgust. Bad as he was himself, he felt, when he grasped this butterfly and saw the gaudy color of her wings rub off upon his hand, that there was a kind, an extent, of wickedness in some humans which would turn Satan himself to a hermit. Durand had an odd poetic element even in his sins,— that he had chased this flying sail only to find a cargo of death! Phew!

He was drifting aimlessly about the river when he heard of Burton's attempt to form a company. He was hundreds of miles from home; no one would ever hear of it; it would be an amusement to become an actor himself for a time, hence his entrance to that boat world where at last he found what real love can be. Durand knew it now. No woman had ever inspired in him such feelings as those which assailed him in Crissy's presence; never in his life before had he despised himself so much, never so longed for some sweet land where people might follow the best impulse of their souls and mésalliances were never thought of. A mutiny began in his restless heart telling him that if he could not have the girl he loved without dishonoring her, he must fly. Nothing except his own will held him there, and yet—and yet.

As these struggles progressed within him came the knowledge that Crissy was not Burton's own child, and the surety, harder still to combat, that Crissy loved him—Durand.

From the instant that Burton began to drink again, everything went wrong, not only in the captain and pilot following his example, but the child sickened. She was not naturally strong; this wandering life, at an age when most little girls are tenderly cared in point of sleep, food and play, told on her. It began, as most sickness does, insidiously; a trifling lassitude, a little fever, an unusual petulance; the mother's anxiety noted this and prepared simple remedies at once. One evening in the very part of the play where Eva's longest scene occurs, the child broke down entirely, and weeping, clung to her mother, sobbing out, "Oh, mamma, I can't; I really *can't* go on!"

"My darling!" pleaded her mother, "try, do try, it is impossible to get through the play without you; do it for mamma's sake!"

"Oh!" cried poor Leoline, "my head hurts so, how can I speak out loud?"

The united entreaties of the mother, Crissy and George persuaded her to make the effort; but when her scenes were over, and they put the trembling, feverish child to bed, their ears rang with the pitiful cries of her delirium. For a week she was too ill for them to even think of having her act.

At this point in their affairs some of the musical young men of the company, growing discontented with the way Burton was running things—if truth must be told, also exceedingly jealous of the influence Durand exercised in the dramatic counsels,—took French leave. This, with the loss of both Leoline and Clara in the cast, made it imperative to stage some light comedies requiring a small number of *dramatis personæ*. Mrs. Burton and Durand looked up plays and got them rehearsed in shape, as Burton was drinking to such an extent that they could not depend upon his assistance at all. The captain, from the time that he himself began to imbibe too freely, declared an open and cordial hating for Durand, saying that it was no wonder business was falling off when they staged such things and put that d—d jackanapes,—meaning Durand—into the leading rôles.

They were now nearing two large cities; these cities were directly across the river from each other, with a fine bridge spanning the stream between them. Crissy was on the hurricane deck looking at the beautiful shores as they steamed past, when she heard voices in angry altercation. It was the captain and pilot.

"Tell you what, Matt, I'm captain of this boat, and I *will* do it!" exclaimed Glockner.

"You're the pilot, but you needn't think you're

God Almighty; you just obey orders, and stop right there," pointing to the town on the right bank of the river.

"Very well!" responded the pilot angrily, "you try it and see what'll come of it; you must be in a precious hurry to git tied up; a pretty fellow you be to want to run yourself right into the lion's jaws; but I'll do it!" he continued, with a quick turn of the wheel. "Nobody shall say as how Matt wouldn't take his orders."

Both men glared at each other fiercely, and Crissy wondered what it was all about. After the evening performance, which was rather slimly attended, Crissy became enlightened. The engineer was getting up steam, busy preparations for departure sounded through the old steamer, when loud voices and oaths from the gang plank—not yet drawn in—met Crissy's ears.

She and Mrs. Burton leaned over the railing to hear what was going on below. A number of policemen's stars glittered in the light of the lanterns. Glockner's and Burton's voices could be heard in tones of angry remonstrance.

"I tell you it's no use," said one of the minions of the law, sullenly; "you don't pull out, Captain, till you settle this amount. You'd better give your orders to stop firing up, for we've got possession and we're going to hold it."

After some more discussion the engineer was informed that they would not start that night, that all hands might as well turn in for a little sleep. Then the angry party at the gang plank could be heard tramping up the stairs. Presently they assembled in the cabin, where a council of war was held until late in the night, or rather far into the morning hours. Mrs. Burton and Crissy retired with all speed, when they heard the ascending footsteps. Lying in their berths, they could distinguish through the thin partition of the state room the words of the belligerents.

After some time they gathered from these the fact that the boat was deeply in debt, as loud imprecations upon "her" testified. "She" was frequently alluded to in disparaging remarks, such as terming her an "old hulk;" wonders as to her value for firewood, etc. Perhaps the rapid passage, from hand to hand, of various case bottles, had something to do with the length of the session held, also the increasing jocularity of the disparagements heaped upon the unfortunate boat. The captain was told, with appropriate oaths, that he had been a smart one to evade the hand of the law up to this time.

Leoline, in her sick, weak condition, clung to Crissy in terror when she heard the rough voices. The girl soothed her into something like rest. At length a compromise was effected between the opposing factions; some of the movable appurtenances of the boat would be yielded to the law. At a certain time the next morning, they would take these from her, and she would be allowed to go her way.

As this went on in the cabin, Mrs. Burton, lying in her berth below the girls, was thinking very seriously indeed over Crissy.

About the time of Clara's escapade, Mrs. Burton had been on the point of telling Crissy that now would be a good chance to make the long promised visit to her mother. Crissy, in answering the letter which contained that providential enclosure, told her mother that as soon as Mrs. Burton could spare her she would go home. But, somehow, weeks of Durand's society had lessened her desire to see her mother immediately, so she said nothing more to Mrs. Burton concerning it. Burton's excesses, the crippling of the company which shortly followed, now rendered it almost out of the question for her to go. Mrs. Burton made up her mind, however, that she would send Crissy home if circumstances should in any way justify the anxiety she felt about the girl. She fell to pondering on the strangeness of the power Durand had acquired; even in her own case, all had gone farther than she intended. It had not been part of her original plan to make Durand's apparent devotion to herself so conspicuous. She felt her anxiety redoubled by the very fact that he had played into her hands so readily. Thinking it over, she was sure that he had some strong motive for doing so. She had no commonplace vanity to mislead her; she knew very well that in his attentions to her he was playing a part, just as he was playing in whatever he had been cast for.

Bad as she knew men to be, and bad as she suspected him to be, no idea of his actual intentions crossed her mind. There was a lawlessness in him she knew nothing about. As she thought, the contrast between George and Durand came to her vividly. George the faithful, honest, plodding, but true-hearted man; why was he so unappreciated? For all George's kind offices to everybody seemed to be taken as a matter of course; even Burton accepted his faithfulness with a contemptuous good nature. She need not have wondered over the plain fact seen all about us, that unobtrusive love and duty, performing its tasks without parade or claim for recognition, is seldom noticed. George received no commendation from the little world around him, because he was of that world; he belonged to it by sympathy, by caste, by the kindly subservience of a desire to please it. But Durand was a type unknown to them,—whence he came, what he was, or who he was, they could not tell. The unexplainable has a peculiar fascination for common minds. There is apt to be more real beauty in some ordinary field or garden flower, than in the loveliest orchid, yet the meed of beauty is always accorded the blossom of the strange plant with its multitude of ugly roots feeding on air. And why? Because it is to us a living embodiment of the element called mysterious. We are too much inclined to measure the worth of a thing by its inscrutability.

Crissy, too, was beset by many restless thoughts. Here was their river experience leading them back to the same old paths filled by dank weeds of debt and drunkenness. From what she had overheard in the cabin she knew that they had passed the town of their summer misfortunes, in the dark of the morning hours, to escape the boat and its belongings being seized for debt. All their undertakings so far had led them to this disreputable wall of shame. Was this the life to fit a young girl to make her mark, to even make a decent living as an actress? Crissy's strong practical sense immediately responded—No! Yet how could she leave Mrs. Burton and the child just now? Even as she thought, through the darkness, like a palpable presence, a graceful figure leaned caressingly toward her; a pair of blue eyes looked into hers with an expression she knew too well. She sighed. Poor child, the chain that held her looked like flowers, but it was really iron. In a short time she would know how hard it was to break it.

The next morning they heard heavy footsteps on the hurricane deck; some men appeared to be carrying something very weighty.

"What *can* they be taking?" asked Mrs. Burton.

Crissy ran out; returning in a few minutes, she cried, "It's the large bell!"

"Oh, dear!" exclaimed Leoline, "are they really taking our beautiful big bell?"

It was too true. The occupants of the boat looked sadly forth as the immense bell, whose musical clangor had so often called their audiences together, or sounded their proximity to some fine town, was borne away. To the women it was almost a sacrilege that this bell should be taken. What would a boat be without her bell? It was like parting man and wife; but law was inexorable and claimed its due.

As they departed from this beautiful city gloom sat upon the brows of all; even George, generally so light hearted, looked depressed. Crissy, on the upper deck with Leoline—who, though still too weak to act, was slowly recovering—could note that the expression of the pilot's eyes, as he glanced askance at the captain, was as much as to say, "I told you so."

The weather was delightful; the quickly rounding weeks had brought them to October. Along the river bank autumn hung her gorgeous banners; the flora of this advanced season, in which the colors of purple and yellow predominated, shone in glowing patches on every open glade. The crisp freshness of the air was full of vitality; the sun had lost his burning heat, but the earth still had its chalice filled to overflowing with the welcome warmth of his golden bounty. The scenery on this portion of the river was wild and grand. The boat sometimes steamed between solid walls of rock, standing up gray and defiant, hundreds of feet above it. Little streams of water, crystal clear, ice cold, burst from the rock in places and trickled over mossy stones into the river far below; the stream rolled on in solemn grandeur tinged with the color of the surrounding rock. This was to be a long distance for them without stopping, as the Captain and Burton had decided not to pause in the journeying till the evening of the next day. Crissy, whose love of the beautiful in nature was an intense passion, could scarce absent herself from the deck long enough to eat. Many of them, not having to act that night, sat about playing cards or reading, yet there was a brooding anxiety in the air. The careless cheerfulness of the earlier weeks they passed together had evaporated. To be sure there was reason for this, especially with the men, who mostly knew what the navigation of the Mississippi was. It could hardly be a matter pleasant to reflect upon that they had a drunken captain aloft, with a drunken pilot at the wheel, and as capsheaf an inebriated stage manager and proprietor snoring off some of his stupor in the cabin.

Durand was as usual reading Shakespeare with Mrs. Burton; George was busily constructing a toy boat for Leoline. It was late afternoon, getting dusk rapidly now, for the days were shortening. Much to Crissy's regret, the grand, rocky shores were passed; they had reached a portion of the river very broad, and studded with islands overgrown by willow trees. The rest were at supper, George came to her to call her in. "I wonder why it is," she said, "that the packets all seem to be taking a different side of the river from us?"

George looked, and sure enough, over in the misty light on the farther side of the river, could be seen a large sidewheel steamer painted white, steaming northward, in their own direction.

"Run in to supper, Crissy," said George, anxiously. "I'll go up and speak to Matt," meaning the pilot.

Crissy was scarcely seated at table before the boat seemed, in an instant — quicker than thought — to strike something; a sudden vibration ran through her, then she stood stock still.

Every one rushed on deck. A look downward disclosed the condition of affairs, they were wedged on a sandbar. The water, beautifully clear in the northern Mississippi, revealed their position at once. The utter carelessness of their pilot was a fact beyond denial; angry oaths resounded on all sides. "Can't be helped by talking about it," remarked the Captain, philosophically; "we'd better go in and finish supper, then see what can be done."

The surprise and annoyance of this event sobered Burton and the Captain. As the supper progressed many plans for their release from this predicament came under discussion. Absurd as it may seem, they concluded to dig her out. As she seemed to be wedged forward, with her stern in much deeper water, they thought that possibly the force with which the great sternwheel might be revolved would aid materially; so by the waning light a dozen men, armed with spades and shovels, could be seen at the hopeless work, standing nearly to the waist in water, digging away at the sand, which almost immediately washed in again. It was soon demonstrated that this would never answer. The boys, accustomed to the river, being good swimmers, one of them took a large rope and swam with it to a certain point considered favorable, where he fastened the rope firmly around a strong tree; then the work on the windlass began. "Boys," said the Captain, gloomily, "you may as well understand that this is likely to be an all-night job, and that every man Jack of you will have to take hold."

Crissy, who, on the deck above, was noting everything with an interest not untinctured with anxiety, heard the Captain's words. The men instantly proffered their services. Crissy's glance involuntarily sought a certain one among them; he was not there. Every man on the boat, except him, was on hand for this summons. She sat alone in the gathering gloom of night and watched the work going on actively below; there was no moon, the stars gleamed frostily overhead — the nights in this northern latitude had lately grown colder — the different colored lamps were lighted over the boat, according to custom. Above Crissy's head a red one was suspended; its light seemed to make wavering pools of blood on the floor of the deck. How well she remembered *that* afterwards. So long as she lived, the recollection of this night never paled in her memory. As she sat thus, absorbed in a reverie, which a troubling vision of her mother seemed constantly to interrupt, she heard hurrying footsteps near her. George's voice sounded sharply from the darkness. "Where is Durand?" he asked; "every man except him has gone to work; we need every soul if we're ever to get out of this."

"I don't know where he is," said Crissy, with such a ring of genuine surprise in her voice, that George, though he looked suspiciously at her where she sat in the red light, had to be convinced.

He ran down the stairs to the front. In a few minutes more Burton came from the rear, just as George had come, as if from a search of the boat. He propounded the same question to Crissy. "I don't know," said the girl, feeling an unaccountable peevishness, "I have not seen him."

Burton, too, glanced sharply at her, then said angrily, "He's a confounded scoundrel and sneak, hiding away when every other man is working like a horse!"

The girl made no reply. Burton, too, disappeared down the front stairway. Crissy felt the hot blood surging over her face; why should they come to *her* to know where Durand was? She felt irritated and singularly ashamed.

Thinking of him brought, by close association of ideas, the thought of Mrs. Burton. The girl rose, and pacing the deck in the darkness, looked through to the lighted cabin or green room at the farther end, the wide doors of the audience room standing open, the curtain rolled up, and the large doors of the cabin back of the stage, also open, gave an uninterrupted view of the lighted interior of the cabin where Mrs. Burton sat at a table in the middle of the room quietly reading; little Leoline was in bed. Mrs. Burton must have supposed Durand was working with the other men; hence was indifferent as to Crissy's whereabouts.

A few minutes later a tall figure glided to Crissy's side, an arm was slipped about her waist, she was quietly and silently conducted to a chair standing rather back of the red light, yet giving to those above an excellent view of the busy men below. Durand, seating himself in another chair close beside her, remained silently contemplative of the creaking windlass. Crissy felt a trembling surprise; it thrilled her with a strange pleasure that he wanted to be alone with her, but yet he had no right to be there. She, true heart, would never have disregarded the call to duty, no matter how hard or hopeless. The sense of this became at last paramount; it emboldened her to speak. "Why are you not helping them?" she asked, with a quiver in her voice. The answer came in a tone low as her own, "Because I would rather be with you."

The girl felt a bewildered embarrassment; he was such a number of years older than herself that it was not the thing to tell him that he really *ought* to do his share; but she would respect him more, she would think him more manly, if he was pushing away at one of those big bars, like the spokes of an immense wheel, as the rest did.

He must have divined her thought, for after a long pause he said, "They will be at it all night; in a couple of hours one of them will fall out dead tired, and I'll take his place." This seemed logical. Crissy drew her shawl more closely around her and said no more. She yielded herself to the peculiar contentment which always came over her when with Durand. He moved his chair still nearer, the encroaching arm stole softly 'round her; sometimes as she turned her head the red light falling full upon her face would show her eyes large and limpid, looking at him with an expression of childlike trustfulness. He sat in deep shadow. An hour passed thus without another word, then he rose softly, and walking noiselessly over the dark deck looked through to the cabin where Mrs. Burton quietly read on. He resumed his silent companionship.

Was it Crissy's good angel or Durand's familiar devil who prompted what came next? Who can tell? He inclined his head more closely toward her, and in a voice—always rich and harmonious—which sounded now like honey dropping through the listening darkness, said, "Do you love me, Crissy?" No answer. It seemed to Crissy as if the throb of her heart had transformed itself into the very air about her; the stars were listening and the red light was a sentient thing. Again the voice, with a gentle insistence in its tones, "Do you love me, little Crissy?"

To answer was dreadful, for she could only answer true. Her lips quivered, and after a struggle she faintly articulated, "Yes." The sheltering arm drew more closely 'round her; not another word was said. What might have been an hour slipped by. He rose reluctantly; she rose too; he drew her to the top of the stairway. "I must help them now," he murmured slowly; "kiss me just once before I go." Crissy could not refuse him, her will seemed bound in a narcotic slumber; that kiss was the first and the last.

She stood under the red lamp and watched him. She saw him step softly from the shadows, and taking the youngest and most wearied looking man from the windlass, put himself, apparently unnoticed, in his place. The men were working now in sullen silence. They seemed to feel the hopelessness in their efforts; the lively talk with which they began work had ceased entirely. Crissy wondered that he did not relieve Burton, so much older and more unused to labor than the rest.

Durand alone knew why he did not. He glanced up once or twice at Crissy as she stood there. In a short time she walked along the guards to the door of her state room. She found, to her relief, that Mrs. Burton had not yet bolted it, and she was thus able to undress and creep in beside the sleeping Leoline. She felt that to speak to anyone that night would be impossible. How glad she was that Mrs. Burton found her book so interesting.

Crissy could not sleep — a novel experience with her — her mind tossed restlessly upon the billows of a troubled sea; a spar or plank to cling to must be somewhere! Then memory — a strange storehouse where the dust lies thick upon so many unused and unwanted things — opened its door to let the light fall full upon some simple words spoken by an anxious mother nearly a year before, — forgotten long, yet closely treasured they stood out in the darkness like printed words before the retina of Crissy's vision, " Remember, that any man who behaves in a loverlike manner to you without asking you to be his wife, insults and would degrade you; if that happens and your heart fails you, recall your mother's words, then run away from him."

Why had she not remembered this before? But

yet until this very night, what need? Now he had asked her if she loved him, but he had not said that he loved her. He always sought her unobserved; he had never uttered such an idea as marriage. Ah! the shame of it! love, anger, pride, held a conflict in that earnest heart which seemed like to burst it. "Then run away from him." Yes, yes, she would. How wise her mother was to know all this beforehand; had her mother been near her she might never have grown to love him so. She could have told her mother everything; she could never, never speak of it to anyone else! The girl writhed in a misery of emotions never dreamed of by the man who caused it. He thought incessantly of her as he worked the windlass. Her love for him, confessed by herself, was now proved beyond a peradventure. He would not stand in the way of fate; it was destiny — he said to himself — which threw this pure affection into his arms. He could not marry her to be sure, but to be with her always — that is until she wearied him, if that might ever be — would do him good. He needed something good in his life; but how to manage it? He must pretend to marry her; nothing short of that would do with *such* a girl. How to get her from these Burtons? He felt sure she would not leave them clandestinely; he knew the river well and many unscrupulous men along shore; some dark night one of his friends would have a row boat close to the old steamer, then on some pretext he would get the girl to the lower deck, a little sudden muffling of her face and voice, and getting her rapidly into the boat. When out of hearing of the steamer, he would explain to her his love and devotion, — his friend, the minister, right there in the very skiff with them — they would go ashore at the first landing, get married, take a packet down river as soon as possible, then away from pursuit and into the sunny south. When day was dawning the creaking of the windlass ceased, the boat quivered, the joyful thud, thud, of the mighty heart of the engine was heard as they slowly got under way. Crissy rose from her sleepless couch heavy eyed, unrefreshed ; the child and woman slept on. The deck was deserted. The men, fagged out by unusual exertion, had thrown themselves into their bunks for much needed sleep ; the captain, pilot, engineer and fireman were at their posts. The gayly painted woods showed dim and dreamlike through the clinging mists in the gray light. A tinge of pink was spreading in the east, laying a carpet for the coming of the royal sun ; soft winds were rustling through the weeds and rushes of the shores ; it was not morning yet — it was only the ghost of it.

Crissy stood with her hand upon the railing, wet with the night dews, and looked sadly at the passing shores; turning her head at a slight sound she saw Durand sitting in one of the chairs where they had sat the night before. She walked slowly toward him ; he patted his knee with a motion which invited her to a seat upon it. The girl blushed deeply, then quietly sat down in the chair beside him.

"Why not?" asked Durand.

Crissy did not reply.

"Why not?" he repeated.

The girl turned her steady eyes upon him and answered, "Because my mother would not wish me to."

Durand bit his lip, half in anger, half amusement. This girl-child talking to him in such a way! He knew very well it was her own mother she alluded to.

He turned a searching glance upon her. He couldn't divine just what it was, but there was a firmness in her face he had never noticed there before. He felt a vague, undefined uneasiness. They sat together a long time, silent as the night before. Crissy's determination never wavered, even with her beloved so near. She would know later that when we pluck the flower of love out by the roots and throw it from us, it is long before order is restored to the torn and empty space it leaves.

Breakfast was late that morning; the company straggled into it very wearily. Crissy was watching for an opportunity to talk with Mrs. Burton alone. She was anxious to do so before rehearsal, which would not be till noon that day; but wherever Mrs. Burton was Durand was sure to be. He had many suggestions to make as to what they would play that evening—the next; in fact, for two weeks to come. All this time he knew that the very next evening, if things went well—the second evening at farthest—he would carry out his plot as to Crissy.

About ten o'clock Crissy stepped softly to the table, piled with play books and written parts, where Durand and Mrs. Burton were deeply engaged. "It would be better," said Crissy, "to play a couple of one-act comedies when we are so short of people; there are some here well suited for you and Mr. Durand. The truth is, my head aches so dreadfully it is not likely I can play to-night."

Mrs. Burton looked up with quick alarm; the girl certainly appeared ill; she was unusually pale, with dark circles under her eyes. She gazed at Mrs. Burton steadily. This lady was gifted with perspicacity; she rose immediately. "Child," she said, anxiously, "you are looking badly; come inside at once, you shall lie down and I'll bathe your head. We'll manage so that you'll not play to-night."

When they were inside the state room, beyond the possibility of being overheard, Mrs. Burton turned a comprehensive glance upon the girl. "What is it?" she asked.

"Just this," said Crissy, "I am going to my mother as soon as I can get there; at our first landing place I'll get off, take a packet down river to a place where I can take the train direct for Chicago.

I wanted to tell you this before the cast was made out."

Mrs. Burton gave a great sigh of relief; she had faith in Crissy right along; that faith was now verified. These women understood each other, though little was said.

"Very well, you shall go if you want to, but it's not likely you can start before to-morrow afternoon. We will prepare in any case by leaving you out of the cast to-night. One thing, however, we had better not mention it—your going, I mean. What with being so short-handed, Leoline unfit yet to act, Mr. Burton, too, would interpose strong objections to your leaving just now; not," she added quickly, "that I blame you for doing it; you are doing what you feel to be *right*, yet we had best keep our own counsel. I'll speak to George that he may quietly find out where it will be best for you to get off. *He'll* never tell, I'll warrant, till we give him leave."

She was correct; though George's astonishment was unbounded when he knew Crissy's determination to go home at once, he took good care to say not a word. He assured the girl that she would not be able to start until the next afternoon, but he would see to everything.

Now came the revulsion of feeling which follows determined action. Crissy was wretched. She had emptied the cup of her happiness. Leaf by leaf she had torn to bits the daisy of her hopes; and what now? A long blankness stretched out before her mental vision. The word duty could not brighten it; even the thought of her mother's love grew dim beside this overpowering anguish. She had deliberately hastened to do what she knew must be done; and now she was leaving *him!* She went to bed for that afternoon, but the ailment was heartache not headache. You will say it was very strange that this girl, whose instincts were for good, should love so bad a man. It is not strange; look about you and see continually the serpent charming the dove. This thing is always going on; it is to be feared it will be, as long as this world shall last. Each soul must struggle from the quagmire as best it may, the quagmire is sure to be somewhere in its path. Durand saw no more of his young friend that day or night. He did not wish to see her. It would be better not to talk with her again until he held her firmly in his grasp. One must use care in snaring such a timid bird. Something in the look of his bird convinced him she had been alarmed.

That night they played in a small place; the next forenoon they would reach a larger one where they intended provisioning up, but would not play, as a large circus was doing a big business there, so Burton had learned from a passing packet bound down the river. After an hour or so at this place, they would steam on to a smart little town, arriving there in the afternoon, and play for it that night.

Durand, after hearing these plans, rapidly

sketched out his own. He knew a fellow in that place who would sell his soul for whisky. All right, then, this chap would have the row boat handy for him; first he thought near midnight; but no, let him keep his boat in the shadow, conveniently near, from the time it fell dark. A certain whistle should be the signal between them. He might be able to spirit Crissy off earlier in the night, and so have a better chance for catching a packet. All this was somewhat risky, but he had run risks before now. Crissy slept well this night, the last one she would ever pass on the old boat. Exhaustion from mental struggle brought repose, she was too young and healthy to lose much rest. When she woke in the early morning, she felt a strange heaviness,—what was this sensation of doom hanging over her? Then she remembered, and the flood gates of her sorrow opened. She dressed, but not to seek the deck as usual. During the day she packed a satchel full of necessary clothing. Even Leoline was not told of her projected departure. George ascertained at the circus town, that about dusk a packet bound down the river would touch at the town where they played that night. He would transfer Crissy and her satchel from their boat to the other, arrange for her transportation, and bid her good-bye. About the middle of the afternoon they arrived at their destination. Soon as the steamer was made fast Durand was ashore, not as one who hastens, but with the graceful carelessness peculiarly his own. As he sauntered nonchalantly toward the town, the Captain and George, standing near each other, at the upper railings, noticed him. The Captain's dark face grew darker with intense dislike. "Look at that man! Who is *he*, I'd like to know, that he must foot it with a manner like a—like a President. I'd like to know why *he* should be allowed to make so free with other men's wives and daughters? By God, if it was *my* wife instead of Burton's, I'd have his heart's blood!"

"Hush, hush!" muttered George, for, looking up, he saw Burton within hearing distance. Burton turned and walked away, but not before the Captain caught a glimpse of his face. Its expression was frightful.

"D—d if he didn't hear me!" he exclaimed, with a hoarse laugh.

This trifling incident worried George; he knew what demons drink made of these men. Even this early in the day, they had been imbibing pretty freely. Somehow a feeling of gladness that Crissy would soon be out of this whirlpool, came over him. The very soul was gone from life without her presence; but it would be delightful to feel that she was safe. He repaired to the cabin and asked Crissy if she had prepared all for her journey. She told him yes. He told Mrs. Burton that she had been wise in saying nothing of Crissy's intentions, for he feared, as matters were going now, that Burton and the Captain were well on the rampage.

Mrs. Burton sighed. "George," she said, "the one who will miss Crissy most of all will be Leoline." George had some doubts of this. "But you will have to take Crissy's place to her. You and Crissy have gone through so many griefs and troubles with us, that it seems as if you really must belong to us in very truth."

George assured her that he would do his best to fill Crissy's vacant place. The short day soon drew to a close. In the dusk George and Crissy quietly slipped ashore, and then to the big packet with her blaze of lights, her whistling, confusion, and noise of many voices.

"God bless you!" murmured the young man. "I hope you'll not have any bother on your journey; be sure and write to us the minute you reach home."

The packet remained such a few moments at these points, that as George left the levee the boat was already in midstream and snorting her way down river. Bending his steps toward the old sternwheel steamer he saw with careless eyes a man in a small boat, rowing slowly along shore in that direction. Everything was in readiness for the evening performance; the audience room lighted, the curtain down, the players preparing in their dressing rooms. Durand's costume needed little changing from its usual gentlemanly neatness, as it was a modern dress the play called for. He was stepping into the green room when he heard Burton's voice in angry expostulation. He drew back from sight and listened. "It's a d—d shame," said Burton, passionately, "to let the girl go just now; sneaking off too, as if she was running away from us. By Heaven, I don't *believe* she's gone!"

"Don't talk so loudly," urged Mrs. Burton, "what I tell you is true. Crissy left for home on the Northern Belle. By this time, she's well down the river. I must hurry now with my dressing; we can talk it over by and by. Don't let Leoline know yet that she's gone, for the child will have a fit of crying over it." With that a door was loudly closed as Burton muttered a fiery imprecation.

Durand walked dizzily through the open doors of the green room, and stepping around the set scene, stood on the dim stage behind the curtain. For a moment he stood there, convulsed with rage — despair — he scarce knew what — such an earthquake of passion seemed to rend him. His plans foiled at the last minute! How could he for an instant have anticipated this? That woman! He hated her! *She* had brought this about! He crossed the stage and stood in the wings where it was darker; he felt as a hurt creature does, who wants to hide itself. First music was beginning; they played a lively waltz; he never forgot that air — a heavy step was on the stage. Burton staggered as if by instinct to the very spot where Durand was standing.

"Scoundrel!" muttered Burton, "you are the meanest villain who ever went unhanged! Let them tell me what they like, *you* caused Crissy to leave us! Not satisfied with that, you would seduce my wife!"

"*Your wife!*" exclaimed Durand, in a voice deep with passion. "She is a drab! I wouldn't give the snap of my finger for her!"

A little fairy-like figure darted upon the empty stage and began an airy pirouetting to the music of the waltz.

"Speak like that again!" cried Burton, wild with drink and jealousy, "dare say that word again and I'll *kill* you if you had *ten* lives."

Leoline stopped dancing as she heard her father's voice.

"You would!" exclaimed another voice, so muffled with rage that she did not recognize it. The men clinched; they fell upon the floor together; a knife gleamed bright and fierce through the dim light; a long groan. Durand dashed past her, his hands dripping blood.

"Papa!" screamed the child, with a shriek of horror so piercing that it resounded high through the music; a curdling cry, which stopped the musicians as suddenly as if it had been the crack of doom. On the lower deck a shrill whistle sounded; in an instant a man dropped, unperceived in the darkness, from the old steamer into a row boat; his companion rowed him swiftly down river, into hiding from the hands of justice.

Crissy was sitting on the deck of the Northern Belle, looking pensively at the stars. Homeward bound after nearly a year of strange wanderings, of vicissitudes unanticipated by her mother or herself, in those fairy dreams fashioned by their hopes. How different was this home-coming from what she had supposed it would be in the early weeks of her sojourning, before the roselight faded from her sky, and the shadows of black reality darkened everything. She was to have returned glowing with honors, confident with success — best of all, able to give the dear mother assistance. Now she returned bereft of every hope connecting her with the stage; even worse, actually compelled to run away from it like a coward or a thief, lest in her youth and weakness even greater ills than disappointment and a wasted year should overtake her. Crissy was mistaken when she thought of that year as wasted; she had learned what was more to her than many years of ordinary school life; she had gauged her own capacities; she had, by the help of God and her mother, conquered her first temptation. That this brought her to a premature womanhood cannot be denied, but the soil that nurtured her soul from earliest infancy was wetted down by tears of sorrow. There is nothing more forcing toward maturity than grief. Perhaps the

Higher Power, which fashions all, knows how necessary this nurture is for some souls.

Crissy had a long, tiresome journey before her, but her mind was so inured to the noise and rush of travel that she felt little or no trepidation when she found herself in the big depot on the lake front of Chicago. She glanced about with pleasure. It was very early morning, the sky was already rosy with delight over the coming sun; the lake, a blue glory, tossed up foamy waves along the shore; the air was crisp and bracing; clear, too, not darkened by smoke as now. She looked around for some means of transportation to her mother's new home. It was a long way out on Dearborn street. She caught sight of some express wagons, and her satchel being too heavy to carry a long distance, she soon arranged with an expressman to convey herself and baggage to the address she gave. Seated beside the man in his humble vehicle, she looked comprehensively on all sides as they jolted along. The man, one of unquestionable Hibernian origin, glanced kindly at the girl as they drove on.

"I'm thinkin', Miss, ye'll be a stranger to this city?"

"Yes, indeed," answered Crissy.

He pointed out to her some interesting buildings and streets. He talked fluently, even enthusiastically, when he described the past and possible future of the city. Crissy listened surprised; this was such an exact echo of George. She discovered later that this was the ordinary discourse of all people who had taken residence in this city by the lake, the air they breathed seemed to fill them with braggadocio.

In Dearborn street great oak trees grew shelteringly each side; the street was broad and clean, and through the advancing day came the bustling hum of great activity; many people of all ages hurried past them to their daily toil. Crissy felt great interest in this city destined to be her future home. At last they drew up in front of a little cottage, where her companion, after helping her to alight, left her. Crissy saw her mother's face at the window, she gave a cry, they were in each other's arms in a minute. Such laughing and crying as followed! such questioning and such answering! such kissing and such hugging! There was her father, too, "quite himself," beaming on her with a quiet happiness. "Dear father," cried the girl, "I never want to go away from you again."

The children crowded around with expressions of surprise that Crissy had grown so much and had long dresses on now, and would she play "paper dolls" with them when they came home from school? When her father started to his work and the children for school, Crissy had her mother to herself once more. She began the long tale of her wanderings, her mishaps and disappointments. At its conclusion her mother said with decision, "Now that I know all this, I could never be satisfied to let you go on with such a life; perhaps this last anxiety which hurried you home to me was for the best. There is no telling what you may have been saved from by being here."

"Ah, mother," said Crissy, sadly, "I only found with strangers the same trouble I left at home. You can see that rum was at the bottom of all our troubles; without that we might have done fairly well, though my unfitness for the profession in many respects cannot be denied, yet I might learn to be a humble worker and fill some subordinate position in that great workshop where I once had the madness to hope I might shine a star; that I am lacking in the attributes essential to pronounced success need not prevent me from earning a living on the stage."

"But," urged the mother, "it would be better to earn a living at something where an ordinary amount of respect would be vouchsafed one; the worst feature of all you have told me is the insult which dogs members of the profession at every turn. To be continually subjected to that, would surely lead in the long run to a total loss of self respect; without *that* no woman can be safe."

A long pause of anxious silence followed. After a time Crissy said, "You are right, mother; what I suffered in leaving *him*, shows me how hard it is to do right where the feelings are involved. Oh! mother dear," cried the girl, sobbing as she clung to her mother, "without the thought of *you* to help me what could I have done?"

"Child," said her mother, solemnly, "if I should die this moment, it would seem to me I had accomplished a great work in having been permitted this influence for good with you. But," she resumed, "let us return to the main point at issue; it will be better for you to leave the stage, and do so at once."

"You are right," answered the girl, "and if 'tis done at all, 'then 'twere well it were done quickly.' It may seem strange to you, mother, but there is a singular fascination in stage life. I have frequently listened to middle-aged persons in the profession talking it over and telling how many they knew who made efforts to leave it, but invariably returned to it again; and you see," concluded Crissy with a sad smile, "once accustomed to being a vagabond, every month makes it more difficult to return to the humdrum of a commonplace occupation."

Thus these two did what all the world is doing at this moment, made their plans for the morrow, unwitting what a day may bring forth. The black shadow of that event which immediately followed Crissy's departure from the old boat, had reached, was about to touch them, for flashed along the wires came this message—

Burton murdered by Durand. Leoline dying. Return at once.   GEORGE.

The mother and daughter never thought of hesitation when they received this message. To their simple notions of duty the voice of anguish was imperative,—Crissy must return at once.

There are some people who, if you called to them from the bottomless pit to throw you a rope by which to clamber out, would only peer over the edge and ask, " Is this any concern of mine ; by what right do you make this request?"

If Crissy's homecoming was sad, how much more so was that other journey that she traveled now in the blackness of the shadow of death. She was enveloped in an unexplainable horror; the wording of the telegram offered the bare, the awful facts. But how to account for all this? That she herself could have been made the pretext for the murder, never entered her imagination. But there was the telegram, read fifty times with the hope of extracting some information or rather explanation. Crissy was melancholy enough on the homeward journey, under those conditions of mind springing from disappointed love and buried hopes, but now —the object of that love a murderer! Oh, how could it be? Now hope was dead indeed. Before the arrival of this message it had been shyly budding in her heart, though she scarcely knew it, but now—. Thus the long hours of travel, filled by distracting thoughts, wore on.

The evening of the next day found her at her destination. George, pale and careworn, was at the levee to meet her; at sight of him her tears burst forth unrestrainedly. "Leoline," was all that she could utter. George looked at her with solemn eyes dimmed by nights of watching.

"Going fast," he answered in a low tone.

Crissy noticed nothing around her; she was not aware that they were walking very rapidly toward a large frame house standing a little remote from others on the high bluff. In a few moments they stood in a large, low-ceilinged room. A slim figure ran to meet them; was it Mrs. Burton or her ghost — that hollow-eyed, sunken-cheeked phantom. Crissy was in her arms.

"Oh!" cried the poor woman, "If you had not left us, Crissy, this would never have happened."

Strange inconsistency; she who had been so anxious to have Crissy go. The girl never heeded, for a voice faint and childish called her. There on a bed lay the little form once so animate with life and motion. Disordered on the pillow lay the golden hair which had been Crissy's pride.

"Darling Crissy!" murmured the child. "How glad I am you came. I was so sorry to think that perhaps I couldn't see you again before I went." She motioned feebly for the girl to sit beside her and twined her thin fingers lovingly through Crissy's.

"Perhaps,—" said Crissy, trying to choke down her sobs, "perhaps, dear, you may not go; we can't do without our little Eva, can we, George?"

The child turned her large blue eyes quietly from one to the other, then answered, with a quiver in her voice: "But I *must* go, and then—then I shall be with poor papa; you will be good to mamma, both of you, I know you will."

Choking with emotion, they could make no reply. The child, weakened by speech, fell into an uneasy slumber. Then, removed from the bed, George recounted to the girl in a low tone the particulars of the tragedy immediately succeeding her departure. The child, sole witness of it, seemed unable to recover from the shock. Of Durand they had heard not a word. Burton lived only long enough to say that he forgave his murderer, but maintained to the last that Durand was a villain who had deliberately planned to seduce his wife and Crissy.

George added that the kindness of the people in this lonely river town was something extraordinary. They had given the woman and child food, shelter, nursing, and more than all, the warmest sympathy. The men of the place provided decent burial to poor Burton's remains in the desolate graveyard on the green bluff; now it was only a question of a few hours when the little girl would be placed beside him.

"Oh! Crissy," concluded George, "if you had failed to come, Mrs. Burton would have been desperate, for Leoline called for you incessantly in the awful delirium which followed her father's murder. She was not quiet then as now; now the fire of her little frame has most burned out."

"The old boat," asked the girl; "where is it?"

"Gone. Burton lived about an hour. The knife penetrated a lung; and as soon as we took his remains ashore, the captain told me it would be best for him to 'sheer off' as the whole affair might be looked into, and make some unpleasantness for him. The boat started northward, and that is all we know or will likely ever know of her."

In the early watches of the succeeding morning, little Leoline's soul departed; the transition was noiseless, apparently painless. Toward the very last she grew too weak for speech, but looked at them all with fond understanding glances. Under this second blow it seemed as if Mrs. Burton's fortitude must yield entirely, but action was imperative. After that golden head was laid beneath the sod, the three faced each other and said, "What next?" George took the lead in every thing. He told them that with winter so near, it would be best for them to return to Chicago as soon as they could, and there procure employment if possible. He and Crissy would be in their homes and that would give them more chance to assist Mrs. Burton.

The kind-hearted people of the river town got together what they could to defray the traveling expenses of the unfortunate trio. Then Mrs. Burton went alone (George and Crissy dared not intrude upon that solemn leave-taking) to bid a last farewell to the graves of her beloved. Below the mighty river sang its sad refrain, the gaily colored trees shook red and yellow leaves upon the fresh turned earth, the restless wind wandered along the lonely bluff, and a slim figure knelt beside the spot henceforth hallowed in memory, though no stone or slab has ever marked the place where those poor forms are lying.

The desolation of this third journey over the same path was something terrible to Crissy. Since she first took it what a whirlwind had passed and made a desert place of the once smiling prospect! Mrs. Burton was silent with the stupor of grief. Crissy was silent with a despair which in the young is always voiceless. George only resembled his old self,—quieter, to be sure, but ever kind, thoughtful, and even cheerful. As they neared their final stopping place, George said he was going to take Mrs. Burton right home to his mother. Crissy gave him a grateful glance. She had been wondering if Mrs. Burton could stand the noise of their little domicile with the children's voices all about her. George said that as he lived on the South Side, Crissy must come to their house first. Then, after, he could take her home; in the meantime, she would become acquainted with his mother and sister.

George was extraordinarily anxious for Crissy to know all his family. So Crissy went with them, and was introduced to the very dearest old whiteheaded lady with engaging manners—just like George's,—and the sweetest of young girls whose dark ringlets fell to her waist in lovely profusion, whose big brown eyes gave loving though shy welcome. Then George took Crissy home, and you may be sure Crissy's mother liked him at once, even though his hair was fiery red, and his form far from commanding; for Mrs. Trevanion's daughter had told her how good he was, and already she appreciated that goodness far more than Crissy did.

The day after their arrival in Chicago, George was out looking up the theatrical people, for work must be secured. Mrs. Burton declared it would make her sorrow easier to bear if she had an occupation, let alone the positive necessity for it.

That very evening, to Crissy's great surprise, George was at Trevanion's house. She was amazed to hear him tell her mother that he had made engagements already, not only for Mrs. Burton and himself, but for Crissy also.

In the grief and anxiety of their recent conversations the girl never thought to tell him about her determination to leave the stage. What was to be done? The contract was signed. George protested that he blamed himself for being so premature, but really he had been pressed for immediate acceptance or rejection of the engagements offered. This was the fact. They discovered later that this management had some difficulty to secure competent persons, and took advantage of George's too evident ignorance of their standing.

A long discussion ensued, Mrs. Trevanion at last declaring that there was no help for it. Crissy's dramatic career must continue one winter longer, and they—the Trevanions—move to the South Side to get her reasonably near what George laughingly termed "the shop."

Crissy acted in many strange places, under many peculiar circumstances, but she now began a new and decidedly odd experience. The gentleman who was proprietor of the extraordinary show of which these three people became members, was a little man with keen blue eyes, red hair, lively disposition and a power over horses seldom equaled. He strangely enough conceived the idea that a show combining theatrics and circus would be a paying thing with that western element comprising the Garden City. In pursuance of this idea he secured a large theatre in Monroe street, ambitiously named Amphitheatre, but popularly styled "the barn." Here the performance opened by an exhibition of trained horses and gymnasts in a large circus ring. After an hour's performance, sometimes longer, a stage slowly rolled forward and covered the ring; then the theatrical part followed, concluding the evening's entertainment.

Fancy this combination! We of the modern times with our chaste tastes gravitating between so-

ciety plays which are all dress, and Black Crooks
and Ali Babas with scarcely any dress at all. Chicago thirty-five years ago might be considered quite
a youthful maiden. Yet, even at that early age
she showed a decided preference for what was genteel. She shook her head dejectedly over this odd
combination of circus riding and stage; she did
what was more important than head shaking,—she
denied it paying patronage. At a time when all
amusements seemed in a languishing condition this
was hardly matter for wonder. This city, young and
untutored though she was at that time, was quite
enough of an anomaly herself without fostering
other anomalies in her very bosom. The specta-
cle of a circus, instantly succeeded by a rendition of
Othello or Hamlet, was too much for even her for-
bearance.

The management, finding that Shakspeare and
circus didn't harmonize very well, put on some of
those wild Indian romances dear to youthful hearts,
— notably Putnam — then came Crissy's period of
torture, for these plays permitted the introduction
of horses, thus giving scope to the equine tendencies of the management. Crissy's limited acquaintance with these animals made her regard them
much as one does an active volcano ; the awfulness
of having to cross the stage every evening on a big
black horse, tearing at full gallop over an extremely
shaky bridge, was something unforgetable. Another
unpleasant feature of this curious coalition was that

the horses' stalls, standing immediately in the rear of the stage, in order to have these beasts handy to lead out at a moment's notice, put the poor Thespians to sad inconvenience, as, for the purpose of getting from one side of the stage to another, they were obliged to run across close to these stalls.

It was an odd sight to see a Roman matron anxiously grabbing up her skirts with both hands, as with frightened eyes she ran past the horses' impending heels; or an elegant young blood of Venice in silk tights, laced and frilled doublet, and immaculate ringlets, muttering oaths of a very modern nature, as he too essayed this delicate task.

But the worst — the very worst of all — was the mingling of these two elements. The stage being a very large one, the whole circus force had to be put on for street scenes and processions. The wrath of the actors over these equinely odored adjuncts, packed closely with them in the side scenes preparatory to going on, may be fancied. It defies description; the circus people feeling themselves despised by the others, fell in their turn to deriding. Many a fierce, though suppressed, war of words was conducted in these narrow spaces, to say nothing of the peculiar compliments bandied in the green room.

It was during the "Siege of Delhi" that these fierce hatreds between the theatric and circus forces seemed to reach a point which threatened demolition to that astonishing combination. However, they got through the winter without bloodshed, which was something in their favor.

When in the course of a few weeks the disagreeables of Crissy's professional life became more pronounced, her mother regretted that accident had placed her in that position ; but the web of circumstance closed around the girl, compelling her to retain this employment until the disbanding of this amphitheatrical attraction.

Her father succumbed during the winter to his old habits, and want as well as anxiety sat around the hearthstone. It became evident that Mrs. Burton would soon pass to that land whence there is no return. She was uncomplaining in her grief and suffering, but the hand laid on her had been too heavy ; her slight frame withered under it. When the spring greenness was on nature again, she grew too weak to think of working any more. She was in correspondence with some of her husband's relatives, who kindly offered her a home. After consultation with her stanch friends, George and Crissy, she accepted the kindness and bade a tearful farewell — a final one, too — to her Chicago friends. She died a few months later.

Crissy's vagabond existence was ended. She secured an employment which gave her some opportunity to study; but destiny had Crissy's future all mapped out. The girl who suffered insult, starvation almost, during her year of vagabondage, was to occupy a position better suited to her lineage and the early prospects of her parents.

At the end of a year, George, like Crissy, determined to cast his lines in other places. He told Crissy confidentially that a fellow needed a tremendous stock of talent anyhow to accomplish anything in the profession. His sister slyly remarked that the removal of a female aspirant from that mighty corps had more to do with his determination than anything else. George was very successful in his new avocation; he was with a growing firm who appreciated his faithfulness. He had one great trouble — it seemed as if Crissy would never learn to love him; he tried to be so patient too. It was months after Mrs. Burton's death that he ventured to speak upon the subject of his love. He hoped the old boat, with its accompanying tragedy, would by this time be a dim memory to Crissy. He hardly more than began to speak when the girl turned to him with quivering lips and said: "I know what you mean, dear George, but I can't listen to you — I can't just yet."

Then he said no more until the War broke out; he was out with the first volunteers. Mrs. Trevanion wept openly at parting from him and Crissy looked very pale. As he clasped her hand in goodbye, he whispered very humbly, "May I write to you, dear?" Then Crissy said he could.

He wasn't much to look at, as he marched off with the other boys, but his heart was just about right, and his spirit as brave as any six-footer among them. The pain of the unwonted absence of a friend so true and unobtrusive, gave Crissy that first little sad thrill which she afterwards confessed to George was the harbinger of the lifetime of love she bore him later. George was only absent a few months when Trevanion sickened. One of the climatic fevers seized him, and found an easy victim in a frame undermined by excesses.

All this time strange things were happening across seas. It chanced that Trevanion's father had a brother who was a bachelor, very wealthy. This man lived to be very old. Why it ever entered his head to select the Trevanion in America to leave his money to, no one could imagine, unless it was that he always heard him alluded to as the "black sheep," the "scapegoat," etc. This bequest reached Trevanion on his deathbed. Too late to help him retrieve the errors of a life, but yet a gladness to light that dark tide he floated on.

When, at the end of his three fighting years, George returned home, he was unscathed, except by some slight scratches, and a private still. He couldn't bring fame or gold to his beloved, but he brought the treasure of an unswerving devotion. It was not long before they were married, for Mrs. Trevanion, who had been George's sincere friend from the first, urged on Crissy to have no more delays.

As years slipped by Crissy renewed acquaintance

with some of the associates of her vagabond year. A few of them became famous; some of them lived out histories sad indeed. Crissy always retained a feeling of deep affection for that profession in which she had the temerity to attempt so much. She made Chicago her permanent home, and watched its growth with interest.

She is a gray-headed woman now, with grandchildren clustering about her; she often tells them how different the Chicago of her youth was from the great city they see now, with its magnificent parks, its elevated roads, its twenty-story buildings, and its great World's Fair. Then the young people look at her very earnestly and think how old dear grandma must be to remember so much.

ALL ON A CHRISTMAS EVE.

ALL ON A CHRISTMAS EVE.

OUR scene opens in the Emerald Isle. It was the close of a beautiful day in early spring; the sun had set, but the fading loveliness of its bright tints remained; an intense stillness was over everything.

On the outskirts of a quiet hamlet two figures, male and female, walked side by side without speaking, until they reached a stile, at which both paused as if by mutual understanding. The man, who might be in his twenty-second year, was of a bright, open countenance, stalwart though not ungainly figure. He appeared in some mental agitation, if his frowning brow, moistened eyes, and compressed lips might be considered any indication.

The girl, some four years his junior, drooped in a plaintive manner a shapely head, adorned by a mass of light-brown hair, fastened with a certain careless grace in a loose knot at the back of her head. She would seem by her attitude to be deprecating some recent remark made by her companion. She was a girl as prepossessing in her appearance as those of her class generally are. She was an Irish peasant. There was a pleading look in her blue eyes, a timid melancholy about her whole demeanor, which had a charm of its own. The passing stranger, who at first might regard her carelessly, would, after a moment, involuntarily turn his head to take another glance at that shrinking countenance, and the sorrowful droop of the young mouth. After a few minutes of silence, during which the young man leaned against the stile, restlessly kicking the loosened earth with the toe of his brogans, the girl said, in a low and tremulous voice, "You know, Dave, dear, that I can't help myself. I must do as they tell me, and go wherever they choose to send me. What can a poor girl like me oppose to the wishes of the only kith and kin she has in the world?" At this the gentle head drooped lower, and tears stood in her large blue eyes.

"And what," answered the man, in a deep, strong voice, "what is to become of me left alone here? Do you think there can be life, or hope, for me in any place where *you* are not? Why, the very sky will lose its sunshine, the birds forget to sing. All will turn dark with you away, Acushla!"

Under the influence of the emotion which possessed him, this man spoke with comparative eloquence; this was not his every-day language. The girl glanced up at him with a surprise, not unmixed with admiration. "Ah, Dave," she cried despairingly, "don't talk like that when you know that we must part, and so soon. Perhaps you can follow us after a while. America is a big country, but

I'm sure you'd find us, and then perhaps there you'd get work, and earn money enough for us to marry and have a little cabin of our own."

"Yes, yes," he responded impatiently; "all that would be well enough, Annie. I'd follow you to the ends of the world, if it was only *myself* to think of; but the ould people, could I lave them suffer? They will never give up their native place, and I cannot lave them. Where would they get the bite and the sup without me? No, Alanna, if you cannot remain with me, we must part, and God help me! That's all."

Then he turned his head away to hide the struggle which seemed to shake his stalwart frame as if it had been a leaf. For a few moments there was silence, and a sense of sadness which filled the space about them like something palpable. After a time the girl spoke again. She touched his arm softly, looking at the intensity of his emotion with something like fear. "Dave, Dave! don't feel like that! Sure we cannot help ourselves, we are so poor and so young, what can we do? But faith, if it will be any comfort to you, dear, I'll promise to wait in America, or anywhere else, unmarried for you. You shall come and claim me when you can, and find me true."

He opened his arms with a sudden impulse, and clasped her in them, but as his face drooped over the gentle head upon his bosom, a shadow deeper than the falling gloom of night was on it, perhaps thrown *backward* from the unknown future, the undefined darkness of what was to be! "Oh, Annie," he said sadly, "when oceans roll between us, when all around you is happiness in that country, where they tell me that poverty and toil are scarcely known, it's little you may remember *me*, or the promises made in ould Ireland. But good-bye, darling; there is no help in the talking of it; God alone knows what is before us!" Then he took her hand, and turning slowly, as the darkness deepened around them, they retraced their steps to the little hamlet.

_

To the residents of Chicago a walk along Halsted street, south of Van Buren, presents anything but attractive features. He or she, as the case may be, being principally cognizant of many bad odors, multitudinous saloons, and filthy sidewalks, over which, at all hours of the day, and far into the night, a motley congregation of people are passing; but as evening comes on this concourse of persons often becomes a swaying mass, including all nationalities and all conditions of life.

Along this street the tired artisans wend their way homeward, stopping only too frequently to assuage their thirst and weariness in one of the many saloons. The busy housewife, often of the Irish or German type, laden down by parcels innumerable, bends her tired feet homewards; the little cash girls, unkempt and dirty, often insufficiently clad, but playful and happy, despite hard work and squalid surroundings, walk along in pairs, or three or four abreast, talking loudly of the experiences of the day. The professional gamblers, generally adorned by large-sized diamonds of doubtful genuineness, hasten along with a contraction of the eyebrows, which denotes the mental calculation which is so prominent a part of the hard work of these gentlemen; gaily dressed, painted cheeked, and bold females, also tread these thoroughfares, and encountering the glances of the dark-browed gamblers, greet them with a smile of recognition or the peculiar badinage of their class. Here, too, upon this busy street may be seen the telegraph and messenger boys in numbers, generally smoking cigarettes, or cheeks distended by great wads of tobacco, their lips swollen, eyes heavy, hands and faces smeared by dirt — exceptions to these sometimes occurring in the shape of some bright-eyed, clear-faced telegraph boy stepping briskly along, head up, mouth smiling, every movement expressive of alertness, you could safely put such a boy down at once in your mind as the darling of some mother or sister, hastening through all the turmoil to a *home*. Through that mass of unsavory humanity, a face of this kind appearing now and then was like the rifted cloud which shows the blue beyond. It may seem strange that respectable toilers in the great city should choose for homes a place contiguous to this brawling, filthy street,—a street so often represented by its habitués appearing at the police dock to answer all kinds of charges from drunkenness up to murder, but so it is; for on many of the streets leading east from Halsted reside persons who, though wage-workers, belong to the class who aim to be sober, industrious, and maintain a decency of living and outward appearance one would scarcely look for in such a locality.

Our story conducts us to one of these streets which, beginning or ending, one hardly knows which, in Halsted, runs thence eastward to the river. The houses upon this street seemed to be mostly frame, in all stages of architecture and dilapidation. In one of these, larger and cleaner than the adjacent ones, two women sat in earnest conversation.

The younger of these women, who was in her twenty-third year, was tall in figure, well built and strong; her hair, of raven blackness, matched the large dark eyes which gave her face, in conjunction with its blunt features and rosy cheeks, a very youthful look; the expression of her countenance denoted a disposition made up of equal parts of goodness and cheerfulness, with the latter quality at present predominating. Her companion was a woman some years older, whose shapely head, with its masses of light brown hair, had a melancholy droop to it, her eyes, large and blue, had a look of appealing sadness. There was something about her which touched the beholder with an involuntary pity.

She gazed fixedly at her vis à vis of the cheerful countenance and said, "So, Bridget, next Tuesday is the day; well, you're the lucky and happy woman to be able to marry the young man of your choice; I wish to God all women could be so fortunate."

Bridget answered in some surprise, "Sure Annie! anybody'd think you afther *envying* me, to hear the way you talk! *you*, too, that are so swate and pritty, with plinty of the young fellows dangling afther you; sure you have only to pick and choose!"

"Yes," said the other, with a touch of anger in her voice; "a pretty lot to pick and choose from! What man-jack is there amongst them could support me like a lady? Haven't I had enough of hard work these long years past, but I must pick up and marry some fool man, who can scarcely scrape a living for the two of us?"

"Is *that* what yer'e talking about?" said Bridget, disdainfully. "If I waited till *my* Jack had money to keep me like a lady, it would be many a year before we'd marry! But I tell you, Annie, I'm willing to work with and for Jack; he's that good and kind to me, we *love* each other so dearly, that by the blessed Virgin I'd sooner be a slave to him than queen to any other man!"

"Oh!" exclaimed the other impatiently, "I understand all that well enough; you can face poverty, worry, everything, because you love the man, but what would be the sinse of marrying all these it you didn't love him—that's what I ask you?"

Bridget looked at her friend steadily, somewhat sternly, too. "Then you mane to tell me," she said, after a long pause, "that you'd marry a man who could keep you like a lady whether you loved him or no?"

The other hung her head, a few heavy tear drops rolled down her cheeks. "Don't be angered with me, Bridget, but it's the truth! I left my heart in Ireland years ago, with a man I'm never likely to see again. We were promised to one another, he used to write to me, but for two years past not a line; perhaps "—this was spoken with great bitterness—" he has found someone more to his liking than his simple Irish girl. Oh, well, it's a world of misery! Why should I remain true to him who has forsaken me? No, the first man who can offer me a good support gets me, even if he's ould enough to be my grandfather!"

Bridget shook her head warningly at this outburst. "It's all wrong, Annie; you must never do it; wait awhile, you are young yet; should you never hear from him again, you may get to love someone else. Tell me now," she continued, with a woman's quick intuition of the necessity of changing the course of the conversation, "how is the ould lady? It's not long for this world she is,

I'm thinkin', so pale she's looking. It's lucky for her that her husband's the kindest of ould fellows."

"She's failing fast now," answered Annie, "her sands will soon be run, it's a good friend I'll miss when she is gone; she and the ould man have been like mother and father to me this last three years, since my own died and left me here in a strange land and you too, Bridget, darlin', what would I have done without your friendship? Now you'll have your heart so set on Jack that it's little I'll be seeing of you."

Bridget laughed gaily. "Never you fear that," she said, "I'll keep a little corner for you yet, alanna, but come now, you must see the wedding gown, and look at the pretty lace veil that I'll be wearing Tuesday next, please God."

₊

Near the little village of Ballyclash, situated somewhat north of Enniskillen, might be seen, about the year 1826, a very comfortable-looking farm house,—that is, comfortable for that date and country. All about this place bespoke a thriftiness and even tidiness most unusual to an Irish farmer. One thing was certain, that the owner of all this exceptional comfort earned it by the sweat of his brow, for he, a gray-headed, tall, and strongly built man might be seen at work when day first peeped from beneath its blankets, still plodding at his toil when sunset painted its flaunting colors along the sky. In the neighboring village of Ballyclash, this man was frequently spoken of as "that careful ould man, John Malone;" to this was added with many a knowing nod, "Ah! but he's the rale hand at a bargain; it isn't much ye'll be gettin' out of ould Malone; and there's his son John, as knowin' he'll soon be as the ould one!"

Now be it known that there was nothing of disparagement in these remarks. Business ability is admired all the world over; the poorer friends and neighbors regarded the shrewdness of father and son with something akin to veneration; where so many strive and so few succeed, the exceptions call for encomiums. John, the younger, was now a man grown; his features, though aquiline, pleasing, his keen, gray eyes, and firm, thin lips denoting the shrewdness inherited from his father. Up to the time of which we write, not a cloud had blotted the domestic or business horizon of the Malone family—John, the younger, being a pattern boy in every respect, entering into all his father's schemes of money-making or improvement with a heartiness which made the old man entertain bright hopes of the future before his son. Old Malone was a man of few words. He expressed approbation or contrary feelings more by significant looks than any spoken avowals. One of the few subjects upon which he was known to converse, except topics appertaining to the farm, was that of what he termed "larnin'." Upon this weakness he dwelt with great severity, maintaining that the man who would waste his means and time upon anything so utterly useless was little more than a fool.

"Look," he would say, "at ould Pat O'Rouk! What does he do but take money enough to buy a fine bit of land, just to send his boy to a place that they call 'college' for a year! For my part, I'm a well-to-do man; you can see all about you what I have done, and divil a bit of larnin' did *I* get, except in the little school at Ballyclash!"

"You, too, John," he would say, apostrophising his son, "see what a fine talent you have for getting on in the world. The village has given you all the larnin' that you need." Then he would relapse into silence, but the lively twinkle of his eyes, the smiling of his well-formed mouth, would show that he was still pursuing the subject in his mind.

It is often to be noticed that anything interdicted or spoken of with disparagement in a family, is sure to make a strong impression on the minds of younger members of the family. The child who is told that the theatre or circus are haunts of the devil, and must not be approached, has a burning desire to investigate; so it was with young John. As he worked afield or in the early dawn made preparations for the day's labor, his mind still ran upon this interesting theme. He thought within himself, "This larnin' must be a fine thing, or it wouldn't cost so dear;" for in his experience of cattle, farming implements and the like, the highest priced was always the best, and as old John would say, sententiously, "much the cheapest in the long run." Now, why this larnin', which was so costly, should be useless, puzzled young John very much. But he kept his fancies to himself, inwardly resolving, however, to look at the thing closely the first opportunity he could get. The chance for this soon presented itself; for one day young John betook himself to Ballyclash to look after some business interests. It was a good time — old John observed — to take, as there was nothing hurrying to be done about the farm or buildings; but Fate, the mischief-maker, had ordained that this was to be a day of days to young John. As he sat in the open and front room of the little tavern, or public house, waiting for the man he was to see about a transfer of land, in steps a young fellow in his thirtieth year, or thereabouts. He attracted John's attention at once. This was not to be wondered at, for he did not belong to the *genus homo* of this locality. Ballyclash had no hand whatever in the forming of this young person. His step was brisk, his movements very quick but graceful, his clothing had an elegance quite beyond description; it seemed to be a part of him. He was handsome in countenance, and his eyes beamed with kindness and intelligence. He sat a short distance from John and called for some refreshment. John looked at him with astonishment and admiration.

"Sure," he thought, "this must be an Enniskillen man; such fruit niver grew on *our* trees."

The stranger seemed wrapped in his own meditations; he thoughtfully tapped his finger tips upon the table before him, looking, as it were, at his own thoughts with that dreamy, inward expression of the eyes which betokens deep consideration.

"Ah!" said John to himself, admiringly, "but his head is full of fine things! pleasant ones, too, mayhap!"

The concentration of John's gaze and observation made themselves felt at last upon his silent companion, for the latter, looking up suddenly, caught John's glance in all its intensity, before the boy had a chance to look the other way. The stranger gave a friendly smile, remarking, at the same time, that he thought everything was looking well through that part of the country. John felt at his ease instantly; the spontaneous kindness of the young fellow found a quick response within him.

In a few moments, with chairs drawn near each other, they fell into a lively conversation upon various matters, only interrupted by the appearance of the countryman John had been waiting for.

During John's conversation with his business friend, the stranger disposed of the refreshments he had ordered, and then, finding John disengaged, proposed that they should stroll out together. To this a glad assent was given. As they walked along the stranger talked as John had never heard any one talk before.

"Why," thought John, "the Priest is nothing to this man; he niver talked half so swately."

Under this magic tongue all things about them took a new meaning to John. He saw beauties in the landscape never seen before. He had a more realizing sense of the possibilities of life; even trifling things, unnoticed by him previously, acquired an interest under the comments and explanations of his new friend.

The stranger could not be insensible to the admiration he excited, or the close and flattering attention bestowed upon his every word.

"It seems to me," he said at length, "that I do all the talking, and don't give you a chance."

"What would be the use of it," answered John, "when I have nothing to say."

"Why should you have nothing to say?" asked the young man in a surprised tone.

"Because," replied John, "there may be many things to talk about, but I don't know how to do it. Howiver *you* can talk as beautiful as you do is a wonder to me."

The stranger laughed. "My friend," he said, "you have a splendid eye and head, you are naturally capable of a great deal, but it is evident that you have not studied—a little book knowledge, even a *little*, will help you to understand your own capabilities—you want learning."

John started! "You want to devote a few years of your life to the acquirement of knowledge. A young man's head is a storehouse, he must fill it from floor to rafter with good learning of all kinds. If he should not need the use of this learning at once, still it will brighten life for him; and when he is growing old, then he can draw upon all the treasures packed away in that head of his, knowing that life, with these at his disposal, means enjoyment of the best and highest kind."

The stranger spoke with enthusiasm. His cheek glowed, his eye flashed, his chest heaved. John felt to his heart's core that the "larnin'" so often spoken of in scorn before him had been basely belied.

Then he told his friend in faltering tones how much he would like to go to some place where this wonderful learning might be had.

The stranger, sympathetic and touched by the boy's earnestness, spoke to him of some good schools and colleges, at a distance from Ballyclash to be sure, but not beyond in price the ample means that John knew his father to be possessed of. Then they parted, the stranger saying that he would be returning that way again in a couple of weeks and would be pleased to see John, and know of his success in getting the old father to his ideas. This young person, whose chance acquaintance made so powerful an impression, John was destined never to see again. What determines us to the most important steps in life may be a chance word, a look, a trifling action. When the soil is ready, the conditions favorable, germination is very rapid. Thus the acquaintance of a day may exert a more powerful influence upon our hidden resolve than those with whom we come in constant contact. Through this young man John had voiced the longing of his heart, and was prepared, by the advice and encouragement of a mere stranger, to enter protest against the instructions of a lifetime. It has been written somewhere, that "there is nothing so catching as enthusiasm," and when that enthusiasm touches a hidden yet strong sentiment of your being, with what force it holds, or with what strength it impels you.

As John walked homeward from Ballyclash, he revolved the question as to the how, when and where he should propound to his father the important proposition for gaining this learning. The more he thought of it the more he dreaded the interview; he knew only too well the stubborness with which his father would cling to an idea which had been so deeply imbedded in his nature. A pet notion, a hobby, too, nursed through many years, until now it assumed proportions so great that it would be like tugging his father's disposition at the roots to advance such a thing to his serious consideration. With John it was this way:

he had of late felt the strange impulses natural to the age he had arrived at. He had crossed the threshold of manhood, that time when the soul, realizing its depths, and somewhat dimly its needs, reaches out for something better than has been its portion yet. Strong yearnings stirred within him; he felt as feels the explorer who stands upon the outskirts of the yet untrodden forest, sure of peril, *sure* of hardship, yet impelled to press forward by the irresistible desire to *know*. John felt that his had been a narrow world, that far beyond its little confines surged an ocean of life that he longed to traverse; that this mysterious "learning" was to be the key which should open the gate to all. As he sat at the simple supper table that evening with his father, mother and two sisters — happy little girls, much younger than John — he felt himself quite weighed down by thought. He stole a few furtive glances at his father's face, but saw nothing there which offered any inducement for him to unburden himself of that which lay nearest his heart. After a short conversation on the business of the day, the different members of the family plied knives and forks with diligence. Silence prevailed, broken only by occasional childish laughter from the girls. The mother, gentle soul, looked at John with some concern, for she, woman-like, felt that there must be something yet unspoken of.

John thought to himself, "I'd better not speak now. I'll take the night to think it over."

Long afterwards he could recall all the little incidents and sensations of that evening. He remembered that just before the sun went down a bird was singing so sweetly in a bush quite near the house, how the balmy wind was blowing through the open doors and windows, with the sweet scent of grass and flowers upon it ; the meadow stretching greenly out below the house, the little stream just beyond it, how peaceful it was ; there was a feeling of holiness in the air, as if every cloud, breeze, tree and bird joined in solemn vesper. Poor John, it was to be many years before his head would be pillowed in that peaceful home again, and then not him, but another quite different. man —careworn, tired, with the flush and hope of youth quite gone. It was late that night before slumber touched his eyelids, so tossed about by feverish anxiety as to what his father would say to him, that he regretted not having spoken to him in the early evening, and having the matter decided one way or the other. After some hours he slept at last— only to repeat his anxieties in dreams.

Early in the morning, as was their wont, the Malone family was astir, the busy mother preparing the meal, the little girls feeding the chickens, the old man and his son in the barn getting ready to go afield. " Well," thought John, " as soon as we ate the breakfast I'll spake to him, for I can't stand it this way any longer."

Breakfast being finished, the old man repaired to

the door-step to smoke his morning pipe before beginning his labors. John followed and sat near by in silent contemplation of his father's fine, though somewhat severe face. He could never remember a time when he found it so difficult to address him, but it was now "neck or nothing;" so he began, "Father I've been thinking there's something I'd like to spake till ye about."

"Well, spake away, bye," said the old man, smoking composedly.

"Then father," said John, "tell me this; have I iver in all my life asked you to give me, or do for me, anything worth the naming?"

The old man removed the pipe from his mouth and seemed to reflect.

"No, John!" he answered, "I can't rightly remember that there is; but," he said this quickly, a smile curling his lips, "if it's the young sorrel mare ye're wantin, she's yours. The mother told me that ye seemed to like the baste very well; so take her John, and welcome."

This good natured anticipation of what his father supposed to be his wishes left John more at a loss than ever how to proceed. In the meantime the mother had quietly stepped near the door, where she remained an unnoticed auditor of what transpired.

"Thank you kindly, father," said John, gravely, "but it was not the sorrel mare I thought of; what I want is to larn something. This is a big world, it's full of things to larn; there's a great world outside of Ballyclash, father!"

"To be sure! to be sure!" responded the old man, promptly; "you're right, boy, the birdlings will always spread wings as soon as they're able to. It's a change ye're wantin; ye want to see other places, and parts of the counthry, and you shall; there's your mother's brother down in Dublin, he'll be glad to welkim ye; go and see him; stir about a little; 'twill do ye good!"

"*No*, father, no!" said John, hastily; "you do not take my meaning; it's not thravel that I want, but 'larnin.' I want to go to some of those grand schools, where they tache everything! It's only lately come over me that I'm very ignorant. I want to be bettered in my mind father: I'm young yet, I can get a dale of larnin if I thry!"

After this outburst from John there was a long silence. The old man's face at first expressed blank amazement; then his brow puckered into frowns, a look of dark and deep determination overspread his countenance.

"This," he said slowly, "is what you want! Afther a lifetime of taching you the uselessness of it, afther hearing me tell you what I think about it, ye'll ask above all things for this! Well, then, here's my answer—I'll not give it to you! I lived a life through without such folly; you shall follow in my footsteps."

"Father," said John, reproachfully, "if you

were a poor man I'd not ask for this, but you have the manes. You own yourself this is the *first* time I iver asked ye for aught!"

The old man turned upon him a look of unqualified anger. "Ye have had your say, John, and I've had mine; there's no more about it, for I'll niver consint to such nonsense!" At this, laying down his half-smoked pipe, he walked away.

The boy felt quite convulsed with grief and anger. A sense of injustice surged within him. He had always been obedient; he had never till this day preferred a request of any importance. Why should his hopes and wishes be treated in this uncompromising manner? He took a hasty step inside the door; his mother stood there, he knew by her face she had heard all. "Mother," he exclaimed, "I'll do the thing I've set my heart on, if I have to cut through solid rock to get at it. I never wanted anything before as I want this. I'll go off alone, and make my way as best I can, but the *larnin* I'll get, if it takes me all my life to do it!"

"John," she cried, "think better of it; don't go away when your father has the heat of his anger on him; all will come right if you'll wait awhile!"

"There's that within me that wo'n't let me wait! I'll make my way to the seaport and sail for America; *there* a man may get what he wants, if he's willing to work for it. Good-bye, mother dear, you've always been the best of mothers to me, but

I must lave you now; I'll kiss the little sisters and go."

"My poor child," sobbed the mother, "don't go like this and break our hearts; sure!" she said this with sudden hope, "I've some money by me; take that and go to Dublin with it; there wait a little. As soon as your father's anger cools he'll send for you and promise all the larnin you want!"

"No, no, mother!" exclaimed John, with all his father's pride and stubbornness shining in his eyes, "I'll ask nothing more of him. I'll lave this counthry and strive for myself. I'm young and strong, and the sorrow of parting from you is all that holds me!"

"Then, John," she cried, "you'll take the money anyhow, for its sorra little ye'll get in the world without the payin' for it. Ye'll write to me by and by how all is with ye. Good-bye, dear! good-bye!"

John made a few hasty preparations for his journey; in less than half an hour he had turned his back on the old home, and with brimming eyes and heavy heart was trudging away.

Youth is the time when execution follows quickly on resolve. Inexperience is full of daring. Hope, the butterfly, just emerged from the chrysalis, with wings as yet unabraded, feels, in its freshness and beauty, its recent liberation from darkness and confinement, that it has long flights before it in the sunshine of life. So this young soul started on his life-voyage full of dreams never to be realized — expectations which could not be fulfilled.

He made his way to the nearest seaport. Finding that within a few days he could sail for America, he wrote some hasty lines to his mother, stating his intention, saying he would write her again from New York.

In those long-ago days, such a voyage seldom consumed less time than three months, often much longer. Long before this time had expired John regretted the hasty action he had taken. Thrown entirely into the society of strangers, and suffering for a while agonies of seasickness on his self-inflicted journey, he had time for plenty of reflection. He began to see that his mother was right in counselling him to go to Dublin for a period.

Changes of a similar nature took place in his father. For a few days the old man went about the farm very proud and sullen looking, pretending to take no notice or be conscious of John's absence; after a while he became affected by the grief which his wife could not conceal, and questioned her as to John's whereabouts. She answered truly that she did not know, for the news of John's sailing had not yet arrived. She had not the heart to mention to her husband the dreaded name "America." After a time the letter came; then, indeed, the father was disconsolate, for the thought that his son would take so extreme a step never entered his head.

It was too late now for regrets on either side. Months of journeying, and the broad Atlantic between them, rendered reconciliation of no avail. When John landed in New York, he found his Eldorado was nothing more than a dreadful mass of brick, mortar and stone, with babel sounds within it, with restlessness, and confusion everywhere; to the tired boy filled with memories of the fresh greenness of his rural home, it seemed at first a haunt of lunacy, and its population hurrying, scolding maniacs. He had little time, however, to mourn the change, for necessity forced him to take the first employment that presented itself. Understanding the care of horses he soon found occupation as a coachman, his obliging manners, youth, health and strength proving powerful recommendations.

After reaching New York he wrote his mother at once, confiding to her his very disagreeable impressions regarding America generally, with New York as a specimen; told her how he felt that he had been too hasty in his manner of leaving home, but he would try to secure that for which he left, and ended by sending his love and duty to his father.

Thus was finished that simple passage in John's life; then began for him its hand-to-hand struggle. With the tenacity of purpose inherent in his disposition, he commenced his efforts toward a liberal education. For a man employed all day in earning what would feed and clothe him, this was not a very easy matter, yet "free education," the proudest, truest boast of the American citizen, was there for the looking after, even for this poor son of Ireland. He found that by stating to his employer the nature of his desires he could procure lessons, also time for study, in the evenings. It was slow work, however; it took many months of steady application to make him feel that he had gained anything at all; study combined with work so filled in every moment of his time that it had one salutary effect,—it utterly precluded the possibility of being exposed to those temptations which beset a young man thrown entirely upon his own companionship and resources. With mind as well as time so entirely occupied, he had no taste for the low pleasures so often indulged in by men of his class; his intellect was so active, his greed for the beloved learning so intense, that months circled into a couple of years before any interests of a more absorbing character began to take the place of those with which he left Ireland. In the mean time his father wrote kindly, almost contritely, begging his return, telling him that he was willing to forego bygones, and allow him the boon he had asked. But pride, that powerful factor in all the evolutions of the human mind, forbade John to listen to these affectionate invitations. When at last a fair-faced girl, with whom his occupations sometimes brought him in contact, began to show by the unequivocal tokens known to women, her attachment for him, the cement which bound him to the new world was thoroughly formed. He promised, however, that in course of time he would return to visit his home, bringing with him one now dearer than all. Time was making many things clear to John; he saw that his father's estimate of learning as to its usefulness was in a crude way correct in the main; of course he felt even now, in this comparatively short time, that he possessed a certain superiority over his father, by reason of his enlarged knowledge and his broader views, but "learning," beyond a certain point, was certainly of little assistance to a man earning his livelihood — for *that*, qualities quite different from learning seemed to be required. John's strong practical tendencies led him inevitably to these deductions; his was the active form of intellect, which wished to put all it knew to direct use and result; the graces of learning seemed to him not strictly necessary. In poetic insight he was lacking; he found it difficult to place in his mind and store away that for which he might never have any real use. Even with all the outward adjuncts in the way of leisure and means, he would never become what is called a book-worm. In spite of these discoveries he kept steadily on; all things considered, he became possessed of a creditable amount of education. Then he met the young woman who was destined to be the partner of his struggles, hopes or failures; following this came months of beatitude. This earnest soul, moved to its depths by so strong a feeling, felt great capabilities stir within it.

Learning *had* been his mistress, she was so no longer; she should now become his tool and should aid the natural activity of his brain to produce a "home." Here in this new world he would build a nest; all that man could do to make that nest an Eden should be done by him. Under the stimulus of this powerful incentive his business talents displayed themselves. Always keen to see chances, where other men might pass by unnoticing, John put his quickness of perception to use. His first employer, at the end of a year and a half, changed his residence to one of the western cities, and John procured employment in a saloon as bartender. It may appear strange that a passion for learning should at last culminate in an occupation of this sort.

So great are the eccentricities of circumstance, that he who steps forth on the journey of life as a poet, may end in becoming the bright particular star of an ale-house; that one who essays the voyage in the stanchest craft ever built, with calm waters beneath him, with cloudless sky above him, may end his existence beneath a stormy sea, or starve upon a desert isle. John left home, friends, comparative affluence, to chase and secure the butterfly of his boyish fancy, fortunate only in the fact that his butterfly, when secured, did not prove a total illusion, and that it still retained some of its prismatic colors, which first allured him.

The truth, however, remained, that he became a bartender; a "slinger of drinks" for thirsty customers. The man who was proprietor of this particular saloon was a countryman of John's. He had, to speak his own language, "been keeping his eye on the young fellow." The keen business man saw that John's strength, sobriety, determination, would make him a powerful auxiliary in a business which required to the utmost good judgment. This new employer regarded the world as a place to make money in. Heretofore his bartenders seemed as fond of drinking as their customers proved to be; this was an inconvenience which sometimes led to serious and anti-money-making consequences. To correct this he engaged John, at a salary too which seemed to the young Irishman almost munificent. All went well; John soon adapted himself to his new occupation, proving much more useful than his employer had hoped for.

In addition to his fine physical build, John had qualities of mind somewhat exceptional. He exercised a strong, though unobtrusive control over his fellow men; he had that inborn power by which some men make themselves a law and influence in the council chamber, or on the battle field.

Keen perceptions, good judgment, total abstinence from the fiery fluids which make so much of this life a hell, made him invaluable in his new line of work. After a couple of years his employer offered him a share in the business for the purpose of retaining him, as rival firms had not failed to observe John's qualities and make tempting offers of higher salary to secure him. It ended in John's being a controlling power where he had begun a poor hireling.

In a pecuniary point of view, John had remarkable fortune; all his ventures turned to money. This pleased him; not because he had anything miserly in his nature, but that money-making was actually an instinct with him; he could no more help wanting to make it than a bee can help wanting to make honey.

John married; he was busy and happy as the day was long, finding the months circling into years all too quickly now. After a few years of married life he found that a disappointment awaited him. At first he did not notice or care, he was so happy with Mary; his home was the Eden he had planned; but no childish laughter sounded in it, no baby hands caressed his face. All he had undertaken to do he had prospered in beyond his hopes in many respects; this one happiness was denied him. His nature was far too generous to let the young wife see that he considered this an affliction.

The wheel of time rolled on, bringing its sure changes. When a lull came in his busy life, John took his wife home to Ireland with him for a visit to the old people. His sisters had grown out of his recollection now; both married, one had a child clinging about her knees; his father was getting old and failing, the dear mother whom he had left so young and fresh-looking was white-headed now. The visit had more of sadness than joy in it, for John, in his preoccupations, had not realized what the inevitable changes of the years would bring.

He had formed a fashion of thinking of those at home as looking just as he had left them. What had been his country seemed a strange land to him now. They begged him to remain, but he could not bring himself to do it. He would come again after a few years and see them, he said, then once more turned his face toward America. The ceaseless wheel of Time rolled on, grinding its victims as it rolled. John's business partner was laid beneath the sod. John became sole proprietor of the establishment.

After a time his wife showed signs of failing health. The doctors advised a change of air. John had heard a great deal of Chicago's business opportunities: he sold out in New York, gathering his household goods about him, and moved westward.

Now the wheel of time was making heavy marks across John's brows, changing the rich brown of his hair and beard to iron gray. Some years after his removal to Chicago he was called to Ireland by his father's impending death. The old man craved to see him once more, and have John's help in settling his worldly affairs. The old mother, who had lost one of her daughters, was so broken-hearted that John begged her after the father's death to return with him to America and make her home there. She would not leave the country of her birth — the graves of her dead. John, by his father's death, received quite an addition to the worldly wealth he had already amassed. This addition, being mostly in lands and improvements thereon, he did not care to touch during his mother's life, as he could not bear to make sales or changes which might distress her.

At the time our second chapter opens, the "ould" man alluded to by Bridget and Annie was the young John whose fortunes we have been following. The beloved wife whose destiny had been joined to his in early manhood was slowly fading away. Some years previously John and his wife met and befriended Annie; her little family had drifted westward, and soon after arriving in Chicago her parents died, worn out by hardships in their advancing years. John's wife, on hearing of the troubles of these Irish people, sought them out. Being kind and charitable, she gave Annie a home with herself and John, after the death of her parents, whenever the young woman was out of employment, which was often, as Annie hated to work for "hire." She did not possess the sturdy independence by which Bridget dignified labor; hers was a disposition which loved to lean against some stronger nature. She was one of those human inconsistencies we sometimes meet, totally lacking in that subtle understanding which knows just where truth ends and falsehood begins. All those she came to know found themselves soon after helping her to struggle against her difficulties, lifting her bodily as it were over the hard spots in life, and feeling well rewarded by a few tear-drops from the melancholy eyes, or a murmured "Thank you," as she drooped her graceful head.

Bridget and Jack had been married about three years. The union proved eminently happy; not a ripple disturbed the sea of their contentment until the fatal days whose events we are about to record. A year after Bridget's marriage, John Malone's wife died; then Annie felt herself orphaned a second time. She spent a great deal of her spare time now with Bridget, watching with interest the comforts and happiness of the young married couple, feeling toward them as a sister would.

After the death of the old man's wife his home was for the time broken up. Bridget's house was now Annie's main reliance in times of sickness and discouragement, these discouragements generally resulting in Annie's throwing up her employment for the time being. At present she was working as second girl in a very stylish mansion on Michigan avenue, where, the labor being light, and having the charm of a little novelty, she was for the nonce contented.

Bridget had married a man who in respect to education was vastly her superior. He was a smart man at his business, too, and commanded a good salary. Bridget wasn't half as wise as her better half in a book learning way, but yet greatly beyond him in good, practical "common sense," and in that comely head of hers she could, as she expressed it, "figure out many things." She realized to the full Jack's youth, smartness and activity. She also knew that these things might not *last*. She had been brought up in a manner which made her appreciate money, its powers and the necessity for it. She said, "A time of sickness and death may come. I must save and be careful, so that Jack and the child may not want."

A little one-year-old Jack Rooney was now crawling about the floor. So Bridget kept a close watch of the financial situation, and after constituting herself paymaster and general manager of all expenditures, saw to it that at the end of every month there was always a surplus to be put in bank. Quite early in their married life she had insisted that they should open a savings account, this account being opened in Jack's name, "as," argued Bridget to herself, "it ought to be, for sure it's always puttin' money *in* and not takin' it *out* that I'm afther! I never want to draw a cent of it without consulting Jack, for why should I care to spend anything without asking *him* what he thought of it?" So the Rooney family, up to this date, had jogged on very contentedly indeed.

Bridget's housekeeping was the pride of Jack's life, her capacity for saving filled him with astonishment and admiration, for this was a faculty Jack himself did not possess; in fact he was a jovial, light-hearted fellow, held in high esteem by his young men friends and adored by all his numerous relatives. On this day, where our story again picks up the fortunes of Bridget and Jack, poor Bridget had received a terrible revelation. It was a day devoted to a general rush of housecleaning, of getting odds and ends together, of having matters tidied up and made ready for an event not so very far distant. Late in the afternoon, after the work of reconstruction in the household department had come to a close, Bridget happened to be looking for some garments in an upper drawer of the bureau, when her eyes fell on a little book. It was the bank book. Bridget smiled, then giving a tired sigh, said to herself, "Well, then, I'll sit me down to rest a bit, and look the book over."

It must be admitted that Bridget took more pleasure in looking this book over than Jack ever had in perusing the wildest work of fiction.

These two natures, Jack's and Bridget's, though so widely different in many respects, amalgamated well; she regarding his higher intellectual attainments with reverence; he considering this "common sense" element of her's the most desirable thing in the world.

Thus poor Bridget took the bank book in her hand without the slightest misgiving. Her faith in Jack's integrity was so perfect, she never thought of going to any considerable expenditure without consulting him, and supposed, poor simple dear, that he would do likewise by her. She had not learned yet that this rule between husband and wife often works only one way. As she turned the leaves of the little book, a look—at first of surprise—flashed over her face, then incredulity— But no! it could not be—she looked again and again to assure herself; yes, there it was. Jack had actually drawn out twenty-five dollars at one fell swoop from the sacred book, and had never mentioned the fact to his wife. But was it recent; perhaps he had scarcely had time to remember to speak to her about it; she looked again, it was dated two weeks back. Her black eyes flashed—so the book had been removed, this amount drawn, the book quietly returned to its usual place, and not one word said to her.

"Very well, Master Jack," she muttered, "It's something I'll be saying to ye."

As the shades of night were falling on this unfortunate day, Jack was wending his way briskly along Halsted street to his home; he had some packages in his hand, little dainties for Bridget and the child. His heart was bright with anticipation of the happy evening awaiting him. In fancy he saw Bridget busied about the neat kitchen preparing the supper. Jack enjoyed these suppers with all the zest of youth and health. He fancied, too, the chubby face of the beloved little Rooney freshly scrubbed to bid him welcome, and the fat dimpled fingers clasped about his own. "Ah!" thought Jack, "it's the happy man I am, with such a wife and child. Was ever anyone more blest. I think I can see those big eyes of hers when I tell her the news about Annie; but sure I'll not be too sudden in the telling; these women are queer creatures anyhow. It might spoil the supper. I'll keep it to myself till the eatin's over and the child in bed, for my Bridget's that kind-hearted that there'll be no holding her when she knows this thing."

Thus musing, he reached his own doorway. He felt somewhat surprised to hear no rush of footsteps to meet him as he opened the door; the hallway was lighted, but very still. Jack had a sensitive nature; the chill of impending trouble seemed to fall upon him, and he opened the inner door leading to the living room in a hurry and with some alarm. There sat Bridget in a rocking chair —her face pale, her eyes dilated; in a corner of the room the little Rooney was whimpering distressfully. The supper table was set, but the air of festivity and welcome, which always attended this simple meal with the Rooney family, was totally wanting. Jack stood in the doorway, a picture of astonishment. "For God's sake, Bridget!" he cried, "what has happened that you look like that? Has the child hurt himself?"

He darted to the corner, catching the child up in his arms. The little fellow sobbed loudly and clung to his father. The truth is, that since Bridget's discovery of Jack's treachery about the bank book, the young Rooney had received some most unmerited slaps and cross words, he being the only present outlet for his mother's injured feelings.

Jack turned to Bridget for an explanation; she rose to her feet, bestowing upon him a look which might have withered him. "Jack Rooney!" she said, "you're a miserable scamp! a low, deceiving fellow, *you* are, to come home to me, your wife, with smiles and pleasant words afther what you've done. It's ashamed you should be to look me in the face!"

Jack *did* look her in the face, however, with an air of bewilderment which was almost absurd.

"After what I've done!" he repeated. At this point Jack took a sort of rapid moral inventory; his sins, so far as he could recall in the hurry of the mind, did not seem so great. To be sure, his memory sometimes served him tricks; he forgot occasionally embassies that Bridget sent him on, or trifles that she commanded him to bring home— especially if it was something for himself. It couldn't be that she thought he had been drinking, for this weakness, easily condoned in an Irishman, was something Jack was not addicted to. Of course he sometimes took a friendly glass with the boys, but never to an extent to unbalance him.

"Bridget!" he said, "what have I done that you talk to me like this? Why should I be ashamed to look you in the face? It's a pretty welcome you're giving a poor fellow after his hard day's work, and me that was so happy in the thoughts of you and the child. Here's what I brought you." He threw his small packages violently on the table. "But I suppose you'll not care for them since you're so angered at me."

"The way *you* talk," said Bridget, passionately, "one would think the blame was on my side instead of yours. But there's one comfort to my soul, as our Lady knows; it is, that *I* never deceived *you*, Jack. I never did anything but what I spoke to *you* about it. I—I loved you too much to ever want to have any *secrets* from you. I'd never be mean enough to serve you any dirty, deceitful tricks, as you have me!"

"Deceitful tricks!" shouted Jack, now thoroughly aroused in his turn by what he conceived to be unmerited reproaches. "How dare you say such things! How have I deceived you? It's lovin' you too much I've been, wastin' my heart upon you, and now you fly into unreasonable tempers with me! Oh! Mother of God!" he groaned, "is this what I hurried home for?"

"Listen to me," said Bridget with deadly earnestness. "You'll not deny the work of your own hands, I'm thinkin'! You'll not tell me that you didn't, like a sly sneak, go to the bank without one word to *me*, and draw out twenty-five dollars? Come now!" she continued, her eyes flashing ominously, "you'll not deny that, will you?"

"Is that all?" cried Jack. "Is that all you're making this fuss about?"

He looked absolutely relieved. The mistaken man evidently regarded this little breach of confidence as a trifle. Bridget gazed upon him with a sort of strained calmness.

"Very well, Mr. Rooney," she said, "since you think so lightly of it, you'll please inform me what you spent the money for?"

Jack passed his hand over his flushed forehead in a confused way.

"What I spent it for?" he repeated. "Oh! I spent it with the boys; sure they're always kind to me and free with me, and it isn't stingy I'd be having them think me."

"With the boys!" screamed Bridget; "he tells me that he spent it with the *boys!* Oh! Blessed Mary, listen to that! when I, the wife of his bosom, toiled and pinched to save it! I, the mother of his children!"

This was not quite correct, only *one* little Rooney adorned the social circle, though indications might suggest that another would soon be added, but Bridget was in no humor to choose her words.

"I must slave and worry," she continued, "wearing my fingers to the bone to save, and he sneaks away with it all to spend on the boys! Oh! Oh!"

At this juncture loud sobs choked her utterance. Jack caught her in his arms and tried to soothe her, whilst the little one, aware that something of an earthquake nature was progressing, added to the distraction by vigorous howling. After about fifteen minutes of this work the storm showed signs of subsiding; the young husband, quite contrite now, vowed never to be guilty of such a thing again. To do him justice, he had not *meant* any breach of confidence; it was a matter of sheer carelessness, and a habit of generosity among his comrades, formed in those early days before he and Bridget became one.

Something like peace settled upon the small group once more; the child, smiling with cheeks yet wet with tears, began to prattle and investigate the parcels. Bridget placed the evening meal upon the table, showing occasional traces of the storm by a tumultuous heaving of the bosom and broken sobs. Jack tried to eat, but these indications of Bridget's yet unsettled feelings filled him with dread lest another eruption should take place. A bright thought struck him; he would remove all remembrance of the late unpleasantness by giving the news he *had* intended to surprise her with under happier auspices. Jack saw that delay might be dangerous. Nothing could hurt the flavor of the supper *now;* so he began.

"Bridget, darlin'! it's something strange I'll be tellin' ye. Something *very* surprising!"

"What may that be?" said Bridget, listlessly; "it's feared I am that there's little can interest me *now*, Jack!"

"Don't talk *that* way, mavourneen," said Jack, coaxingly. "Sure you're the light of my life. It kills me to see you feeling badly. Then I'll tell you. I met old Malone this afternoon, and he told me that this day two weeks he and Annie will be married."

Bridget started as if she had received an electric shock. She sprank to her feet, ran across the room, and took down a shawl hanging there.

"What are you about?" Jack said in alarm. "Where are you going?"

"I'm going to see Annie this minute. I'll save her from such madness. To think of her marrying a man old enough to be her father. Oh, Jack, it is dreadful. It must not be."

"But, Bridget," he remonstrated, "you can't go so far after all you've suffered this night."

"It isn't far," she answered, "for she'll be at Mrs. Corrigan's to-night, and that's but four blocks away. Let me go, Jack dear," continued the impulsive Irishwoman. "Let me go and talk to her. Let me show her what a wicked thing it is for her to do. Take care of the child, it isn't long I'll be away."

Before Jack could interpose another word, she had thrown the shawl over her head, was out of the door, and hastening down the street. After traversing a number of blocks quite unnoticed, a woman with a shawl over her head being a familiar figure in those thoroughfares, she halted before one of the dingy looking habitations, indigenous to that region. Entering without ceremony the front door, she pushed her way into a low ceilinged room, where a number of women sat sewing and chatting together.

"Good evening to you all," said Bridget, hurriedly; "where is Annie?"

One of the women nodded toward a door at the back of the room. Bridget opened it, and found herself alone with the girl she had come to see. They stood looking at each other for a few moments without speaking. Each had an intuition of what was passing in the mind of the other. Annie turned very pale, and seemed to brace herself as if for a struggle. Bridget spoke first.

"Annie," she exclaimed, as her breath came in heavy gasps, "Jack has told me something that I don't want to believe is true. It surely can't be that you are wild and wicked enough to intend marrying a man old enough to be your father?"

"Yes," answered Annie, sullenly, "I do. He's a

good man,—one who is willing and able to take care of me. I'm *tired* of living the wretched life of kicking about from one service to another. I'll marry the old man and be my own mistress!"

"Oh!" cried Bridget, "you only look at it *one* way Annie, and there's two sides to everything. You harm the man you marry as well as yourself when you wed without *love*."

"Love," said Annie, angrily, "who bothers about *love?* There's no such expectation. Malone is too sensible a man to look for it. He knows it's not in nature. He only wants what I can give, which is duty and faithfulness. It's no use talking, Bridget, my mind's made up to it."

"You're just like a child walking in the dark," said her companion anxiously. "You don't realize what you are undertaking. There's nothing but love can take you through some of the trials of married life.

Then remembering the stormy scene at her own fireside that night, she added passionately: "Be warned in time, Annie! Go to Malone; tell him all about the young fellow you loved in the old country, and ask him if he wants a woman whose heart belongs to another. Be *honest* with him. He's too good a man to take you unless you're perfectly willing."

"I'll do nothing of the sort," said Annie. "I *am* willing, for I'll never see Dave again, so why should there be any fuss about it. As for telling the old man, there's small need; the past is dead and done with. He never needs to know. This day two weeks we shall be married, and you and Jack are bidden to the wedding."

All Bridget's reasonings and entreaties proved futile. With a heavy heart she soon afterwards retraced her steps homeward.

∗

When John Malone began to think of taking Annie to wife, which was only a few weeks before the marriage was decided upon, he thought of the matter from quite an unlover-like point of view. The truth was, that with his Mary he buried the one love of his life. This in his inmost soul he knew. If Annie had not been left a charge and trust upon him, he would never have even dreamed of marrying again. His wife, upon her dying bed, commended Annie to his care. The girl had been a companion to the sickly woman for a number of years. John's wife, with the keen insight the dying seem to possess, was aware that a girl of Annie's temperament was peculiarly liable to temptation and misfortune. The girl's utter loneliness drew strongly upon the sympathies of the old woman, so she solemnly charged her husband to care for the orphaned girl, and let no harm befall her that he could avert.

After his wife's demise John's home became a sorry place indeed. The old woman employed by him as housekeeper devoted all the energy she had to drawing her monthly stipend and getting through her daily duties with as little work as possible. Annie, whose lively step and pretty figure had been such an adjunct to the home-like influences, did not stop in his house at all now. Under the circumstances it might have seemed an impropriety for her to do so. She gave most of her spare time to Bridget and some of her other female friends. Thus the old man, whose home life had been so much to him, became very lonely. He had his books, his pipe, his business calculations, but with no sympathetic presence near these things lost their charm.

It must be confessed that months before *he* thought of such a thing, Annie had taken into very serious consideration the idea of marrying him, and by her adroit remarks first brought such a thought to him. She would go to him with little tearful complaints about her hard destiny. Sometimes she would blushingly tell him, with a touch of scorn, too, that such and such a young fellow had asked her in marriage. "But," she would say, "no young jackanapes would ever get *her!* If she *ever* married, she would want a steady, sensible man of mature years, whom she could look up to and respect; that she despised these young fellows with their conceit and selfishness."

Now Malone knew, by what his wife had told him, that Annie had refused several offers of marriage. Not knowing anything of her love passages in the old country, he came to the conclusion that Annie was likely incapable of that passion in its romantic phases. So, when the notion of marrying her began to assume tangible shape, he saw no particular objection on account of the disparity of years. She would of course outlive him. He could leave her a handsome provision to maintain her in comfort all her life. He had no near relative now in the wide world except his old mother, soon to be gathered to her loved dead. In marrying the girl he would wrong no near ties, but on the other hand, he would make a friendless woman happy and independent, besides giving himself a reviving interest in life.

The native kindness of his temperament asserted itself. The unfortunate, poor, lonely girl had the strongest claims upon the generosity of his disposition. Had she been happy — well to do — he would never have given her a second look or idea. Malone brought to this union the feelings of an indulgent father toward the girl he married. In spite of Bridget's prognostications, the early part of the wedded life passed along with the greatest smoothness.

Something strange had happened three weeks before the marriage. Annie never mentioned this thing to Bridget. It chanced that Annie, on the death of her mother, had stored the little household effects owned by the old lady in Malone's house. Time slipped by, and Annie had almost forgotten these trifling belongings of her mother's until three weeks before the wedding, when Malone asked her to go over the house with him, and see what refurnishing she would like to have done, for the old man knew that a young woman would prefer to have things bright and modern about her. This house itself was a substantial brick one, owned by Malone, who, foreseeing Chicago's possible growth, had purchased some good pieces of realty.

He said to Annie, "You'll have to go over the place from attic to cellar, for it all needs looking after.

In a small attic room two hair-covered trunks, studded with brass nails, stood in a corner, while odd articles of old-fashioned furniture filled most of the remaining space. Annie clasped her hands, the tears stood in her eyes. "Poor old Ireland!" she said, "how it brings everything back to me to see these things again. I'll take a look through them before they're moved." So after Malone left her, she knelt down by the old trunks, and for the first time since her mother's death looked over their contents.

It is sad work at best to handle the garments once worn by one passed away from earth forever; to lift the trinkets one by one, once so treasured by the dead. Many a sad token of her childhood and early girlhood met Annie's eyes; then she came upon a small package of letters. They looked quite yellow with time and their long incarceration in the mouldy old trunk. She turned the packet carelessly in her hand. "It's best," she thought, "to burn written things, they are no longer any use, but mayhap I'd better look them through." So she untied the string about them. She found them to be mostly scrawling letters written to the father and mother in her school-girl days by herself; then an envelope which seemed literally covered by black stamping, which denoted that it had been forwarded through many postoffices.

Annie was puzzled, the address was to her mother, the envelope was dirty and ragged; this, too, was the condition of the letter it enclosed. She opened the enclosure with trembling fingers and an odd, faint feeling; she looked at the signature. It was that of a stranger to her—a man; the letter ran thus:

NEW YORK.

DEAR ANNIE,—A friend of mine, a helper here in the hospital, writes this for me. They tell me here that I am dying, so I must try and get a line to you before I am no more. I came to this country to search for you, and claim your promise to be my wife. Your people had moved to some other city, I could find no trace of you. I hunted everywhere, and worried so that at last I fell sick. Have been in this hospital for many months.

Last night the doctors told me I couldn't hold out much longer, so, darling, this is my last good-bye. I trust to God and the Blessed Mary that this letter may reach you. Take with it the love of him who was yours till death.

(Signed) DAVE.

Annie's tears fell fast. He *had* been true to her after all. He had not forgotten her or learned to love another woman, as she supposed. Why her mother concealed this letter from her, unless to save her from pain, she could not imagine; but here, yellowed by age and travel, the proof of David's fealty lay in her hand.

After the first burst of grief had subsided, a strange calmness came over her. If she had experienced any shrinking from the marriage with Malone, that was over now. Dave gone forever, it mattered very little with whom she spent her life. In telling Bridget she would never see Dave again, she told what this letter had conveyed to her. From this time forth he was a recollection, no longer a living hope.

Annie had an ease-loving nature, though she gave careful supervision to her household matters, and kept Malone's home delightfully neat and charming for him. She enjoyed to the full extent the many accessories to comfort with which he provided her. She became plump and rosy-cheeked, her face beamed with health. At last some of Bridget's rugged cheerfulness seemed to dawn upon her. Malone regarded this improvement with delight. He would look upon her proudly and say inwardly: "I am father, brother, and husband to her, she shall henceforth have all in me, her path shall be as easy as money and carefulness can make it."

When Bridget would run over for a friendly call upon them, Annie would get her into a corner and say, archly: "How do you think the old man gets on with his young wife? Does it look like an unhappy marriage?"

Then Bridget, smiling, would have to admit that it did not. Thus a year slipped by, and a happiness Malone had never dreamed could be his came upon him — a baby boy was added to the household. Here in his old age came something to love and cherish beyond all else; a boy, to inherit the worldly gain, the houses and lands he had accumulated.

It seemed as though he would never tire of looking at the young, fair-haired mother with her baby in her arms. It was indeed a pretty picture, and Annie's devotion to her child, and pride in it, lovely to behold.

Annie and Malone would call on Jack and Bridget, and compare notes on the relative charms of the young Rooneys and infantile Malone. Then Jack would pinch Bridget's cheek and say, "See now, mavourneen, what came of all your fretting; they're just as happy as we are!"

But Bridget would shake her head gravely, and say, "No, Jack, not quite."

All this while Malone was busy and successful. He had purchased a good bit of ground a few minutes walk from one of the finest parks, and had now in course of construction upon it a large brick building with stone facings. This building was high and imposing looking, the lower story finished up in fine style as a saloon, the upper stories arranged in elegant apartments. These he intended to have Annie furnish to suit her taste as soon as the building was completed.

He argued that this place was a good investment in real estate, that it would be an excellent business stand, as it stood near what would be the terminus of the cable road, and a place connecting with the dummy line and electric road. Added to these advantages, the location was very healthy, which would make it just the thing for Annie and the babe, particularly in the heats of summer, when the fresh winds from the prairie west of him would refresh them, and the contiguous greenness and shade of the park be equal to having an elaborate flower garden of their own. He often drove Annie out to see what progress the building made, unfolding to her during these drives many plans for her future happiness.

"As soon as we get settled there," he would say, "you shall have a nice little carriage and pony of your own. In that big house you must have additional servants, Annie, for my little wife must not work too hard. Then too, you need a stout young girl to help with the care of the child. He's getting to be such a big fellow."

At this Malone would gaze adoringly upon his child, then sigh to think how in nature it could never be his lot to see that child grow to manhood.

Malone was still in robust health, stout of figure, red cheeked, bright eyed; his hair and beard of iron gray rather improved than detracted from a countenance which had always been handsome.

His look of capacity and honest fearlessness was as pleasing as ever. He retained that controling power and magnetism which made him so universally liked in his younger days.

Time passed uneventfully on. The fine house near the park was finished, all was got in readiness for its occupants. As soon as they moved into it comfortably, there was a grand house warming, to which all the Irish friends were invited. You may be sure Bridget and Jack appeared there, dressed in their best to do honor to such an occasion; in fact Bridget was so gay in her new gown and red ribbons, that Jack—sly fellow—whispered to her that he "was falling in love with her again," whereat Bridget pinched his ear and bade him mind his manners. The young Malone was brought out and exhibited to the admiring glances of many old Irish ladies, who pronounced him the "finest child" for miles around, and then drank deeply to his future health and happiness. This young scion of the house was now strong on his legs, running about the fine apartments of the new mansion with a liveliness which filled his father with admiration and caused the young mother some alarm. She declared that for mischief there couldn't be a child on earth to match him.

Annie had the carriage and pony now, the extra servants, in fact every necessity and comfort that the old man could devise for her.

⁎

A woman who was now a part and parcel of Malone's household was named Nora Nolan. She was ostensibly the cook, but wherever Nora went, she made herself something more than she was called. Though termed cook — in itself a profession which is growing in respect, since so many aspire, and so few attain proficiency in this accomplishment — Nora was the universal eye of the establishment. Her senses of order, cleanliness and economy, being fully equal to her culinary ability, made a strong combination in one individual. She was, as she herself was wont to say when occasion required, "A woman not to be trifled with."

In personal appearance she was not much, unless wrinkles can be counted as adornments, she was small, thin, and decidedly old. No one in looking at her could fancy a time when she might have been young, or even passably good looking. From this diminutive woman issued a voice so grandly deep, so like the first solemn roll of an organ in some dark and lofty church, that the unused listener invariably started and looked about in bewilderment. Nora's voice, added to her tremendous will power, made her undisputed mistress in any kitchen where she took up her abiding place. She was known as *Mrs.* Nolan. Young and irreverent persons sometimes hinted a doubt that a *Mr.* Nolan had ever existed except in Nora's imagination, that is, a Nolan married to Nora. Fancy had to be wild indeed to bring Nora to the mind as a blushing bride during any period of her life.

These hints were never breathed to Mrs. Nolan herself, no living soul had the courage to do that; these doubts gained color from the fact that it was only an average of twice a year that Nora ever mentioned the defunct Nolan. These periods— the Fourth of July holiday and Christmas week— being the only times when Nora ever relaxed her silent dignity, for she was a woman of few words, as if, knowing the power of her voice, she was saving it. At these times she was wont to seek a slight exhilaration in the "flowing bowl," then she would shed a few tears and make some guttural remarks about that "poor, dead, dacent man Nolan," then, shaking her head mournfully as if to imply some mighty romance if she would only choose to tell it, retire into the silent realms of thought.

She had been a faithful ruler in all Malone's domestic affairs up to the death of his first wife, that is, dating from the taking up their residence in Chicago. Malone used to say laughingly that she must be a strictly Chicagoan growth, one of those mushroom anomalies that the famous city can boast of. Nora's antecedents being shrouded in mystery so dense and silence so impenetrable, certainly gave plausibility to this theory. When John's wife was buried Nora disappeared with this speech—a long one for her—to John: "Good-bye, Misther Malone; it would be improper for a lone widdy to be livin' in your house now." With this farewell, pronounced slowly in her awful voice, she vanished and was seen no more by Malone till after his second marriage.

This shows conclusively that Mrs. Nolan had a strong sense of propriety, though she need not have feared the breath of scandal, her appearance quite precluded the possibility of even the veriest trifler ever speaking of her in such a connection. Mrs. Nolan was heard to say once—shortly after this, when the "flowing bowl" had affected her otherwise stately reasoning powers—that she had taken the only proper step left to a lonely woman like her, and she felt sure that poor, dacent man Nolan would smile in his grave, God rest him, to know she had done right!

One morning, a few weeks after Annie and Malone had been married, the cook, a stout, red cheeked Irishwoman, ran into the dining-room almost breathless, crying out, "Oh! Mrs. Malone, there must be a crazy woman in the kitchen, a little tiny thing, like a dried leaf she is, with the most dreadful voice in the world. She ran in at the door, which was standing open to let the smoke out. She grabbed the skillet from my hand and said, 'Stand aside, you miserable thing, you're ruining these pancakes in the frying!' and there she is, turning the cakes over and browning them as if she was the lord of everything."

At this Malone began to laugh. "It must be Nora," he said, and straightway repaired to the kitchen. The instant Nora caught sight of him, she waved him back with a lofty gesture of her hand, saying in her unapproachable voice, "Wait till I serve the breakfast."

From this moment Nora established herself in her old capacity of cook *par excellence*, and general manager of the running machinery of that part of the housework which pertains to what is called its drudgery. From the minute of her advent, order, quietness and perfect service reigned.

Annie, knowing Nora's thorough value in these respects, was right glad to have her firmly enthroned in the kitchen. When they moved into the handsome new residence, Nora of course went with them. Her management and industry made the working part of the new home as noiseless and complete as any one could desire. Thus Mrs. Nolan again became a "power in the land." With such a dragon—albeit a small one—as Nora to guard his domestic treasures, with Annie and the boy in perfect health, with his business matters thriving, Malone had only one pressing anxiety just then: this was nothing more or less than his difficulty in securing a bartender who could be relied upon. Owing to his varied and scattered business interests, frequent absences of days, sometimes weeks, at a time from his saloon, made it imperative that he should leave these matters in the hands of some one who could be depended upon.

He would say to Annie, "If I could have the good luck to get a man in the bar-room as trustworthy as Nora is in the kitchen, I'd be in clover."

It was now about the middle of December, and Malone was obliged to go to New York on a matter of pressing importance. Often as he had performed these journeys, he could not remember to have had such an intensely anxious feeling as that which now beset him. His mind naturally reverted to the inefficiency of the man in charge of the saloon business.

"If," he thought, "I had some good man in place of that careless Joe, it might not fret me so much just now to leave home. However, I'll look about among my old friends in New York, and see if they can furnish me a man worth his salt."

He did not confide to Annie his unusual depression and anxiety, thinking that it might worry her, but the evening prior to his departure he made an expedition to the kitchen, where, finding Nora alone, he said to her with great earnestness,

"I'm off to-morrow, Nora, on a journey. You're the only one on top of earth I have enough faith in to leave my wife and boy in care of. Look after them well, and the blessing of God be on you." Nora took one of his large hands in her little shrivelled palms, and pressing it kindly, answered in tones low for her, "I'll *die*, sir, ere harm shall come to them. Be quite aisy in your mind on that score."

Then John felt somewhat comforted. When Nora made this promise she did so with her whole soul, for there was no living being so reverenced by her as John Malone was. His thorough goodness had penetrated to the depths of her erratic mind like an all-pervading essence, and the one fine quality of her strange brain — a dog-like devotion and tenacity of purpose to aid the object of her regard — made her promise to *die* ere harm should befall her charge — a literal truth, to be proved to the uttermost if necessary.

Despite Malone's anxieties all went well, even the shiftless Joe developing better qualities under the responsibility imposed upon him than could have been expected.

Annie passed the time in John's absence by driving over more frequently than usual in her neat little phaeton to call on Jack and Bridget, by adorning the pretty sitting-room with some fancy articles of her own manufacture designed to surprise her husband on his return, and playing with her child, who, with his rosy cheeks, golden curls and pretty features, was what Nora declared "A angel! like those painted around the altar!"

Thus time passed till the evening of John's return, previously announced by telegraph to his wife; then great activity could be noted in the handsome new building. Nora's efforts in the way of supper that night would have tempted an anchorite. Annie and the child appeared in bright, new garments; good-for-nothing Joe gave an extra polish to the glasses; even Kitty — Nora's faithful, and it must be confessed often terrified, coadjutor — donned a new gown with snowiest of aprons. All shone out bright, cheerful and welcoming.

The instant Malone arrived the observant Kitty saw that he was not alone. A young man, tall and slender, was with him.

"Mrs. Nolan," cried Kitty, excitedly, "sure the masther has a gintleman wid him. I can't exactly see his face, but it's handsome he is, I know!"

Mrs. Nolan regarded the giddy assistant with gloomy silence. John, leaving the stranger with Joe, was already up-stairs exchanging greetings with Annie, and smothering the boy with caresses.

After a little time he said, "I 'most forgot to tell you, Annie dear, the good luck I've had at last. I've secured a man to help me here that's after my own heart. True us gold he is, and steady as the sun. Oh! you rascal" — this to the young Malone — "you needn't be searching my pockets for the Christmas presents; they're in a big bag down stairs. I think, Annie, it was good I could get home in time for Christmas with you. It seems to me," he continued, jokingly, "that I'll have to give the new barkeeper to you for your Christmas box, Annie!"

"I know by that nonsense, John, that it's some extravagant thing you've been buying for me," answered Annie, laughing, "How often must I tell you that you shouldn't deck a foolish woman like myself with jewels!"

John's eyes twinkled with pleasure. "Never mind!" he said, "if there's aught else for you, you'll not see it till to-morrow morning."

When supper was over John went to the kitchen and recommended the stranger to Nora's kindness. "Feed him well, Nora!" he said. "He's a good young fellow, and a countryman of ours."

On returning to the sitting room he said: "This young chap that I picked up in New York is poor and lonely, Annie; he has not kith or kin this side of the Atlantic. He tells me that he has some friends here who came over before he did, but he has never been able to find them. I am sorry for him. He seems very sad for such a young man. My old friends spoke highly of him as being steady and industrious. I'll have him up by and by and introduce him to you. How thankful I am to find that you and the boy kept so well in my absence. Do you know," he added, tenderly, "that I found it harder to leave you both *this* time than ever before? But my mind's easy now. I'm hoping," he continued, his thoughts again reverting to the other subject, "to help this young fellow along if he proves what I look for; so we'll treat him sociably, for he's not quite the common sort, like that senseless Joe."

John being a reticent man, this was a good deal for him to say at one time, but Annie was not listening very intently, for her mind was occupied by lively speculations as to what manner of Christmas present John had brought her. She knew by past experiences that his generosity was equal to any tax his affections might put upon it. A woman who was young, healthy, happy, and far from indifferent to her personal adornment, was likely to take considerable interest in speculations of this description. A short time after this, as Annie returned to the sitting room, having just bestowed the little one, drowsy with sleep, in his crib, she found a stranger occupying a chair opposite her husband. The stranger's back was to her, but she supposed immediately that this man must be the new assistant John had secured. John looked up smilingly on hearing her approach, and said, quietly rising as he spoke, " Let me introduce to you my wife."

The stranger stood up and faced Annie. The man and woman looked steadily and intently upon each other as they had looked years ago beside that stile in Ireland. In the eyes of each shone out instant remembrance of that parting hour. There was a moment of silence — how long it seemed — then a hasty and cold salutation of bowed heads and a few mumbled words from Dave.

Annie felt herself sinking into a chair with a strangely faint feeling, yet even in that supreme moment the instinct of hiding any outward manifestation of agitation was strong within her. Why she should aim at concealment of any former acquaintance with this man she herself could not have told. There was no reason why she should not have said to her husband, "I have met this gentleman before, he was a friend of mine in Ireland."

If Dave felt any surprise at her course in affecting not to recognize him, he was conscious that it would be a rudeness in him to call their early friendship to her mind by any spoken word; so, after some commonplace remarks upon their late journey and the weather, he continued the conversation with Malone which Annie's entrance had interrupted. In a short time Annie stole, softly, unnoticed from the room. She sat in her chamber window in the dark, looking wearily out along the lamp-lighted street; the wind whistled through the bare-branched trees, cold and shrill; a light tracery of frost was forming on the window panes; she fancied that there was a sense of desolation on everything. Here was Dave, not dead, as she had for nearly three years supposed him to be, but the Dave of her youth, only paler, thinner, more gentle and refined looking, with the refinement of grief. His faithful and fruitless search for her had laid some heavy marks about his brow and mouth.

As she sat there thinking, suddenly, through the heaviness of her heart, darted one dreadful thought — what would he suppose! He found her here the wife of another man. He would think that she had not loved him! The very supposition of this — which would be far the best thing under the circumstances for Dave to believe — made her feel quite wild. Oh! she could not let him go on thinking *that!* She must let him know some time that she had supposed him dead, though here Annie had to admit to herself that she had consented to marry Malone before she received what she supposed to be *proof* of Dave's death.

Within the large house that night two people passed the long hours in wakefulness. Dave walked his room incessantly, living over in memory all that had been between him and Annie in early youth. He recalled the agonies of his long search for her, the fatality which attended every effort put forth to find her, and *now* she was found — a married woman, and lost to him forever. At this his grief overpowered him. He wished he had not come here. It would have been better never to have found her at all. This, then, was her love for him! *She* had not been faithful like himself. But even as these angry thoughts beset him came recollection of that long look exchanged the instant of their meeting,—the expression of her eyes, which betokened anything except indifference. Then, like an arrow, he was pierced by the knowledge that she was married to an old man, old enough surely to be her father. Why should he judge her? She surely never wedded a man of that age for love! How could he know what impelled her to take this step. No, he would not let himself think harshly, but yet — ought he to remain here? How could he live where he would see her often; and this old man, who was so kind to him, was the soul of honor and generosity. It would be better to go to him, frankly tell him all, and abide by what the old man thought it best for him to do. But no, he couldn't do that without Annie's consent. After all, why should he fret on this score? Annie, as a married woman, would not permit herself to give one thought to him. They would live in the same house, to be sure, but quite unheeding each other.

Poor Dave! his was the common error — to dream that the hopes and passions of years would yield thus, even to what seemed the inevitable. So the fatal conclusion was arrived at—that he would say and do nothing in this matter, but, trusting to his own and Annie's integrity, go on as if there had never been a *past* in their lives.

As Malone slept the "sleep of the just" beside her, Annie's distracted thoughts traversed the years since her parting from Dave. How she cursed the day that she had been weak enough, for the sake of worldly ease, to marry Malone! She, in whom a lifetime of devotion could scarcely compensate Malone for all his goodness to her, did not realize what he had done for her, with that large gratitude which Dave bestowed upon the old man after one short week of acquaintance.

"No!" she cried to herself, in her love and anger, "what right had he to marry a mere girl like me! how could he tell but what some time I might meet and love a young man!"

It was monstrous to think of giving up love for her whole life, and for what? A house and servants! To think how happy she could be with Dave. Oh, misery! misery! and so the long night wore away.

It was a great misfortune, just at this point in the affairs of the family, that Mrs. Nolan should be afflicted by one of those periodical lapses from the straight path to which she was sometimes subject. Had she been what she called "herself," her lynx eyes would have noted a rather "strained" coldness between the young mistress and the new member of the household. But Nora, though outwardly betraying very little of her potations, was, when under their influence, very impervious to impressions. When feeling thus her dignity was more appalling, but her intuitions not half so keen. Her overscrupulous care of the kitchen at these times caused Kitty many retirements into secret places to shed some private tears.

"Oh, missus," Kitty would say to Mrs. Malone, "It's hard to plase her when she's sober, but when she's the other way, divil a wan of me can do it."

Annie had no great tax upon her self-control the first few weeks, as she saw little of Dave, he and Malone being very busy in the saloon.

Dave's quick perceptions made him ready to John's hand in many ways. He entered into all his employer's plans with the sanguine liveliness of youth, and he evinced no desire whatever for the ordinary pleasures of young men, seeming content to be always on duty.

When some weeks had passed there was a slow, almost imperceptible change in Annie's daily habits. She had been lively and fond of visiting the girl companions of her unmarried days, but now she spent much more time in the house, devoting many hours to some intricate kind of fancy sewing.

The young Malone had taken a strong liking to the stranger, insisting with loud screaming upon spending much of his juvenile time down stairs with Dave or his father; so Annie would often go down with him when the place had few or no customers in it, and sitting behind a screen, where the winter sun slanted its rays through a window near her, go quietly on with her sewing, now and then looking up to admonish the child. This became her daily habit, she exchanged scarcely a word with Dave, but watched him shyly from under her long lashes. He would go on with his usual avocations as if totally unconscious of her presence, all the time feeling her as near him as if she had been standing close beside him. Thus without words, with averted glances, these two derived an odd sort of happiness from being in the same apartment.

If company—as was sometimes the case—detained Annie upstairs for a day, Dave would experience a keen dejection, then when she returned with that interminable sewing in her hands, and sat quietly on the far side of the room, with the sun glinting on her fair head, a delicious contentment would steal over him; he felt that he could live this way forever, satisfied to know that she was near, though ever so unnoticing. Annie appeared, to any ordinary observer, wrapped up in her child. When she raised her eyes it was to look at and talk to him; however her proximity to Dave he was never absent from her mind; her contentment was not in the same ratio as Dave's, one haunting anxiety was always present to her, the anxiety to clear herself in his regard; right or wrong, she *would* speak to him some day to make him understand how all this had come about.

Dave in the meantime had no lack of kindness

and encouragement from the others. The old man treated him with great consideration. The young fellow employed under Dave to assist in the laborious work of the place quite idolized him, thinking his word was law in everything. Kitty did not try to conceal her rather ardent regard for him, and even the stern Nora unbent, pronouncing him "very dacent for a *young* man."

It happened one day as Kitty and Nora worked busily near each other that Kitty came to a dead stop in her employment and said, evidently to herself, though speaking aloud, "It's a wondher to me what has tuk the misthress; its never so quiet she was as now, since I've known her."

Nora looked up with an expression on her face which made Kitty tremble. "Kitty," she said, sternly, "It's going on with your work you should be, and lave alone the talk about your betthers."

Notwithstanding this Norā took a mental note. Her observations the next few days did not corroborate Kitty's suggestions, for Annie was in unusually high spirits, owing to a three-days visit from Bridget and the young Rooneys. Jack being in the country, Bridget was lonely, and "tuk the chance" to spend a little time with the Malones. It is needless to state that Annie's boy, in conjunction with the baby Rooneys, almost made the house a howling wilderness, Nora being quite beside herself when they organized foraging trips to the kitchen.

During these days Dave saw little or nothing of the mistress of the house. On being made acquainted with him Bridget bestowed upon him one of her frank, good-natured smiles, remarking that he must be much the same age as Mr. Rooney, and that she hoped her husband would become acquainted with him; to which kindness Dave responded gratefully.

The months ran their rapid course from that eventful Christmas till the end of May, yet never by word or look did Dave strive to break the coldness and silence that lay between him and Annie. As she furtively looked at him she would sometimes think, "Perhaps he doesn't care for me any more, perhaps he ceased to love me long ago." But something within her repelled that idea. At all events, if he no longer cared for her in that fashion, he certainly did not seem to care for any one else. The blandishments of the pretty rosy-cheeked Kitty appeared to fall quite harmless on him. So far as could be seen, there was no space in his mind for anything but business.

Malone was absent frequently three or four days at a time during these winter months, yet Dave never took advantage of these absences to speak one word to Annie beyond the commonplace remarks which usually passed between them. This irritated Annie exceedingly; she surely would tell him some day what she wanted to, but she was too proud to break into his cold silence. What was the matter with him—was he angry or indifferent? How she wished that she could know.

The spring was remarkably early, the trees began to show a tender verdure, the grass was green, long days of sunshine coaxed the bashful wild flowers into blooming; little blue violets began to blossom in the meadows west of the tall house, nature tripped smilingly about her work, scattering wonders as she went.

Part of these sunny days Annie spent in the park with the little one. She found a bench sheltered by tall shrubs, where she sat with book or work held idly in her hands as the child ran about picking, with constantly renewed delight, the dandelions.

One day, as she sauntered homeward from one of these expeditions, Malone came out of the house to meet her. He was very pale—there was a look of deep trouble in his eyes. Annie became agitated. She asked with alarm what had happened. Truth was, her thoughts flew to Dave—could anything have befallen *him?*

Malone said sadly, "I've just received word of my mother's death. You know what that means to *me*, Annie! I shall have to go to Ireland at once; it will be too severe a journey for you and the child. The boy must be older and stronger ere we take him across the ocean. It will likely be a matter of months before I can return."

Annie felt her heart give a refractory bound, a

horrible fear had attacked her when Ireland was mentioned lest Malone would expect her to go with him. Some hurried preparations for departure ensued, then a number of consultations with, and directions to, Dave relative to the management of the business; John saying, "Dave, I know you'll look after things as carefully as I would myself. I trust to you implicitly."

Then he was gone; the whole thing passing so quickly that it seemed to Annie like a dream. The suddenness of this departure had left her no time for that mechanical arrangement for future actions which takes place in almost every mind when any change is planned which makes an alteration in the daily modes of life. She only felt to her heart's core that she was alone. A strange joy took possession of her. Would she need to study every action and look now? Must she continually droop her eyelids for fear her love should play truant, and peep from beneath them? Would the days ever seem so long now? She would lose that restless fear lest in her dreams she might call aloud the name forever in her thoughts. Hail, happy mornings, and thrice happy days! She was free, if only a few months—yet it was heaven to even think of. She kissed the child passionately, murmuring, "Yes, little one, we shall spend our days with the sunshine and flowers; we shall be alone to think and dream; the summer shall be ours, ours only!"

The couple of weeks succeeding John's leaving passed uneventfully. Dave was so extremely busy now that he scarcely glanced up when Annie passed through the place. She had gradually given up sitting inside with her sewing, spending most all the bright daytime now in the park with the child whenever the weather allowed.

Dave was troubled by a strange uneasiness. He felt that the husband's absence made it incumbent on him to be more careful than ever in Annie's presence, yet in spite of himself she seemed to draw him : he was literally wrapped around by her personality. After she passed through the doorway he would go swiftly in that direction; to feel that his feet trod the same spot just passed by her, than suddenly standing still, a deep blush would suffuse his face, as he turned back with a sigh. Annie's mind was acting upon his ; her steady determination to speak to him affected him, though he was unconscious of the cause.

One lovely morning in June Annie and the child came down, as usual, attired for walking; Dave stood at the open door. As she came toward him his heart beat violently. Annie paused near him, turning her eyes full upon his, her eyes saying plainly as eyes can talk, "Follow me; I *must* see you; come,"—then she walked slowly toward the park.

Dave trembled from head to foot ; he ought not to go, but should he not—perhaps she would be angry. Oh! he must not make her angry with him! It surely could be no great sin to talk with her alone just once—only once—for he was quite sure she would only wish to see him this one time. He ran hurriedly into the yard, and calling in the young fellow who helped him, said, "Here, take charge for an hour or two, till I go out on some business."

Making a hasty toilet, he started. It must be confessed that he took a very roundabout way to go a short distance. His sense of guilt made him fancy that the very pavements had eyes. The trees, too, seemed to nod to each other as he passed near them and whisper "Traitor." He knew well the very spot where Annie would be; in his occasional leisure hours the child had led him to it, and patting the bench affectionately, had claimed it as "mine and mamma's."

Yes, there she sat, evidently expecting him. As he came near she rose to her feet, a deathly paleness overspreading her countenance. The look of love and anguish that he gave her made her forget all that she intended to say to him. For a few moments both seemed incapable of speech. The child was playing at a little distance among the late dandelions. There was a mellow stillness in the warm air, broken only by the warbling of a thrush close by.

At last Dave spoke; there was reproach in the tone of his deep voice as he said sternly, "My years of searching for you have ended in this; from sickness, only lived through by the hope of meeting you, from sorrow and poverty, I came here to find that the woman who promised to be true to me had forgotten all and married another man."

He paused, his chest heaved; there was a choking sensation in his throat. Dave had not intended to speak to Annie so severely. In his secret thought he was only too kind, too forgiving to her; but the sight of her, pale and drooping before him, made him thoroughly conscious of his own weakness. He hastened to affect a greater sternness than he felt; in order to mask his struggle between love and duty. Annie was so overpowered by his tone that she could only reply by putting her hands out toward him with a deprecating motion, then covering her face with them, burst into a passion of sobs and tears. Dave, in his turn overcome by her unexpected emotion, conducted her to the bench, and gently compelling her to sit down, stood anxiously and patiently before her.

"Dave," she sobbed, "I always loved you; I love you *now*."

"Annie," he answered, with sudden determination, "you have no right to love me now, nor I to hear you say so. It is just torturing you and myself to talk about these things. Let us be strangers to each other, as we have been all these months past. We will go our ways, noticing each other no more."

"No!" cried Annie, wildly, "you shall not go away till I have told you all; you shall sit here beside me, and know how I thought you dead."

Dave started violently. "You thought me dead!" he exclaimed.

"Yes," said Annie eagerly, as she saw his resolution to leave her was quite shaken; "sit down and listen. Oh! I have so much to say to you."

Dave sat down and listened as Annie told the story of those memorable years, toning down her part in all—adroitly, as women do. Months of repression gave an impetus to the conversation. Time passed unheeded. The child, wearied by play, crept unnoticed to Annie's feet, and leaning his curly head against her dress, fell fast asleep. At last Annie, with a sudden recollection, looked at her watch. Two hours had passed. When Dave saw the time he was startled; he rose hurriedly.

"This will not do," he said, "I must go back at once."

"Not now," cried Annie; I haven't told you *half* yet."

"And I," said Dave, reproachfully, "have told you actually nothing."

"Then, come again, Dave; don't make me wretched by saying no. What harm is there in our talking sometimes over what is done with for ever?"

It is hard for a man to say no to a woman who loves him, but when he loves her——.

Dave strode hurriedly away, but Annie knew he would come again. She was intensely conscious of her power over him. The summer weeks seemed to have borrowed wings with which to fly so fast. The meetings in the park became a customary thing, the only change being that they increased in frequency, and in a short time a more distant and sheltered bench was found. In the large house all went about their usual duties and pleasures without a suspicion of the real state of affairs, Annie's arrangements for secrecy being perfect.

In the presence of others her manner toward Dave relaxed a little from its former stern severity; she would chat with him carelessly now and then. After awhile he was allowed to drive her and the child out; but Annie frequently now drove out alone, leaving the child in care of Nora and Kitty. These changes took place so gradually that they attracted no attention, all knowing that Dave had been left in sole charge of the business. It was natural that he should have many things to speak of to the mistress.

When Annie drove out alone, Dave frequently joined her in some retired side street, then they would drive through unfrequented roads, with ample time for these unending conversations.

As all this was going on Annie saw little of Bridget, the Rooney family being just then in a state of transition, for the precious bank account — since a certain evening never interfered with by Jack—had at last borne fruit. After mature consideration the young couple concluded to invest these savings in a home of their own, with—as Jack said, gayly—"a fine yard to it, where the young Rooneys should play in the dirt as much as they wanted to." Thus it happened that Bridget, busied with moving into and decorating her little cottage, and making extraordinary plans for the beautifying of the "yard," had been unable to call at the big house as often as heretofore. The appearance, too, of another young Rooney since the early part of the Spring, kept Bridget closely at home, so that, as Annie said, the "calling" had to be all on one side.

One day, about the end of August, Annie declared her intention of going over to see how Bridget was getting along. She took the child with her—Dave driving. As they approached the cottage—a neat little place with a small lawn in front adorned by some flower beds—sounds of laughter struck upon their ears. Dave assisted Annie and the child out, then securing the horse, quietly followed them to the door step where a pretty picture presented itself. Jack was seated on the floor laughing immoderately, while two young Rooneys of the male persuasion, with little fists clinched, pummeled their father in sham fight. Near by sat Bridget in a low rocking chair with the newest infant in her arms, a lovely little girl, who was looking at the good-natured belligerents on the floor with baby terror. Bridget was gazing upon the happy group with love and admiration when, looking up, she beheld Annie standing in the doorway. There was something in Annie's face, as she stood there surveying the group, so different from its usual placid expression, that Bridget felt alarmed.

Jack sprang to his feet to welcome her, whilst the young Rooneys swarmed about the little Malone. Jack was soon engaged in converse with Dave, whilst Bridget, hastily depositing the sleeping infant in its crib, turned a look of questioning upon Annie. "Well," said Annie, in a peculiarly *hard* tone, "I thought I'd take a drive over to see you in your new home, Bridget. I needn't ask you if you're happy! you, with your *young* husband and little children all about you! God knows you have enough to make you happy!"

"Oh! for the matter of that," answered Bridget carelessly, but with a feline glitter in her eyes, "you're the woman who should be talking of happiness; you who can wear gems, and drive about like a queen in your own carriage; you with a husband who dotes upon you, and a child as beautiful as a picture!"

On hearing this Annie made a strong effort at self control, but the heaving of her bosom — the look of anguish in her eyes — could not escape the observation of the woman who had known her from early girlhood. Bridget turned her glance from

Annie to Dave, who sat a little distance off talking to her husband. There he was, slender, handsome, owner of the "indescribable" charm of youth. Bridget possessed remarkable perspicacity. In an instant she knew nearly all.

"Annie," she said, with a commanding look, "come here."

She led her into an adjoining room and closed the door; then she turned upon her a flashing glance, and speaking in a low voice, quite hoarse from anger, said: "I have known and loved you as girl and woman for many years; if ever some great trouble overtakes you, come to me, I shall be *your* friend till death! but never — so long as you and I shall live — never dare to bring that man to my house again! Whatever secret you have is safe with me, but never bring that man again!"

Annie trembled violently, but made no reply. Bridget returned immediately to the other room, leaving her alone to recover her composure.

The men talked on, unaware of the tornado blast which had whistled past them. Bridget, when unobserved, cast some lightning glances upon Dave, expressive of strong disfavor. Annie soon ended the call by declaring that they really couldn't remain any longer, then, escorted to the phaeton by Jack and the admiring young Rooneys, took their departure.

Dave was distressed and greatly surprised on their way homeward to find Annie taciturn and gloomy. Having yielded to his passion and her own, his conscience, once so active, seemed steeped in an intoxication of happiness. This was the first time she had seemed to feel unhappy when with him; he regarded her with anxious looks. Of course he could form no idea of what was passing in her mind. Those few dreadful words of Bridget's had given Annie the first realizing sense of the degradation of her position. She recalled bitterly now the warnings Bridget forced upon her before her marriage. She had never told Dave anything of *that*. In the madness of her love for him, she had not told anything which could make her inconstancy seem other than the force of circumstances. She was deeply angered with herself for having in that unguarded moment dropped the mask — and before Bridget of all women; Bridget, who had tried so hard to save her from the chance of this. Dave tried vainly to elicit from her the cause of her changed manner. This day began between them misunderstandings and quarrels which embittered months to come.

Malone had written to both Annie and Dave very frequently, detailing to Annie the delays and annoyances he met with in selling off the property in the old country, telling her that he felt it would be better to remain long enough to convert all this into money, for re-investment in Chicago, than to leave any of his pecuniary interests in Ireland in the hands of agents. He hoped to return in September. More delays occurred. Finally Malone wrote that he would surely be home by the end of September. When Dave knew this, his brow was like a thunder cloud; in consequence of the nearness of the husband's return a fierce quarrel ensued between the lovers.

The idea that Dave had entertained since the hour of their downfall, now took tangible shape, leading to those recriminations which are the bane of illicit connections. Dave besought Annie to fly with him, to leave her husband forever. He had remotely hinted at this before, but now, rendered desperate by the thought of John's return, he urged this step upon her, pointing out what their mutual misery would be under the circumstances of having her husband with them continually, arguing that having sinned so far, they could not do worse. In answer to all this Annie pointed to her child. She would not give up her child. Dave said they would take the child with them. Annie reminded him that Malone would never part with the little one, but would follow to the ends of the earth to recover him; that he could by law take him from her. The quarrel was protracted and bitter, ending in Annie remaining firm in her determination, in Dave foiled and desperately angry, threatening to leave her entirely and never to see her face again! since she loved her child better than him! at which, Annie weeping and reproaching him, the conversation ended. These angry scenes only concluded, or rather, it might be said, were suspended, by the return of Malone. The pressing necessity for concealment produced a lull in the storm of irritated feeling, and things settled down in their old time régime.

Malone was delighted to return. He had so much to tell and hear about, he saw no indication of the blight which had fallen upon his domestic life. He was pleased by the manner in which Dave had attended to the business in his absence, for Dave had faithfully endeavored to make up for lapses in other respects by keeping all the business well looked after. Malone's thanks and praises seemed like searing irons to Dave. He listened with an apathy which concealed raging fires of self-reproach. His opportunities for seeing Annie privately seldom gave him a chance now to express to her the distractions of his mind. The Christmas holidays again approaching, took his remembrance to that time a year ago when the love of his life stood so unexpectedly before him the wife of another. Again and again, he asked himself why he had not followed the impulse of his soul, which bade him then to either tell the truth to Malone or fly. What could excuse the folly of actually keeping himself in the way of temptation. All this agony and shame would have been prevented, and *now* he could not leave Annie—no, he would try yet to undermine her resolution, and make her run away with him. Cur that he was! he felt that he could not do anything worse than he had done already!

Life now became a veritable hell to the guilty ones. Malone aggravated their torments by his unvarying kindness, which made Annie feel that it would be death itself to have him know the terrible reality. The winter was passing away, and somehow, when Annie sat near the sunny window and sewed, Dave, though he loved her madly as ever, no longer saw the aureole around her head, and she had lost the timid joy with which she used to look at him and listen to his voice. There had been a happiness in those days of innocence, which no after raptures could equal. They knew that *now*, both of them; and yet the chain that bound them heart to heart grew stronger with the knowledge, as sorrow and despair, twin sisters of sin, led them ever onward toward the shadowed path ahead.

Now Spring came on again — the careless, happy Spring — smiling upon their agonies with that sunshine which a year ago had led them by pleasant places to taste the sugared sweets of love. Malone had often spoken to Annie of his good fortune in securing such a man as Dave, who had more than met all his expectations.

"If he keeps on like this," said Malone, smiling, "I'll surely have to give him an interest in the business. I had struggles myself when I was a young man; I know what appreciation can do to help a person along."

Then Annie would smile faintly, and remark that it was a good thing that he felt pleased, and — did he notice lately how the child was growing? Then, as she spoke, she would twine the boy's golden ringlets around her finger, to distract John's attention from the theme she hated to have him mention.

Annie began to look very pale as Spring went on; she moved slowly and listlessly about the house, for she was nearing her second confinement. Dave, when unobserved, watched her anxiously; yet at this period, through all his anguish, shot a gleam of hope. Perhaps after the babe was born she would be willing to admit that he had now a double right to her. Perhaps she would then leave Malone's child and fly with him. Then, far from the scene of their first guilt, they would live for and with each other always. Buoying himself up with thoughts like these, he patiently watched the weeks crawl by.

In the occasional absences of the old man, they privately met and talked to each other. Both were sad and downcast. Annie inwardly hoped, though she dared not breathe this hope to Dave, that she would die in the approaching crisis. She had not the courage to think of leaving Malone, and to live like this. The savor of the Dead Sea fruit was always in her mouth now. As it had ever been with her, she considered herself more sinned against than sinning. She would say to Dave, he was wiser and stronger than herself, why had he listened to the importunities of her affection? Had *he* been firm they need not be ashamed and miserable now! Dave would hang his head at this, without one word of remonstrance.

On the last day of May Annie gave birth to a boy. The weeks succeeding her confinement she seemed to have very little vitality, taking scarcely any notice of the infant or what went on about her. Malone regarded this lassitude with apprehension, and sent for a physician of note. He prescribed, shook his head, looked grave and muttered something about being strange in so young a woman. Still Annie slowly, very slowly, regained her strength.

After this confinement, that neglected portion, her soul, seemed to awaken; the magnitude of her errors stood before her in undraped deformity. Like the Undine of the story who could never gain a soul except through the love of a human being, so Annie had never realized *her* soul save through sin and sorrow. If she had determined before never to run away with Dave, her resolution was even more firmly settled now.

****

Changes quite undreamed of by Dave took place in Annie's sentiments to him. From the moment of her conversation with Bridget, in which the latter had divined her wretched secret, Annie had experienced the sudden revulsion of feeling common to weak natures. Now that she realized all she had sacrificed, and how much more even Dave expected from her, a chill fell on her passion. The frequent quarrels with her lover produced a strong impression on her.

In all the years she had known her husband, a harsh or even impatient word to her had never escaped his lips. The contrast between his gentleness and the anger with which Dave was often goaded to urge his wishes on her, made her hope that Dave would go away and try to forget her.

Why, she argued, should he wish her to give up her child, her reputation—all, to fly with him to poverty and open shame? It was with ideas like these that she began to avoid every occasion for private conversation with him. Her sole effort now was to retrieve all that she had lost. There was the hope that if Dave would only be reasonable and trouble her no more with his importunities to fly with him, this part of her life might pass away like some bad dream. So Annie, who, like a gambler, had hazarded all, would fain regain all by the throw upon one desperate stake.

She did not know—how could she—that her Nemesis stood just outside the gates, ready with her tongue—not hands—to pull the house down on the guilty pair. Within pleasant walking distance of the Malone mansion lived a middle-aged woman named Carnrody. Mrs. Carnrody, who, by the way was a widow, lived in comfort in a neat cottage of her very own, bequeathed to her by the late Mr. Carnrody. Now, this amiable lady had so very little to do in attending to her own affairs that she felt obliged to take an absorbing interest in those of her neighbors. She retailed all the gossip, not only of her own locality, but even that of distant thoroughfares. When she was seen wending her way from house to house, her friends would sarcastically remark that "Carnrody was afther gettin' up one of her rale illigant stories consarning her neighbors."

People who had enjoyed Mrs. Carnrody's acquaintance, and knew her, shunned her as if she were the plague, declaring that she had the ability to tear more characters to pieces than all the courts of law could patch up again. This woman had employed some of the aforesaid leisure to watch Annie, with a result easily imagined. Many of Dave's and Annie's secret meetings had been known to her. Having carefully gathered the venom, she was now prepared to distribute it, her impelling motive being a deep-seated animosity toward Mrs. Nolan,—the Carnrody's efforts toward forming a friendly league with the kitchen inmates of the big house having failed signally, owing to Nora's determined stand against her. When, shortly after their installation in her neighborhood, Mrs. Carnrody called, and, introducing herself with many smiles, claimed acquaintance as a countrywoman and near resident, supplementing all with the remark that Mrs. Nolan, being a widow, like herself, would doubtless feel the need of neighboring with her, Nora regarded her with a stare calculated to have the effect of the far famed Gorgon's head. She measured the woman with a glance, concluding that her enmity was safer than her friendship. So it would have been, had the young mistress of the house been what Nora supposed.

It was nearing Christmas again. Annie remembered bitterly that two years ago on Christmas eve, she and Dave stood silently looking into each other's eyes their inexpressible surprise and woe. Now, what a horror of blackness settled around her, recalling all that had happened since. Dave, too, remembered with a sullen misery, born of his inextinguishable love, his late remorse. A determination was forming in his mind that in a few days he would force from Annie a final answer, and after that—but he dared not look into the gulf beyond.

In these souls about him, teeming with conflicting thoughts, Malone moved, the central figure. With the crystal clearness of his mind luminous by contrast, his probity of soul seemed to shine through his open countenance. Not the faintest suspicion ever sullied Annie in her husband's thoughts. Being a man—a man in an occupation which often showed to him the most degraded side of human nature— he looked upon it with pity, yet repugnance, knowing that awful evils existed. He gazed upon them as the wayfarer looks upon the mud beside the path, which nothing will induce him to put his foot near. Upon the sacred altar of his home, his own dear woman stood spotless and glorified. That sin or shame should enter *there*, no more came to his mind than the possibility that a kneeling penitent should rise from his prayers to pull down and smirch the gentle-faced Madonna before whom he made obeisance.

That Annie was all he could wish her to be in disposition, he knew was not the case, in comparison with the gentle being who shared his younger years, the incense of whose sweet charities had risen perpetually about him. Annie was selfish and unsympathetic, but against all this stood out the charm of her motherhood — the mother of his children! To John, unversed in woman-lore, this very motherhood seemed an explanation of the little interest she bestowed on the anxieties of mortals less favored than herself. Why should she — bound heart and soul in the care of her babies — look beyond, to see if any sat weeping by the outer wall? Thus John, happily oblivious, beamed his earnest way through the mazes as Fate drew all her forces toward the closing struggle.

On the afternoon of the 23d of December, Bridget was a very busy woman. She was constructing, slyly with her own strong hands, a most wonderful garment, to be presented to Jack on

Christmas morning. It was the regular and proper thing to give Jack a stunning Christmas surprise, but it must be always something made by herself. The care of the house and small Rooneys made this enterprise very difficult; especially as the little ones had grown to an age when their discretion did not keep pace with their inquisitiveness, so that they could not be trusted with even a whiff of the secret, and for Jack to know anything before hand! Oh, that would never do! She was amazed just as the last light of day was waning to hear Jack's step at the door. So early for him! She bundled her work out of sight in a moment and ran to meet him.

"Well," cried Jack gayly, with a poor assumption of his ordinary manner, "here I am, ever so much earlier than usual, because my better half must share the worries as well as joys of my life."

He threw himself into a chair and looked at Bridget with a contracted brow.

"Soonest told, quickest done with," answered Bridget serenely.

"Bridget," said her spouse gravely, "I've heard this day things that I can't let myself think can be true. A woman named Carnrody has been circulating most scandalous stories about Annie and Dave. My God! think what this will be for Annie's husband. It must be stopped — this talk — at once."

A violent tremor shook Bridget. It had come at last then. From the moment she guessed that guilty secret, she felt that there might be some dreadful ending. She looked at Jack with a horror in her face, and began to wring her hands in a helpless manner quite unusual with her.

"Bridget," said Jack, thoroughly startled by her look, "you can't think there is any *truth* in such stories? Annie is never so wicked as that. Perhaps she has acted thoughtlessly or foolishly. You must see and talk to her at once. Malone is so good and just a man that he must not be trifled with."

Bridget had never breathed a word of this matter to her husband. He had expected fierce anger on her part when hearing of aspersions on Annie's fair fame, with violent speech against the calumniators, not this ashy face and dead silence.

After a long pause Jack said, "Being so far to go, it is too late this evening, but you must get to her first thing in the morning. Talk to her like the sister you've always been to her. Try to make her understand all that she owes her husband. I can't tell you," continued Jack, choking a little, "how I feel for Malone; I love him as a father."

Bridget never could forget the dreams she had that night. Once she roused, screaming, for she seemed to see Malone — his hands all red with blood — standing over Dave, who lay dead upon the ground. Very much shaken by the nature of her dreams, she dressed herself with trembling hands, and hastened out to Annie's. Soon finding the chance for undisturbed conversation, she came to the point with that directness which was part of her character. Annie was thoroughly terrified, she had supposed her secret safe, now — Dave *must* go. Bridget insisted this was all that could be done, if "Annie had one grain of decency left." Bridget put it to her in this extremely plain way—she must send Dave away, never to look upon his face again. With Dave away, these stories might cease, and never reach Malone's ears. "Unless," said Bridget, bitterly, "you want to bring utter ruin upon your husband and children — to kill with shame the man who has done everything in the world for you!"

Annie drooped like a withered flower under these invectives. She said, helplessly, "I will *try* to make him go away; I will indeed!"

"At once," said Bridget, firmly, "there must be no lingering; tell him this very day, and *make* him leave you!"

Annie sighed. Bridget having done all in her power, hurried home.

This day being the one before Christmas, was a time of extra activity with Mrs. Nolan; her "bump of order" must have grown to a tremendous size by the constant exercise it received. The day before Christmas this bump became particularly rampant, in consequence, Kitty was reduced to a state of submissive agony; her "feet," as she dolefully expressed it, "seemed most *wore* off." From the attic to the cellar Mrs. Nolan seemed to literally ride—like the old woman in Mother Goose—"on a broomstick." No corner was safe from her investigations, no dust-covered nook escaped her quick eyes; resembling some ugly little demon, she appeared to be everywhere at once.

Late that afternoon Kitty sat for a few fleeting moments resting her weary feet, and watching some Christmas dainties "baking off." She felt emboldened to this brief respite by the surety that Mrs. Nolan was at that moment in the very top of the house. Looking wearily up, she espied coming toward the open kitchen door no less a person than Mrs. Carnrody. The kitchen door stood open because it was very fine weather. It was one of those "open" winters Chicago frequently enjoys. The grass was still a vivid green, though dead leaves lay thickly under the big trees in the park; the breeze, which blew them lightly along, was balmy and summerlike. Bright sunshine irradiated everything. Nature seemed to join the universal holiday rejoicing, making up her mind that she would no longer be reproached for frozen toes and blue noses or a coldness of demeanor, but would show Chicago what she could do in helping along the holidays if she just took a notion to.

Had Kitty been less tired and disquieted, she might not have been pleased to see Mrs. Carnrody, for in her heart she really didn't like her very much; but she was young, fond of gossip, and Mrs. Carnrody could furnish her with the latest news of the neighborhood. Mrs. Carnrody, on entering, gave an apprehensive glance about the room.

"Mrs. Nolan is upstairs," said Kitty, divining the lady's thoughts. Mrs. Carnrody openly declared herself glad to hear that Mrs. Nolan was upstairs, for she, Carnrody, had come there for the express purpose of seeing Kitty and telling her that she was working in a house where no respectable girl should be. She, Carnrody, had no feeling of pity for Mrs. Nolan, who was old enough to have her eyes open! but Kitty was young and innocent, and knew no better!

Then this good woman poured into Kitty's horror stricken understanding all that she had suspected—all that she had seen—every damning circumstance connected with the young mistress.

In the meantime, on the dark staircase, behind the door, which was not entirely closed, stood an unseen listener. Mrs. Nolan being very small, also lightly slippered, had a noiseless way with her. She arrived upon the scene in the middle of these revelations. She stood stockstill and listened, making up her mind at the same time what to do. Mrs. Nolan had a way, to use common parlance, of taking the bull by the horns. She waited until she knew, by the unguarded sound of the voices, that the speakers had forgotten everything except the subject talked of—then she pounced on them, grabbing Kitty by the shoulder. She shook her violently, asking her what she meant by standing there listening to a parcel of lies about people whose bread she was eating. Then, turning a flashing glance upon the Carnrody, she bade her begone!

Nora's face at this juncture was frightful beyond description, added to its native homeliness, the distortions caused by rage gave it a twisted appearance; she seemed almost to "spit fire" like the dragons of old!

The Carnrody was a coward at heart, she recoiled before this impish figure—actually turned and fled. Kitty tremblingly shrank from the range of Nora's eyes. Just then the Carnrody—it could be no other—was heard shrieking! Nora rushed to the window and looked out. "Glory be to God," she exclaimed, "the dog has got her by the leg!"

It was indeed true. Mrs. Carnrody, scurrying in great excitement through the back yard, had failed to notice a savage looking dog fastened near the entrance to an open shed. As she passed unwarily close to him he seized the intruder by the leg and held her till one of the hired men rushed to the rescue. Owing to the ample nature of Mrs. Carnrody's petticoats the dog inflicted little more injury than fright. Nora surveyed the situation with a grim smile. "It's little help she'd get from *me*," she muttered, "if the dog had eaten her up."

Mrs. Nolan bethought herself that it would be as well now to say something to Kitty. She turned, but that damsel had also fled. Poor Kitty was so overcome by all she had heard that she locked herself into her chamber, and leaving the Christmas cookery to its fate, indulged in a long fit of weeping. Nora, who through every misfortune never lost sight of the necessary incidents of life, took charge of the baking, *thinking* hard as she did so. Though she affected to regard these tales as fabrications, she did so with the instinct which makes the mother bird simulate a wounded wing to distract the attention of the intruder from her secret nest; in her heart all this came to Nora with the force of conviction.

We pass through dark places with an uneasy sense that dangerous things may be about us, it is not till a beam of light penetrates the blackness, that, looking backward, we discern all, and shudder as we gaze. In the landscape of Nora's mind one stood in bold relief—Malone—the world, the *only* world of good that she had ever known; the kind master and friend of many years! To let this disgrace come to him; it must never be. For Annie she cared nothing. That any woman could treat the master that way was astonishing. Nora's harsh mouth curled with scorn at the thought; nevertheless, through Annie and Annie only, could she try to right this wrong.

She would undertake the work at once. The afternoon was waning fast, something impelled her to essay the task immediately. Carefully completing her culinary preparations, she laid her apron off and donned a snow-white one, as was her custom when she entered the rooms of the mistress. Then she went slowly and meditatively upstairs.

Annie sat alone with her infant, the boy was down town with his father. Nora tapped gently at the door and answering Annie's summons stepped inside. She walked over to the mistress and gave her a penetrating glance. Annie was so alarmed by the interview with Bridget that she read this look as if it had been printed words. She felt no surprise that Nora should know—she had a bewildered sense that at any moment it might be placarded upon the very walls.

Nora's deep voice said to her exactly what Bridget had said; that these tales must be hushed up; that Annie must insist upon Dave's leaving the house and city, making up her mind to save her husband by seeing him no more. Mrs. Malone must pledge her word to Nora that at *once*—this very night—she should tell Dave this.

Annie humbly promised and Nora returned to her usual avocations. Then in a long spell of reverie Annie said to herself, "even if I wished never to part with him, I couldn't help myself *now*, he *must* consent to bid me good-bye forever."

By this time the Christmas eve was falling darkly; lights flickered along the lamp-lit streets; the hoarse cries of the street venders had ceased; from the window she could see the dark tops of the almost leafless trees in the park, standing black and solemn against the sombre sky, their shadows lying still as death within the yet unfrozen ponds. She shuddered as she looked, thinking how quietly one might lie beneath that placid water. After all, to *live* was a dreadful thing; a heavy burden. Why should people yearn to preserve this grievous mystery of life? She heard a step, and turning found Dave beside her. There was something—or did she fancy it—she had never noted in his face before.

"Do you remember," he said, looking at her steadily, "that it is Christmas eve? Two years ago to-night I met you after my long search. You know how madly, how wickedly I love you; how long I have implored you to leave the husband you do not love and live with me. To-night again, for the last time, I ask you. You are killing me by your refusals. I must have a final answer now."

Annie answered fretfully that his pertinacity was ruining her; that already their intimacy was talked of; that, in short, he must leave her at once and forever.

Dave's features expressed his anguish. He looked at her with an expression which seemed to say that she had been willing to sin, but not to sacrifice for him. Annie felt the mute reproach and turned her head aside.

There was a long silence. Dave said in a muffled voice, "Look at me—look me in the eyes—tell me, is this your final answer?"

Annie slowly gazed at him, replying, "Yes."

Would she ever forget the look he gave her? There was a meaning in it she could not fathom. It filled her with a strange alarm. She tried to frame some words of excuse, farewell or explanation, but they died upon her lips. Dave stepped quickly to the sleeping infant, bent over it with one long look of tenderness, kissed it, and was gone.

Annie sat there pondering, the darkness closed her in. Along the streets, carriages and wagons rolled with their freight of people, carrying parcels full of anticipated happiness. The street cars clattered by filled with a happy throng, all holding the inevitable Christmas packages. Through lighted windows little Christmas trees could be seen, covered by fantastic decorations. The humanity of the great city was all astir and bustling for the best holiday of the year; while in the big house, the dejected figure sat at the window in the dark, Mrs. Nolan pondered gloomily in the kitchen, and Kitty tried to wash the tear marks from her face.

When Malone and the little boy returned an hour later, the child nestled closely beside his mother, and described, with glowing cheeks and sparkling eyes, the glories of the State street stores, telling her, with a child's extravagance of fancy, all the pretty things he would buy for her, interspersed with ardent guesses as to the nature of the surprises Santa Claus might have in store for him.

Annie looked from the child to Malone, from Malone around the room, furnished with all the accessories of comfort. A vague wonder came over her that she should by her insane folly have put the torch to this domestic peace—for what?

A mournful wind was rising. As it wailed around the house, it seemed to breathe an answer to that inward question. The burden of its song was, always, "the wages of sin is death." What was this heaviness that settled upon her spirits? Not the remembrance of Dave's agony. Somehow that did not touch her as much as she feared it would. The child's prattle made the supper a cheerful meal; otherwise, with Annie so silent, the lively Kitty, who was generally all smiles, waiting on the table with a face of ghostly pallor—it might have been depressing.

Nora did not appear; she had been so agitated, that—to use her own words—she "partook a little." It may have been a *little,* but its effect was to make of Nora a walking automaton. Taciturn at all times, she became under these influences silence personified, walking about with an air of lofty abstraction quite terrifying.

John went down stairs immediately after supper to assist Dave and the boys, for it was a time of great activity in their business.

As it drew near midnight, John secured the opportunity he had been looking for to have a word alone with Dave. People had dispersed to their homes. The night, bright and warm, seemed to speak its message of peace to the wide world. Malone approached Dave with a face beaming with kindness. In his hand he held a small box covered by russia leather. "As things have quieted down," he said, "it gives me the chance for what I've been wanting to say to you. You've been my right hand man, Dave, ever since you came here. I haven't said anything to you of what's in my mind, but for all that, you've been appreciated. I've noticed how steady and industrious you are. To-morrow we'll talk things over and you'll know that I'm going to do what will advance your interests. It is Christmas eve," at this the kind soul fidgeted somewhat bashfully over the box in his hand, "and being the season of the year when we like to express our friendships in little gifts, I brought you this. I hope," he added, rather timidly, "you'll like it." John added this because he saw something in Dave's face, as he took the box from him, which puzzled him.

Dave opened the box, and there, reposing on a' bed of purple plush, lay an elegant gold watch.

"Open it," exclaimed Malone, flushing with pleasure, "and see what's engraved inside for you." But this Dave's trembling fingers could not do, so the old man did it for him. Inside the case, in beautiful characters, was Dave's own name, followed by "Presented as a token of esteem from his friend, John Malone." Dave trembled more violently, still. He said, in a hollow voice, "Mr. Malone, I haven't any words to thank you for this and all your goodness the last two years. There is only *one* return I can make you, and—" here Dave looked him full in the eyes, "I will do it."

Malone shrank back, there was something so incomprehensible in Dave's eyes — so strange a look that John never, to his dying day, forgot it — that he bade him a hasty good-night and left him.

As the old man went up stairs, he experienced a feeling of disappointment. He had looked forward to Dave's delight in receiving this gift. He had lived the scene through in his mind in anticipation, but the scene in his fancy had not at all resembled *this*. So with a sigh, he thought to himself, "I fear he wasn't pleased with it after all."

Soon lights in the large house were extinguished, except in one room where Dave sat writing. Whatever he wrote cost him much thought, for he sat with his head leaning upon his hand and pondered deeply between every word. When the writing — which took him a long time — was finished, it amounted to only a few lines addressed to John Malone. Upon this, which was carefully placed on the center of the table, Dave laid a paper weight, then turning out the gas, he stepped softly to the hall outside, closing the door noiselessly after him.

That night Mrs. Nolan slept not. The "little," so far from benumbing her senses, roused every faculty. She turned off the gas in her room, having previously arrayed herself in a warm woolen gown, shawl and close bonnet. Then she paced the floor softly and restlessly for over an hour, seeming by occasional muttered interjections to be striving to combat some inward yearning. At last, as if yielding to an irresistible power, she felt in her pocket to be assured that her latch key was there, then, closing and locking her door, she too departed. These excursions in the "stilly night," only indulged in by Nora when under the effect of her potations, had nothing wrong about them excepting their uncanniness, consisting only of rapid walking in some sequestered places, where she would address fearful adjurations to the moon and stars, meantime smiting herself upon the breast with many lamentations over the depravity of her nature. She generally returned to her home just preceding or in the first faint dawn of day, where, after attiring herself in her customary morning habiliments, she would be found at a later hour busied in the kitchen, with an air of impenetrable dignity.

As the cold gray dawn of the Christmas morning began to break, Nora made her way through the southwest corner of the park—which was the shortest cut to the big house—quite recovered now from the effects of that "little"; she felt shivering and depressed. As she walked rapidly through a small grove of trees near the greenhouses, she stumbled over something. Regaining her equilibrium with some difficulty, she was surprised to see that she had stumbled against a man lying at full length on the grass.

"Poor fellow!" was her first thought, "sure he's been drinking like myself."

She stooped in the dim light to look at him, then recoiled with a cry. It was Dave—a bullet-hole was in his temple—his right hand clutched a pistol. Nora knelt beside the prostrate form quite sick with horror. She laid her hand upon him—he was stone dead.

Yesterday she had hated him and wished him dead, *but now*, at the sight of his useless atonement, the woman in her nature caused her to utter a loud wail.

A policeman slowly sauntering at some distance heard the cry and hastened to the spot. The policeman examined the man calmly. "I think," he said, "he has been dead some hours." Then, as the daylight, growing stronger, revealed the countenance plainly, he too started, exclaiming, "Why, it's Dave, from Malone's place!"

All the people thereabouts knew the good-natured young Irishman very well. The policeman surveyed the form in astonishment.

"I never would have supposed," he declared, "that Dave was a *drinking man*."

Nora begged him to remain with the corpse till she should tell the master. Then she sped to the house. Tapping at Malone's door, she begged him to come outside, she had something important to say to him. The old man, astonished and alarmed, was dressed in a few minutes, coming out immediately, knowing that Nora would never bring such a message unless it was really something serious. She told him in a few hurried words that Dave was lying dead by his own hand, and bade him go to the scene at once. He was incredulous; she urged him to convince himself. He went, which was what Nora was desperately anxious he should do. She wanted to prepare Annie. She knew that it would be better for her to be the only witness to that scene.

Annie, greatly alarmed by this sudden summons, sat up in bed looking anxiously toward the door, her fair hair falling unbound about her shoulders. Her large blue eyes sought Nora's with a world of questioning in them. Nora locked the door, then, grasping Annie firmly by the hands, told her the truth. After the first few moments of actual stupefaction, Annie rent the air with shrieks so horrible that Nora, thoroughly frightened, begged her to bethink herself, to remember her reputation, her child, everything. But the desperate creature, springing from her bed, made for a knife that lay upon a table, and would undoubtedly have ended her life that moment if Nora had not overpowered her! Foiled in this, she dashed her head against the wall, only yielding to persuasion when too exhausted for further motion.

The heavy perspiration rolled from Nora's forehead when she at last succeeded in placing Annie in the bed again, telling her in a firm voice that nothing but disgrace would come of giving way to these transports! She *must* be quiet!

Kitty was knocking at the door, begging to know if the mistress was sick. Nora opened the door, telling Kitty that the mistress was very ill, and not to leave her for an instant till she—Nora —returned. Then she went quickly to Dave's room, where, opening the unlocked door, she saw with one comprehensive glance the paper on the table. She read it, and after a few seconds of consideration, thought best to leave it. All it contained was this:

CHRISTMAS EVE.

MR. MALONE:

Dear Sir,—When you read this, you will know what was in my mind when you spoke to me so kindly. My object in writing this is to have it understood that I deliberately take my life with my own hand; that *no blame is to attach to any one except myself.*

I thank you from my heart, Mr. Malone, for the great kindness you have always shown me.   DAVE.

By the time Malone reached the scene of the tragedy quite a crowd had assembled. There is scarcely a spot on earth where a crowd will get together more quickly than in Chicago. It is a marvel how they can arrive as fast as they do. Many of them were neighbors who had known the dead man. As Malone stood unnoticed on the outskirts of this gathering, he heard one of them say, "It's easy telling why the poor fellow shot himself; he was dead in love with old Malone's wife!"

John staggered! Was this the explanation of Dave's strange looks last night? Everything turned black around him.

"Hullo!" cried a voice, "here's the old man himself! Look out for him, boys, he seems to be fainting!"

When they led him home a little later he was as white as the corpse that the men were bearing on a litter. He walked feebly upstairs and went into the room where Annie lay and looked at her. She was quiet now, her eyes, widely dilated, staring straight in front of her, seeing nothing. Her breath came in heavy sobs. He looked at her in silence, then sighed as he had never sighed in his life before, and slowly quitted the room.

Nora observed him anxiously; she thought at once that he must have heard something; she dared ask no questions. Had Nora been able to leave Annie alone long enough to go outside, where excited groups of people clustered around the house, seeming all to be talking at once, she would soon have understood that John Malone could scarcely fail to hear the story of his shame; for on this sea of scandal the Carnrody ship sailed triumphantly, with all her canvas spread.

To leave Annie entirely without attendance was out of the question; her life was trembling in the balance. When she fell into a frightful stupor, from which nothing could rouse her, Nora sent for the doctor. He left drugs to be administered, saying that it would be dangerous, night or day, to leave Annie alone, and he would return again in a few hours. Kitty was almost helpless in her grief for Dave, for whom she had conceived a strong regard. Bridget came to them as soon as she heard the terrible tidings.

John Malone and Jack, closeted together, quietly arranged the details of the funeral. It was murmured around that Dave's remains should not rest in consecrated ground, owing to the suicide. Malone said sternly that the man who had lived in his house and broken bread with him, should have decent burial, whatever his sins might have been. Nora noticed with alarm that Malone never approached Annie again, or even asked about her.

The funeral was set for the morning of the 27th. On the evening of the 26th Jack and Bridget returned to their home, promising to be over next morning. Bridget spoke to Nora of Annie's state. She was still lying in that deadly comatose condition. The doctor came after dark and drew Nora aside, telling her that toward midnight he thought Annie would rouse; to guard her then most carefully.

It was fully two o'clock in the morning when Nora, drowsing uneasily at Annie's bedside, with one hand clasped on the slender wrist of her mistress, heard a faint whisper. She started. Annie's eyes, wide open, regarded her with a look of recognition. Nora bent her head to catch the low tones, "Where is he, Nora?"

Who could Annie mean? Nora's eyes looked the question.

"Dave," murmured the woman, "where have they put him?"

"He is not buried yet," answered Nora.

"What room?" persisted Annie, "where?"

"It's in the back parlor, but you mustn't think of that, Macushla!" whispered Nora, hurriedly, for she seemed to have immediate perception of Annie's desire.

"I must see him," said Annie, sitting up, with eyes fairly glowing through the dim light, "I *will* see him! you shan't say me nay! *How can I believe*, unless I see him?"

"But the watchers!" objected Nora.

"Send them away!" Annie commanded.

Nora saw that remonstrance was useless, and softly left the room. The watchers sat in the front parlor, sound asleep. Having satisfied herself on this point, Nora quietly closed the doors of communication.

Returning to Annie's apartment she found her standing in the middle of the room, in her long white night dress, like a ghost. Nora, throwing a heavy shawl about her, silently led the trembling creature to the room of death, warning her, "for God's sake, to be quiet!" In that room, where they had met, two years ago, lay the coffined form.

Annie looked down upon the icy face and pressed her lips upon the unresponsive mouth. "It was for *me* you did it!" she muttered, "for me! for me!" Then she whispered something to the senseless clay. "Come," urged Nora, "come away, you are satisfied now!" To her surprise Annie yielded at once, falling soon after into a quiet slumber.

A week had passed since the funeral. Annie, who had been up and dressed for a couple of days, moved listlessly about her room. She had not seen her husband or boy since Christmas morning. To Nora's astonishment Malone had sent the boy to Bridget's house immediately, and he had been there ever since. On this day Annie, for the first time, asked to see her boy. She did not mention her husband. Nora answered with some constraint that the boy was with Mrs. Rooney. Annie regarded her with surprise, but said no more.

During the week Nora's quickened observation had noted many things; the snowy whiteness of the beloved master's hair; the deep furrows in his countenance, always stern and unsmiling now; the slow and heavy step. Then she knew in her soul what it meant. Malone would never condone his wife's sin. The home he had built about him would be a thing of the past. She looked at Annie, on whom no intimation of this had yet dawned, and wondered.

On the afternoon of that day Malone beckoned to Nora that he would speak with her. He told her to go to her mistress' room and mention that Mr. Malone and Mrs. Rooney wished presently to confer with her. She did so. Annie received the message calmly. In a few minutes the old man and Bridget entered the room. The old man did not sit down, but stood looking at his wife with a stern dignity of manner she had never seen in him before. Bridget was very pale and downcast.

"Mrs. Malone," said John, with something of a quiver in his voice, "You will understand at once what I wish to speak of. It is to make arrangements for your future. After all that has happened it would be impossible that you should reside any longer with *my* child and *me*. I have made arrangements for a comfortable home for you in the country, where all your wants shall be supplied, no expense being spared toward your maintenance; your friend"—he looked at Bridget—"will arrange all details with you."

He turned to leave the room. "Stop!" exclaimed Annie, springing to her feet. "Stop! and tell me this— do you mean to take my boy from me! Am I never to see my child?"

"You have your infant," answered the old man, sternly. "The boy is *mine!*"

Without another word he left the room. "Bridget," cried Annie, wildly, "he can't *mean* it; he can't be cruel enough for *that;* tell me he don't mean it! I'll do anything he wants me to, if I can see my boy sometimes; no penance will be too heavy for me, only not that! not that!"

"It's no use," said Bridget, sadly. "We both tried — Jack and me — to persuade him to forgive you, but he's so proud nothing will move him. I didn't think he had such iron in his nature. Oh, Annie!" continued Bridget, in a flood of tears, "how could you, *could* you bring all this about?"

But Annie did not weep. There was a despair upon her that no tear could moisten, no cry give vent to. Without her child! and she had hoped that little hand might save her yet, and lead her on to Heaven. Whatever Bridget argued or explained Annie never seemed to heed, but sat in a stony silence. At last Bridget had to leave her. The night began to darken around her. Nora slipped into the room with food and light. Annie never noticed; when spoken to she appeared not to hear. Nora undressed her and put her to bed that night, for she was as weak as a baby. No word or token of any kind escaped her. The next morning Kitty and Nora, in turns peeping into the room, found that the mistress still slept. It was getting very late. A vague uneasiness possessed Nora. She would see why the mistress slept so long. She pulled the blind up gently, and, turning the light of morning on the fair face, saw her mistress lay there — dead!

They found afterwards, concealed in the bed clothes, the remainder of the poison she had taken.

⁎

Since the time of which we write the snows of winter and the sunshine of summer have twice lain upon the beautiful park. On the spot where Dave's life's blood stained the grass happy children are picking dandelions. Through the shady walks where he and Annie wandered lovers go arm in arm, and far apart, in their dishonored graves, lie the principals of this little tragedy.

In the doorway of the large house near the park an old man may sometimes be seen looking out upon the now busy thoroughfare. He seldom smiles. There is a settled sadness in the lines about his mouth and eyes, even when he looks fondly down upon a beautiful, golden-haired boy, who, clinging to him, calls him father.

Nora, who has grown palpably much older, looks tenderly after the wants of the young and the old master.

In their quiet home Jack and Bridget, surrounded by an ever-increasing brood of young Rooneys, live their happy lives.

A PIECE OF LAND.

A PIECE OF LAND.

There lived in a large city two brothers, named Romulus and Remus. Now don't imagine that we are going to give you a page from ancient history, for we aren't; our page is from prosaic modern fact.

If it was the perusal of Roman history which led Mrs. Ellinthorpe to bestow these names upon her boys, it certainly was the only history she ever perused. She must have read it at a very early age, for her life, from a period when she was extremely young, was devoted to providing herself with the necessary bread and butter, her education being circumscribed to the arithmetical problem connected with the gaining of said subsistence. When she reached her twenty-sixth year, and had so far solved that problem that, by industry and saving propensities, she was established in a little business of her own, she became luxurious and committed her first extravagance. That is to say, she married. She was not a sentimental woman, not at all; that she should do such a thing as this, had never entered her calculations. But somehow this step is not always a matter of calculation; in some cases it is one of speculation; with Mrs. Ellinthorpe it was a sudden, a most unaccountable one of affection.

Mr. Ellinthorpe brought to this union a little money and considerable ability. He put both of these requisites into the business and it flourished like a green bay tree. In due course of time Mrs. Ellinthorpe presented her husband with a baby boy, and when she asked her consort his opinion on the name of *Romulus*, that gentleman, who had never heard the name before, pronounced it a "high sounder," saying, "give it to him, my dear."

When little Romulus was nearing his third year a baby brother was added to the family group. Then Mrs. Ellinthorpe, having a faint remembrance of brotherhood between Romulus and Remus, declared her intention of bestowing the latter name upon her youngest offspring.

Her husband pointed out to her that there was only one objection ; that both his sons would have names beginning with the letter R, which would make a mixed up state of things when it came to signatures. Mrs. Ellinthorpe proved equal to the situation, declaring that Remus, having the shortest name, could always sign his in full. In this way the difference of opinion was settled. When Remus was four years old, everything in the business was going on finely. Mr. Ellinthorpe had speculative tendencies and branched out in the way of expenditures for the improvement of the business which his wife thought rather daring. She remonstrated, but he figured it out to her so conclusively as to the ultimate benefit to be derived, that she reluctantly yielded to his ideas.

These ideas were progressive—in fact, excellent—if Mr. Ellinthorpe had not made one slight mistake. He had not calculated on the possibility of dying before his plans could be carried out. But die he did, at a most inconvenient time, leaving his widow with the charge of the two little boys, and a business with a debt upon it. Mrs. Ellinthorpe treated this misfortune as she did those of her younger days. She immediately put her shoulder to the wheel; she also put her boys into public school as soon as their ages permitted. She worked hard with both brain and hands. She would try and keep her boys at school till they reached fourteen or fifteen years of age, then they could help her in the business. So, after a fatiguing day in the store, the mother would sit near her sleeping youngsters wearily patching their clothes. Then, as she stitched, she planned. She would see herself walking along the street a white-headed old lady, neatly dressed; on either side of her walked a son, tall and handsome. She would see herself a white-headed old lady, sitting in an elegantly furnished house on a fine street. Opposite her sat the sons. Grown men now, fashionably dressed and stylish looking, they caressed and praised her, telling her that in her old age she should work no more but live in luxury. Then the mother would smile in these waking dreams even as the tears coursed down her face, and look tenderly at the sleeping children.

Being brought up in so hard a school, Mrs. Ellinthorpe had an exaggerated idea of the value of money. She had, in early youth, of necessity, formed the habit of denying herself things which involved the expenditure of cash. What she had at first done under pressure of circumstances, she now did as a habit,—even after the liabilities which came upon her with her husband's death had been discharged, and she began to accumulate something in bank,—she still kept up her strict retrenchment of expenditure. She intended to give the boys a good start; she had borne the burden and heat of the day for them; they should not work under every disadvantage as she had done; she would teach them as they grew up; all that she had learned by such severe experience she would instil into them,—those money-making doctrines, which had placed her in the position to give them so good a start.

At seasons of the year when business was brisk she confiscated many of their play hours after school, sometimes even Sundays as well as Saturdays, to helping her in the store. By this she hoped to train their understandings. Romulus took to this kindly enough, but little Remus frequently rebelled. Under these disadvantages church and Sunday-school proved things that the boys only knew of by hearsay.

One Sunday evening, in the fall of the year, when the days were shortening fast, the little boys — Romulus was then in his tenth year — coaxed the mother to take a walk with them. The night was darkening around them. They came presently to a large edifice most brilliantly lighted; as they were passing, ravishing strains of solemn music rolled through the open doors. Romulus clasped his hands together ecstatically. "Oh, mother," he cried, "how beautiful it is! Is it a theatre?"

"Hush, child!" said his mother, in a scandalized voice, as she pulled him along, "it is a church!"

Put one idea before a child from infancy, educate him to it as he grows older, inculcate it constantly by "precept and example," and that child will have the thing as thoroughly branded into him, as ineffaceably marked upon him, as is the brand upon the wild cattle of our plains. It becomes a part of him, just as much as the food he eats and the air he breathes. It is a singular fact, however, that the same precepts may produce widely different results in differing individualities.

Romulus had been brought up to think that money or property — money's representative — was the *summum bonum;* that to obtain and hold this was the aim of life — all that existence contained worth the having. He proved very pliant to these doctrines. His mother would say to him, "The great principle is this — hold fast to all you can get and grab for more." She would add, "Make people, as well as inanimate things, useful to you. If you are half way smart you can make people you are thrown in with work for and with you; a little judicious flattery, which is always inexpensive, goes a long way and brings large returns. It is commendable to quietly and slyly take advantage of those you meet; always bearing in mind," she continued, "that they would do the same by you if they could get the chance."

Mrs. Ellinthorpe's success with Romulus was extremely gratifying. He followed her instructions to the letter; even in early boyhood he developed traits which filled her with proud joy. In games with other boys he came off victorious, especially in those games where a sharp lookout for the "main chance"—a gentle sleight of hand, a cunning which at times became almost unscrupulous—could aid him; the result was that his pockets bulged with marbles, pennies, jack-knives, bits of elegant twine—all those things prized by youth.

We regret that as a truthful historian we are obliged to record one unpleasant fact connected with these youthful smartnesses; that is, that few of his boy associates liked him; after a few games with this genius his financial prowess rather alarmed them, and they "fought shy" of him.

Remus was a sad proof of what different results may spring from the same course of training. It was very strange; he had been educated to habits of actual stinginess; the coin of his country was placed before him continually as the shining goal of all ambition; those valuable precepts to which the well-regulated mind of Romulus leaned naturally and gracefully, had been carefully bestowed upon Remus with results which caused his mother anxious pangs for his future. In very early boyhood Remus began to display his improper tendencies. He saw that money was very hard to get; consequently the instant he secured a piece of it he spent it, arguing that as it was unlikely he could get any more for sometime to come he had better make the most of his opportunity. This wrong principle he applied to everything; if he had an extra supply of cake, marbles, etc., he ran off to share with his boy friends. In all games of chance, in which he was remarkably successful, being blessed with a large stock of what is usually termed "fool's luck," he would turn around immediately and divide with the ones he had gained from. Of course all this had the sequence which might be expected. Remus, who was not half so smart as Romulus, not near as good-looking, soft-voiced or affable, was everybody's darling, His playmates would hang in large numbers about the back door waiting and calling for their favorite. Whatever good thing was going, they invariably saved some of it for Remus. If they owned some elegant retreat under a sidewalk, fitted up with old barrels, boxes and bits of carpet, stolen from their mothers' backyards and kitchens, Remus was invited to join this select circle and become president of their gang. Here, smoking cigarettes and short clay pipes filled with the foulest tobacco, with an occasional swig at some beastly beer, they would play cards and tell stories at times when the parents never dreamed of their dear ones being engaged in these pursuits. Here Remus would share all his earthly possessions with the boys; when he did not give them more, they knew it was because he hadn't it. He would fight for, as well as with them, which proofs of affection they returned in kind. Yet Mrs. Ellinthorpe, in spite of these irregularities in Remus, couldn't help loving him very much. If she felt ill Remus would spend every cent he could procure to purchase some little dainty for her, expressing his affection for her in looks and caresses as well. The coldest nature would melt under the geniality of his "ne'er-do-well" disposition; then the poor woman would sighingly reproach herself for loving this boy so much when his brother was in every respect so superior to him.

Mrs. Ellinthorpe could feel that even in matters of the affections Romulus was cold and calculating, when he bestowed a smile or caress upon his mother it was invariably the preface to some request. This became more pronounced as he grew older. She experienced that curious contradiction of feeling which makes us rather regret the rapid advancement of the pupil who has gone beyond our teaching.

Romulus loved power; if Remus had been as calculating and selfish as himself he would have found in him a powerful opponent, as it was, his brother's good-natured follies made a smooth way for Romulus. He became what from childhood he had aimed to be, his mother's sole friend and adviser.

In early manhood she confided to him that she had managed to accumulate some moneys; that they lived in a mean and close way as a safeguard; that with Remus's extravagant notions it would be as well to keep him ignorant of the real state of their finances; that the world at large was always on the lookout to take advantage of those possessing any substance and wrest it from them; that knowing this, she and Romulus would keep their own counsel and go on making and hoarding just as much money as they possibly could. To all of which Romulus yielded a ready assent, particularly to that portion relating to Remus. He had twofold reason for this; one was, that Remus, careless spendthrift though he was, had useful qualities. He liked — actually *liked* — to work hard; he could do the physical work of a man when only fifteen years old. The really *laborious* portion of their business fell upon the shoulders of Remus, and what extra help they had to employ in the busy seasons.

Romulus hated to work with his hands; to sit hours at a time with a bit of paper and pencil before him, figuring out the possible or probable profits of an investment, was just what suited his peculiar genius.

He represented to his mother that he was much more useful to her in managing her pecuniary affairs—reducing her expenditures by the simple process of getting as much as he could for as little as possible, arranging for the investment of means not needed in the business—than he could be at mere drudgery, which they could hire done at a very low figure.

To all such representations his mother yielded more and more. The other reason was, that by keeping Remus in ignorance as to their real financial standing, it would hold that young person as his mother's willing servitor; his affection for her would preclude entirely the notion of leaving her so long as her circumstances seemed strained; then, too, Romulus would in all respects "hold the whip hand."

The years, rolling steadily around their circle, had brought Romulus to his twenty-third year, when a new anxiety came upon Mrs. Ellinthorpe. It seemed to her a sudden thing, yet indications of it had been in the air for some time. It was in the Spring, a warm evening of the Sabbath day, that sitting beside her son on the front porch she noticed him start whilst a deep blush overspread his fair face. She looked for the cause, which proved to be merely a pretty girl on the other side of the street.

A distracting light flashed on Mrs. Ellinthorpe, a long vista of probabilities opened before her with a marriage altar in the perspective. This was a serious outlook. She must take a little time to think it over; for Romulus to marry would be to shatter that golden fabric she had reared in her imagination. Where would that rich old lady, with the white head and the adoring sons, be then ? When a young man had a mother who was devoting herself to his interests, his advancement in life, all that he needed to be happy, why should he wish to marry ? No, it would never do! She must quiet this bugbear of her mind by exacting a promise from Romulus that he wouldn't let himself do anything as unnecessary and absurd as marriage. But how to speak of it ? Such subjects had never formed matter for their conversations. How could she bring it about ? It must be done, and soon too, else he might thoughtlessly allow his affections to become entangled. She did it the very first opportunity she got to talk to him alone ; she did it with a suddenness that almost took his breath away.

"Romulus," she said, "you must never marry!"

A burning blush suffused the young man's face and he made no reply.

"Romulus," she repeated, anxiously, "you must not think of such a thing! You know that every effort of my life has been, and is, for you; think of the expense marriage would bring you, of the preoccupation of mind. You would not care to help your mother through her difficulties then; your heart would be all on your wife."

"Mother," said Romulus,— he had by this time regained his composure,—"you need do no fretting on that score. I think," he continued, reproachfully, "you have found me faithful to you so far. Have I ever hinted a wish to marry? You know I haven't."

This was true, but she did not feel quite satisfied yet.

"Promise me then that you won't," she insisted. "You know that it is for *you* I am saving and scrimping. I want you to be rich and respected. (Mrs. Ellinthorpe could not disassociate respectability from wealth). If you, as a young man, should marry and hamper yourself with a family, it would be dreadful."

"Oh, well!" said Romulus, rather moodily, "I'll promise not to, if that will satisfy you."

It was harder for Romulus to promise this than his mother knew, for he was already rather deeply involved in a young man's first passion. With his usual reticence, he had kept the matter to himself, more especially as he had persuaded his mother to put some of her spare capital into some real estate ventures, and saw that marriage was an extremely remote prospect for him. He had also, with his customary cunning foresight, given the object of his passion to understand that this might be considered flirtation on his part, nothing more; that is, he had given her to understand this in *words*, but *actions*, in these cases, have more effect than talk. When the young man of her preference looks ardent love into a girl's eyes, takes every opportunity of meeting her, conveys affection to her in every way except language, she generally feels quite sure that she will secure him soon.

In thinking about it, Romulus felt the wisdom of the course he had pursued with Luella in never asking her to be his wife; to be sure, he had accepted many gifts from her—pledges of the young girl's real love for him—but then, in his estimation, that was nothing. Of all this his mother had been profoundly ignorant. He would take his time to it, since it must be done, breaking his romance with Luella slowly and gently. Then he shed a few tears over his own disappointments.

His was the kind of nature which hardens under such a shower; every tear he shed strengthened his determination to end his amorous difficulties. For him to marry was out of the question; his mother, in her anger, would disinherit him, and love without money to ease the way—pooh! he couldn't think of it. He was a coward at heart; he dreaded to face Luella's grief when he struck the final blow. He would postpone it as long as possible. Circumstances favored this design, as his sweetheart was obliged to leave the city for the best share of a year, to accompany an ailing relative to California. The poor girl went away quite happy, feeling that Romulus really loved her, and that the rest was only a question of time. They corresponded, too, in a strictly Platonic fashion. Romulus was very careful in this respect, for he had heard something of suits for "breach of promise."

The worry of this love affair being temporarily laid aside, he turned the efforts of his intellect into their favorite channel—money making. Like his father, he had strong speculative tendencies; he had, into the bargain, a pretty high opinion of his own smartness. A man who is cunning and unscrupulous is seldom long at meeting his match. With the vanity of youth, he could not resist talking to the men he met about what *he* would do if he had the means; how much there was in this venture and that.

One day a cunning old fox came in his direction; he listened intently to the brags of this beardless youth, then quietly spread a net for him. This white-whiskered fox had had many experiences with youths like this; he knew just how to catch and fleece them. The cunning of the young man was a coarse thing beside the oily craft of the older one. He drew his game so gently toward the net, with manipulations so quiet, yet so sure, that the other never knew he was caught until the older, having secured what he wanted, threw off his mask. That was how Romulus came to be owner of a piece of land comprising forty acres. Such a bit of land, regarded from a farmer's standpoint, wouldn't amount to much. The soil was gravelly and yielded a growth of stubborn weeds. It was nothing to look at, being only a piece of extra desolateness set in corresponding loneliness upon the prairie on the outskirts of the city; but the fox had dressed it in prismatic colors. He had shown where streets would run through it, where churches and schoolhouses would be built upon it, where a depot would be placed; how in a short time—say two years at farthest—this land would be parcelled off into building lots, selling at prices to yield an enormous percentage on the original cost.

The fact was, the fox had more than he could carry, and wanted to unload, but Romulus didn't know this until later. The young man had assured himself of one thing before purchasing, that was that a railroad line was actually surveyed through this locality in such a way that said road would bound his acres on one side. This was a large purchase considering the limited means at his disposal. He induced his mother to mortgage some property she owned in order to meet the expense of this. "It will be only a little while, mother," he said gayly, "when it will be returned to you seven-fold."

His mother, carried along the stream of his sanguine hopes, was delighted, and she listened with keen interest to all his plans. Together they prepared a receptacle for the golden showers which would surely fall their way.

All this time Remus rollicked carelessly and cheerfully through his days of laborious toil. He spent most of his evenings with the young fellows of his own age, laughing at his serious brother, who pored over papers and plans and figured away incessantly, yet never seemed to grow any richer. They kept the light-hearted boy in profound ignorance of all their investments and hopes; in the meantime he took gratefully the simple pleasures his condition in life afforded him.

The year of Luella's exile was nearing completion. A newer and deeper interest now possessed her recreant lover. He fancied that he felt the throes of the tender passion again. In this case his feelings needed no restraining hand, as he was positive that his interest, as well as love, would be gratified without the bogy of marriage to terrify him.

The lady who brought all this about had grown into his existence so gradually that he could scarcely recall the time of her coming. A lady of fine figure and graceful manners had frequently called in at his place of business to make purchases. He could not quite tell how it was that they fell to conversing with each other. He was cognizant of an atmosphere about her differing from the women who usually frequented the place, an intangible air of refinement. She talked with a kindness which seemed a part of her everyday life; she was earnest and unaffected, yet had a softened sadness about her. Romulus, who was always keen in his notice of such adjuncts, saw the diamonds at her throat and on her fingers, the unstudied elegance of her apparel and her lavish use of money. She spoke frequently of her loneliness—her husband was absent a great share of the time; she had no children; time was heavy on her hands. She told him that she envied people who had keen interests in life, imperative duties therein. This drew him to telling her, with the bombastic frankness of youth, that few young men had so many cares and poignant anxieties as his; that measuring years by the worries and responsibilities they carried for him, he often felt he had reached the mature age of a hundred. She smiled softly, yet sympathetically, at all this, looking at him meanwhile in a way which bespoke profound interest—flattering attention.

Romulus dropped unconsciously into the smooth currents of these personal discourses, gliding easily on, as one sails blissfully on the bosom of some untried river, knowing nothing of shoals and rocks beyond. He was all the more at ease because his new friend, being somewhat his senior, treated him as one treats a favorite child with a sort of gentle tolerance of his youth—a free hearted manner, too, which had nothing of boldness in it.

She was a type of woman previously unknown to him. Frivolous girls who giggled and chattered incessantly, staid matrons with constant suggestions of cookery about them, ladies of slight reputations with rouged cheeks, bold eyes and voices— all these he had met and conversed with, but never before this a woman whose conversational powers embraced all subjects, who spoke of worlds of literature and art hitherto unheard of by him, who could dress even the commonest incidents of life in a language where pathos and humor sat side by side and never jostled, yet withal arrogated nothing to herself, making him feel—he scarcely knew why—much better satisfied with himself, much prouder and more hopeful during a talk with her than he had ever felt before.

He passed weeks and months in a state of sweet complacency. From the sky of hope one bright star shone on him with a steady radiance. He never said to himself what that star was, but in his soul he knew it was the certainty that he would sometimes see and talk with *her*. This feeling was the more insidious that it partook of nothing in the nature of desire, he never looked for her coming with the feverish unrest which characterized his love for Luella, no blushes heralded her approach—only a tender contentment, a quiet though intense joy. Luella's return at this period was like a harsh vibration, a sudden break in the finest part of some splendid anthem.

An unpleasant business confronted Romulus; he must break with Luella at once, and prevent the possible chance of these ladies meeting each other when seeking his society. Imaginary pictures of Luella in hysterics and his other lady friend looking on with that slow, peculiar smile upon her lips, haunted him. So he sent a nice little note to Luella as soon as he knew of her return, asking her to meet and walk with him next day in a sequestered place, as he had something very important to say to her. The poor girl was delighted beyond measure by this proof of his regard. When she appeared, all blushes and smiles, to meet him, he was surprised to find what a cast-iron strength had grown into his heart during the last year. He told her with cruel distinctness that their meetings must end with this one; that his mother discountenanced anything of the sort. He could never! never! do anything to *distress* his *dear mother!* At this point Romulus shed tears.

Since the days of our first mother, whose unfortunate curiosity led to those events which excluded us all from Eden, it has been very much the fashion to place the blame of most shortcomings and misfortunes upon women, particularly *mothers*. This fashion, like others, has many contradictions, for woman, serving so frequently as the recipient of contumely, is at other times "lauded to the skies" with a most lavish expenditure of vocabulary in regard to her virtues.

The mother, poor dear soul, is put to many uses that she wots not of. We all know the ordinary duties assigned her—the controling of her domestic and social matters. She is the homely, grubbing, comfortable soul who flits genially about the dining room and kitchen, carrying to the senses of her family and friends the aroma of well-cooked dinners and bountiful picnic supplies. But more than this, she is the "kicking post" for the whole family, so that if anything is lost or missing a demand immediately ensues upon "mother," with expressions of incredulity and anger should she fail to know of its whereabouts. Likewise in any domestic difficulties, there is always a generous desire on the part of the rest to allow mother her full share of the blame.

On the whole the life of mother is anything but rose color; from morning till night her patient feet perform their endless task; her anxious brain plans, her tired hands execute. The men of the household getting home from their daily avocations, take the easiest chairs and read the evening papers till mother summons them to supper; then, when enjoying with keen relish the viands carefully culled from the housekeeper's stores by the thoughtful soul who presides not over but at the meal, they uncork the vials of their wrath—that is, the accumulated annoyances of the day—upon the devoted head of mother.

All this mother may in her secret soul object to.

She seldom does so verbally, such scenes are not unexpected to her. If the meal passes in peace and joviality, as it occasionally does, she nibbles on these crumbs of comfort, feeling grateful for this short respite. That the catastrophes of the family in general should be laid at her door does not surprise her any more than the fact that when her sons, daughters, or husband are in an agreeable humor, they load her with commendations quite as extravagant as their usual fault finding. Mother is used to all this, she makes very little outward manifestation as to any feelings she may have. There is a portion of mother's life where she is very conspicuous, in reality the principal actor upon the stage of every emotion, yet she is totally unconscious of the part she plays. When her son, with glistening eyes and thrilling eloquence, is telling his young lady friend that *his mother* is the noblest and sweetest woman upon earth, the poor soul alluded to is sitting in the back room darning his hose and trying to remember when he last kissed or spoke kindly to her.

A mother is a handy thing to have in some instances. Romulus found his mother a great convenience in this case. A few months of more congenial society had made him heartily tired of Luella anyhow; he was in no hurry to marry even if his mother had not interdicted it.

As we are telling a *true* story, without a grain of romance in it, we must admit that Luella didn't even faint when receiving this blow to her affections; she wept copiously and told Romulus that she could never get over it, and that she considered his mother a hard-hearted old woman! Romulus shook his head in apparent dejection, and said it was their destiny, it couldn't be helped; they must be the slaves of circumstances. Then he said how he would appreciate her love for him, but she could see that it was out of the question for them to enjoy each other's society any more. Then Luella, who was not lacking in pride, told him that she should certainly never seek his company again, at which statement Romulus felt in his heart a secret relief. Then they parted for good, and we are happy to say that at the end of another year Luella had so thoroughly recovered that she married an estimable young man who was worth a dozen like Romulus, and "lived happy ever after."

For some months succeeding this, all ran smoothly. Mrs. Ellinthorpe was surprised by the good nature of her eldest son. Like most geniuses—financial or otherwise—he had been subject to spells of irritability; all this appeared, for the time at least, modified. He dwelt with elaboration on his schemes for the land, telling his mother it would not be long before she'd be riding in her own carriage. The Fox having deluded Romulus, he in turn deluded his mother; she listened with admiration. It is so easy to believe what we want to, besides her faith in his discernment; his aptitude for turning everything to advantage, was very great.

The new friend made the year following his parting with Luella very pleasant. She talked, she even walked with him quite frequently; she presented him with gifts commemorative of their friendship; she marked the date of their first conversation with each other by a diamond ring, of their first walk together by a ruby scarf-pin; she did these things in a way which conveyed a subtle flattery, a delicate, melancholy admiration for him, which quite thrilled Romulus. He used to accept these gifts as he had Luella's, with a fancy that he would some time reciprocate. This notion of liquidation in a dim, uncertain future is very much in vogue with some people. It may seem a matter of surprise that Romulus should keep his "dear mother" from knowing anything at all of his amorous proclivities. To be sure, he was only applying to his love affairs the same principle which regulated his pecuniary ventures; his mother had educated these principles into him; yet, strangely enough, he could not say to her with brutal frankness what he certainly said to himself very often, " This woman loves me; she is a married woman, consequently I couldn't marry her if I would; there is nothing to prevent us from loving each other, if we maintain a decent amount of secresy. If there is any right or wrong about it, that is *her* lookout, not mine; no man should be fool enough to pass the blossom on his path without picking it."

It may be seen by this that Romulus was perfectly willing to love and be loved, yet the object of his affection — if we may call it by that name — maintained a certain boundary line between them which he found impossible to cross. During the second year of their acquaintance he had progressed far enough to hold her hand for half an hour at a time, as he looked inexpressible things into her eyes. This, of course, was very enchanting, but then it was illusive and dream-like in its nature. He was inwardly chafing, yet dared not give too distinct an idea of what was passing in his mind; he was like one who attempts to snare some little bird, with strained eye, with hand upon the bait with which he hopes to draw the victim on — yet afraid to move, almost to breathe, in case some sudden fright might cause his prey an alarm, when it would fly, never to return.

Things remained in this condition for another year. Romulus was astonished and chagrined; he did not know that in this game of hearts he had an opponent worthy his utmost skill. With the ready vanity of youth, he had taken it for granted that this lady would never have singled him out for her friendship or society unless she loved him. He did not realize that this woman of the world was playing her little game, too; that with adroit flatteries she was luring him on to lay his nature bare:

that she derived a secret amusement from picking up these specimens, as one lifts some odd insect gingerly on the top of the finger, steadying it, meantime urging with pin pricks the helpless thing to fresh manifestations of its actions under those circumstances.

This woman had for a long time been engaged in seeking a cure for a wound. She had been suffering since the first two years of her married life with a complaint which is alarmingly prevalent — the heartache. People seek strange cures for this disease. Many of them apply the poultice of religion, others the black draught of reform; very many the madness of dissipation. None of these harsh remedies suited this lady, so she drifted aimlessly about, and the ache grew harder. It so happened that she caught the ache in this way — she loved her husband with the deepest, strongest love that woman can experience. You will say that was all right; so it was, but, unluckily, there must have been a mistake somewhere, for, though he certainly loved his wife at first, he seemed, after awhile, to weary of what was always all his own, and looked too longingly after forbidden fruit. To this his wife closed her eyes — she was too proud a woman to let him or any one else see her sufferings — she never reproached him, never interfered with him; she wore her gay mask with thoroughly deceptive grace, only removing it in the deep loneliness of the night, when she stood face to face with her soul in the darkness and uttered her wretched wail. If she had been fortuuate enough to bear a little child, she would have satisfied the hunger of her heart on it. Even *this* happiness was not hers. If she had been forced to toil for a subsistence, she would have found some natural outlet for her restless sorrow, but not even this. She lived sumptuously in her elegant home, she trailed about in silken garments over her velvet carpets, and the ladies of her "set" praised and envied her. The men called her a noble, stately woman; the only one she loved on earth hurried away to chase his newest butterfly. Then she sought amusement.

There is a frightful bitterness in the kind of heartache she suffered from, which makes one take pleasure in seeing others suffer in the same manner. She began to amuse herself in this dangerous way some time before Romulus met her. The first time, the party she selected was about her own age. His vanity precipitated an inglorious defeat. His masculine mind could only draw one inference from the fact that the lady showed a preference for his society! He had the temerity to hint this inference. He departed very hastily from the blue flame of her wrath, and wondered—stupid fool that he was—what the world was coming to.

At this period her soul grew so sick that it clamored for a holiday. She sent for the family physician; she told him plainly that her malady required a change of air, for instance, a trip abroad

— he, dear old soul, took his large fee and instantly prescribed the remedy suggested. Her husband consented willingly; at home or abroad, it mattered little to him, so that she didn't bother him. Even this was not much of a distraction — heartache is such an obstinate disease.

On her return she found herself improved in health, but then — all this was the prologue to her acquaintance with Romulus. What first attracted her attention to him was his youth. That other hateful experiment was old enough to be really wicked; perhaps a *young* man would be her friend in very truth.

This fallacy concerning youth is indulged in by many; when we see pictures of angels they are always young. Did we ever see a representation of angelhood which was middle-aged or old? Yet how much innocence do we really find in youth?

During the second year of her friendship with Romulus this lady made some singular discoveries as to that gentleman's mental calibre. There was a meanness in his cunning which amazed her. When he talked with conceited verbosity about his mother — revealing himself in the light of a martyred victim to his deep love and reverence for the author of his being — she drew him on by an approving silence which concealed her real understanding. This "mother" business was nothing new to her; she had heard so many youths descant after this fashion, she had not the implicit faith in his statements he supposed.

Remus was having some little experiences about this time, but nobody ever thought of taking much notice of anything *he* said or did — the only regularity in his conduct being his punctuality at meal time. He had a masculine appreciation of the necessity of "feeding up," which made his mother sure of seeing him at least three times a day. His conduct after business hours — being after six in the evening — might be called erratic; he was much given to nocturnal rambles. Some three hours after Romulus had fallen into the sleep of virtuous repose, the careless steps of Remus could be heard entering the maternal mansion. In early boyhood his mother had tried remonstrance, even beatings, to cure him of these irregularities, but in vain. There is nothing so hard to argue with or convince as a thoughtless good nature; dogged obstinacy may yield under determined assault; the merry good humor which receives your scoldings with a smile or kiss, then goes its way, is irresistible.

Mrs. Ellinthorpe found resistance useless; then, woman-like, she made the best of it, saying to Romulus that his brother would soon outgrow all these improper likings, at which Romulus shook his wise head gravely and answered that Remus had bad tastes and was evidently going to the dogs.

Under ordinary circumstances it is expected that after a young man turns his twentieth year he is liable to fall in love and wish to marry — it is just as natural for all this to come about as for him to eat, drink or breathe. Somehow Mrs. Ellinthorpe had never associated this idea with Remus; she had, as we have noted, felt anxiety concerning Romulus. This was inconsistent, for Romulus, being a pattern of propriety, she should have felt that he was not likely to do anything so unreasonable, so much against his interests as well as his mother's, as to marry; whereas Remus — who always did exactly what he felt inclined to do, "without rhyme or reason" — was, in the very nature of things, the one who would first fall into this serious error; and of course he did, desperately, too, for it was never his disposition to do anything half way. So into love he fell, head over heels, a pretty girl of eighteen having captured him. For a year he lived, figuratively speaking, in heaven. An unaccountable, ridiculous happiness marks the first stages of the fever called love. Remus had a capacity for loving which kept pace with all his other unrestricted capacities, and he never thought of stinting himself. When the young girl had promised to marry him some day, and love him for ever, he went about with such an air of beatitude upon him "that he who runs might read," but they didn't read or care. The people who look continually for gold can seldom see any other brightness. That Remus was so occupied by his own affairs that he didn't bother them, or show a disposition to pry into their money-making schemes, was a consolation. Meantime Romulus dwelt with great severity upon his brother's manifold shortcomings, thus seeking to strengthen his own influence, yet Remus being in a measure indispensable, they must hold him to the business. This was more imperative, for Mrs. Ellinthorpe was breaking down in health; she could no longer participate actively in the work as she had been wont to do. The strain of those long years was telling on her; then, too, old age was coming without the little comforts and luxuries with which love endeavors to surround it. She became a sufferer from that too strict economy she had inculcated. She discharged the household duties unassisted; this—even for the small family of three—was often, very often now, a tax upon her strength. When Romulus found her pale and exhausted from the preparation of a simple meal he would cheer her up with promises of a future without work or care.

One can't live exclusively on promises; to one fainting from weakness by the wayside it is small help to know that a bountiful repast awaits a mile or so farther on. Mrs. Ellinthorpe had a dim, uneasy perception of this, so when Romulus insisted on putting the profits of the last year's business into a new speculation, "just the thing to double itself if they waited a couple of years," she resisted vigorously. She reminded him that in her estimation the time had come for them to realize on these numerous investments. A few more years of this pinching and straining would bring her to death's door.

Romulus assured her she was all right; she only lacked patience. It would be better for her to put things in his name, or give him power of attorney to act for her, if she felt the strain of the business too much. He was willing—he remarked with a self-sacrificing air—to take *all* on his shoulders. He was young and strong, and for her sake would bear it. His mother was not yet broken enough in health or spirit to do this! The wily guardian of her interests had to practice the patience he had so strongly enjoined upon her.

It was particularly unfortunate that she should prove so unexpectedly obstinate just now as the purchase of the forty acres had cramped him, and some ready money *must* be raised. How was he to do this? It required reflection, and he hit upon a way at last.

This unlucky day, when all was going against him, the Fox appeared. Romulus was feeling excessively cross, the Fox suggested the necessity of improvements upon these acres. He was interested in them, as they adjoined his land—it would be to their mutual advantage to make the land more attractive. Romulus asked sarcastically if he wanted it set out in parterres with a beautiful fountain in the centre? The Fox remarked gently that his young friend seemed irritated; that he—the Fox—being a practical man, only desired the expenditure of a hundred or so in sidewalks and shade trees. At this Romulus gave full rein to a temper naturally violent. He consigned the Fox, in flaming language, to a very warm region! The Fox was inwardly delighted—this was what he had come for—a final rupture. Perceiving the humor of his dear young friend he kept applying the goad, which led to their parting with mutual curses and openly expressed determination to have nothing more to say to each other.

The Fox retired from the field laughing to himself. He knew what Romulus didn't—that in a very short time the assessments on these acres would be something enormous. The Fox chuckled with rapture; he was all right—having plenty of capital to swing his ventures—but his egotistical young friend—raising money by mortgage and forced loans and paying big interest! Oh, it was too funny! The Fox laughed till the tears ran down his face.

A week later Romulus hastening to his supper, after a delightful tete-a-tete with his lady friend, found his mother presiding at table with a gloomy brow and distraught manner. Remus full of talk and gayety saw nothing. He rushed off in his usual heedless way as soon as the meal was finished. His mother looked moodily after him. "*He* is bad enough," she exclaimed—"but *you* are worse!"

"Mother," said Romulus, as a dark flush passed over his face, "what do you mean?"

"I mean," she answered, "that I know all about your trying to raise a second mortgage on that property of mine; *you* didn't tell me, but an old friend, who thought I ought to know, did. Look you," she continued, severely, "*you* may call it what you please, but most folks would term it rascality! Never try such a thing again."

"You wouldn't help me out of a tight place," said Romulus; "a fellow can't figure *everything;* unexpected expenses come sometimes; one can't drop *all* for the sake of a few extra hundreds involved. If you want to manage matters entirely by yourself, just say so! If you won't wait for the land to grow into value—why, throw it up, that's all!"

Mrs. Elinthorpe was alarmed; without Romulus she could do nothing; he had been the controlling power so long that she would not be able to get on without him, she must condone this—his first offense. She did; but this experience left her much older, much sadder.

Some weeks after came that surprise from which the Fox had so discreetly retired. Romulus was assessed for sewers, water pipes, grading, etc., on his piece of land. That this would come about some day he knew, but so soon, and at such great expense, he had not figured on that.

A great author has written in one of his books, "You are sure to succeed; if a man's foot obstructs your way—stamp upon it; do you think he won't remove it?" Romulus would succeed exactly in this fashion; he would stamp upon anything which hindered him, just as he had stamped out the little flame of Luella's love when he no longer required its warmth. Mrs. Ellinthorpe recognized at last the peculiar mixture of shrewdness and meanness she had spent so many years in modeling. She felt a pang for which there was no balm; she grew cynical and cross as her perception of this truth increased, and now came Remus to her with his tale of love. Love! she hated the word! She told him angrily, almost fiercely, to look around him, did he see the bare walls, the uncarpeted floors, the poverty, and dare think of a wife. Ah, it was like him to be so unreasonable as to want to marry! Was this the return for her years of toil, that as soon as he reached man's estate he must love some woman more than his own mother? Let him go and tell this girl—since he had been foolish enough to ask her to be his wife—that he could not marry —that he had no way of supporting her—that he owed a duty to his mother! Then Remus, quite crushed, quite broken-hearted, obeyed. He did not postpone the fatal declaration of his woes; he went to his beloved at once with the whole story. The girl, who truly loved him, looked at him with her beautiful eyes full of tears and said, yes, he could go, he could give her up since it was his mother's will. She would be willing to share poverty, *anything*, with *him*, but if he thought it *right* to give her up, he must do so. She turned away with choking sobs, but Remus, fond, foolish fellow, caught her in his arms, saying he would live and die with her, he wouldn't give her up for ten mothers! Then they both vowed to wait for each other if it was for ever. So ended the first part of Remus's love story.

Romulus was getting on very slowly in his private love venture. The lady who had not been much given to obtruding her husband into their conversations, found occasion to mention him quite frequently of late. If a number of weeks slipped past without Romulus seeing her, she had been obliged to remain at home rather closely, her husband being of a jealous temperament. If Romulus, grown impatient, proposed a drive or walk, she would have to put it off till some other time when her husband might be out of town. Romulus privately gnashed his teeth and cursed the husband. Meantime my lady, who was heartily sick of her "amusement," would have given it up, only that she wanted to play the little game out, and demonstrate the meanness of her ardent young lover. His avaricious propensities being well known to her—she decided to throw a golden bait, then suddenly remove it, and watch the result. To this end she talked of some thousands she had in bank, asking, with a delightful unconsciousness of manner, if he could recommend some way of using it. She carried large sums of money with her which she carelessly displayed to him; she supplemented all this with some handsome gifts. In her heart she rather hoped that he would *steal* from her,— she believed him capable of it. She managed all this with a demeanor which would have fooled men older and more worldly wise than Romulus.

The train was ready laid; the next meeting with him she would touch off the fuse and explode the mine; she would come to him in great distress with a tale of financial ruin and beggary—pretending to throw herself on his generosity. The *result* she was assured of,— he would discard her friendship with many soft excuses. She shook with inward merriment, even as her lip curled with scorn, fancying the scene. This lady dove, with the wisdom of the serpent, didn't really know which she despised the most, Romulus or herself.

It was the night preceding the last grand experiment of her love game with this modern financier. An unusual restlessness was upon her. She walked incessantly about her dressing room, her slippered feet fell noiseless on the soft velvet of the carpet. The windows of the dressing room, situated in the third story of the house, looked out upon the street; she pulled aside the silken curtain and gazed, bright stars gemmed the broad arch of the sky, the lamps flickered in the fitful gusts of wind which blew along the boulevard; it was silent and deserted except by an occasional carriage rolling swiftly over it. Beyond it, the lake tossed its white crested waves; why was she so excited and restless? she could not sleep, read or write, she would think until she became drowsy enough for bed.

Years after, this night stood silhouetted against her memory, a black figure of fate on a lonely expanse. She sat beside the window, bringing into mental review the years of her acquaintance with Romulus; all that had come of it was a comparatively innocent love making, there had been no guilt in their intercourse, but had he *really* loved her — had he been all that she at first supposed him — could she answer for the result? She was glad that he had proved a scoundrel; her husband's infidelities could not be urged as excuse for her. Then her mind reverted to her husband — who, all the time she was making an excuse of him to Romulus, was out of the city — she remembered the happiness of their early married life, her trust in him, her hope for the years to come. Then the blankness — the pall that settled over her when she knew the truth. She could distinctly recall how, in those weeks of her first overpowering anguish, was lovely weather, how the sun blazed at her with a searching light that seemed to mock her, how the flowers shook gaudy colors at her. How balmily the wind was blowing, how the black death in her soul cried out against the garishness of life. She shuddered, remembering all this.

Ah, was not her sorrow dreadful in the bearing, a nobleness compared to the low pursuit with which she strove to heal her wound? Her tears burst forth, for the first time in many months she was drenched by the rainstorm of her emotions; torn by sobs and convulsive moanings — with her jeweled fingers clenched in her long, dark hair — she lay upon the floor as the wretched hours wore on.

About one o'clock in the morning she was roused from this lethargy of despair by a violent ringing of the bell, the patter of servants' feet along the hall, excited voices; then she was hastily summoned. They tried to break it to her gently — her husband had been badly injured in a railroad wreck, it might be unto death — she must be composed; yes, she could go to him; in two hours she could get a train. A mad whirl came into her brain, if he should die before she could see or speak to him. Oh, fly, hasten the preparations for her departure; what ailed the lagging horses? the slow train? Off she went, with Romulus forgotten as completely as though he had never lived. Thus ended the second love passage in this young man's life, for he saw her no more.

Mrs. Ellinthorpe never renewed that first active resistance to the encroachments of her son. "Hope deferred" had made her heart too sick for anything — even when connected with the gold she loved so well. Romulus grew crosser, too, as the passing months brought in their train accumulated worries. The sudden and complete disappearance of his last lady-love amazed and chagrined him beyond expression. He could not shake off a fancy that at any time she might stand before him with her handsome presence, her slow, strange smile. He began to think he had really loved her and to condole with himself accordingly. He had little time, however, to fret over this sudden turn, for "ways and means" claimed his incessant attention. That piece of land — uneasy venture — was a vampire which drained his purse. If something could be done to make it more accessible, perhaps he could sell to advantage. He was not the only one desiring this, as a number of men largely interested in real estate had holdings near his own. He talked with them. The railroad was now in course of construction. If, when it was running, the railroad company would place a depot near this land, it would be a fine thing for all interested. The older men suggested that Romulus wait upon some of the railroad magnates, lay the case before them, and by his representations and their combined influence, bring about "this consummation devoutly to be wished." He — puffed up with importance of holding consultation with these older and moneyed men — willingly consented.

Whilst Remus plodded away at the business, and his mother lived on hope — she had precious little else to live on — Romulus haunted the railroad offices, chased after and humbly waited on the president of the road, and at last, by dint of cringing, pushing and begging, got the measure through. It took months to do this, and when it was at last accomplished Romulus bragged long and loudly. His moneyed friends, to whom also it was a great boon, complimented themselves on having gained it without any outlay of time and trouble on their own parts.

The little god of love is represented with his eyes bandaged. There is a proverb extant about the blindness of this passion. However this may be in point of truth, love certainly had the opposite effect upon Remus, for under its influence he noticed many things which never came to his observation before. He wondered why Romulus, always keenly alive to business interests, should spend so much of his time away from the store, yet render no account, so far as he knew, as to the why and wherefore. Why, when Romulus was there, strange men, having no connection whatever with the business, should be frequently calling to see and talk with him on subjects Remus heard nothing about. He began to think that this brother, with whom he had fought in boyhood and always had dubbed a sneak, was trying to pull the wool over his eyes. The happiness of another was at stake, the girl who had promised to wait for him, would do so till she was grayheaded and toothless if things kept on the present way, for the business appeared to yield nothing more than a very insufficient living. Remus, thinking that "all is fair in love and war," took the earliest opportunity to solve his doubts. A gentleman coming in hurriedly one day—evidently not knowing Romulus by sight—addressed the brother. "Mr. Ellinthorpe, I believe?" said the stranger.

Remus nodded gravely; he had a perception that it was a mistake. The person who spoke was a tall young man, with a face prematurely aged by nights of poker playing and other genteel vices: he wore his hair parted down the middle and arranged in front in the sweetest beau-catchers imaginable; with such curling embellishments—his hat carefully placed on the extreme back of his head—these attractions, further aided by a blonde moustache, elegantly waxed, he was quite a distracting figure.

Remus saw all this with a glance; the stranger hooked the forefinger of his right hand into the second top buttonhole of Remus's coat. Holding him thus, he poured out a torrent of volubility which Remus's understanding had to take long strides to keep up with. From this vortex of words —interspersed with the choice oaths affected by young men of his class—Remus at last gathered something to this effect: that the person before him could bring unexceptioual references as to his abilities; that hearing how Mr. Ellinthorpe and some others wished to employ a pushing, go-ahead, energetic man to take charge of a real estate office on their subdivisions, he was just the fellow for them; that he could talk purchasers blind—Remus readily believed this—that Mr. Ellinthorpe's large landed interests needed a painstaking, competent, rushing hustler! These words ran, raced, fairly tumbled over each other in the stranger's eagerness to get them out; Remus caught his breath in surprise; with affected carelessness he said that the trifling real estate *he* carried could hardly need so much looking to.

"Why your very last purchase," exclaimed the other, "that piece of land on which they tell me a fine railway station is being built, that alone needs careful supervision; a good man right there can make things just hump, I tell you!"

Remus having discovered all he wanted to, dismissed the voluble young person with a promise to "think about it."

He went to his mother at once, coming to what he wished to say with his usual straightforward manner. That he was very much angered could not be denied.

"Mother," he said, "from the time we were little boys you placed more confidence and love in Romulus than in me; being some years younger than he I uttered no protest against it. Though I've been a harum-scarum, heedless young fellow, I have worked with and for you ever since I had the strength to work. Then, when I grew to manhood, when I came to you and told you of my betrothal to that young girl, when I begged your sympathy and encouragement, you urged me on the score of your poverty—my duty to you—to break my word to her. The happiness of two lives must be set aside that you and Romulus should go on accumulating land and money. You told me," he continued, bitterly, "to look around me at the poverty and discomfort, but you didn't tell me of your acres, your hoarded thousands, this piece of land which I heard of to-day. It is wrong—all wrong!"

Remus ceased talking for a moment, quite breathless from his angry agitation. His mother began to weep. "It is quite true," she said, through her tears, "you seemed such a spendthrift, as you grew up, that I couldn't trust you. But we are not rich, Remus; far from it. Every cent, and borrowed money besides, is in these investments. We are tied hand and foot, and if I wished ever so much to help you to marry I couldn't."

"Mother," he answered, with an impatient wave of his hand, "we will put the question of marriage aside. I will only say this about it—that I didn't break my troth with that girl, that I'm glad I had manhood enough to keep my word to her. We are as much engaged to each other now as ever. The point I would come to is this—what are you doing this for? Why do you seek to accumulate at such dreadful sacrifices? You are growing old and weak, and if you had taken reasonable comfort and pleasure in life as you went along you would now be stronger and happier. Romulus is to blame for this with his sneaking plans, all for himself and what he calls his *ambition!*"

At this unlucky juncture Romulus appeared upon the scene. A fierce storm of words ensued, in which Remus told his brother, in very forcible language, exactly what he thought of him. The presence of the mother, instead of restraining, inflamed these combatants,—for Remus felt, with justice, that his mother had been the greatest sufferer.

"Go," he said passionately, to his brother, "take your way and I'll take mine, since you'd drain the very life blood from my mother with your folly; I'll not stand by to see it. You've got things in such pretty shape with your plans, your investments! A little decency, as one goes along, is worth all your prospective riches! Mark my words, when at last—if ever it comes to that—you are worth all the money you want, you will have nothing else, you will stand alone upon your pinnacle of gold with not a pleasure left you, except what gold can buy; then you'll be surprised to find how many things there are that money *can't* buy!"

He paused for an instant, as Romulus hurled some highly colored imprecations at him, then continued, "If I could do any good to *you*, mother, by remaining with this hell-hound here,"—a

scornful look at Romulus marked the sentence—
"I'd stay, but it would be only working for him to accomplish what is really meant for *himself!* Let him talk as he will to you about his love for you, he takes a queer way of showing it. You are the chisel with which he seeks to open his golden door, that's all!"

Remus rushed out, with a vicious slam of the door to emphasize his feelings.

"He is a fool!" snarled Romulus. "He'll never *have* anything or amount to anything as long as he lives. Of course, to cap all, he'll up and leave us now just as we need him the most. I hoped we could hold on to him a little longer; hired men won't look after things as well as *he* does, and I'm obliged to be away so much of the time."

This speech jarred upon Mrs. Ellinthorpe. Its cold-blooded tone of calculation coming just after Remus's fiery denunciations was like a cold trickle of ice water.

"He may be in the right," she murmured. "After years of toil and struggling, where do we stand? I am old and tired. I have trusted all to you, yet nothing is realized. I long to fold my hands and rest."

Romulus talked to her of the future, the certainty now that they would soon have plenty. She must not fret over the violence of Remus; he had always been headstrong and unreliable; if he was determined to go, let him go! He—Romulus—

would keep his hand upon the wheel and steer her in safety through her troubles.

He left her only half convinced; she felt that Remus was right in the main; she could not retrace those steps of a lifetime; she could see plainly *now* the blunders by the wayside. But Romulus held all. His wheedling had overcome her doubts over and over again. He had managed to get so much of her property into his name that he held her fast. Henceforth her fortune *must* be cast with his, and Remus left to work out the enigma of life by himself. Ah! that they could be little boys once more, she would do so differently. She saw that what Remus had called the "decencies" of living should not be despised,—the church, the social intercourse, the nice home, the becoming attire,—none of these should yield to mere money making. Thus thinking, and weakly weeping, she picked up the burden, grown much heavier now, and trudged her weary way.

Remus proved true to his word, he instantly looked about him for a position, being sternly determined he would eat no more of that bitter home bread leavened with deceit. With the "fool luck" which helped him in his youthful games, as well as the affections of his comrades, he soon found employment where, though the wages were low to start on, he was promised higher as soon as he demonstrated that he would work well and faithfully. His labor was lightened by the thought of the reward. He talked it all over with his beloved, and she assured him that with him she was content to live on the humblest fare. After a few months he would have saved enough from his modest salary to furnish a few rooms with housekeeping necessities, then they would get married. He procured a cheap temporary lodging near his work, but did not entirely neglect his mother under the pressure of these new cares. He went to see her two or three times every week. Having expended his wrath on Romulus, he soon forgave her part in the unpleasantness. He felt anxious, too, as to her health, for he could not help noting her increasing feebleness. Mrs. Ellinthorpe mentioned to Romulus the fact of Remus's calls, then Romulus cursed his brother so fervently that she took pains never to allude to Remus again.

The station upon his piece of land being in process of construction rendered Romulus comparatively happy. He never wearied of talking over the hopefulness of the situation with his real estate friends. They all said this was the time to push things; it would be better to build a little wooden office out there and put a smart agent in it, and the expense could be shared by all. They employed the identical young man who had buttonholed Remus by mistake. This gentleman, arrayed in a linen duster with a pen behind his ear, made an interesting picture as he sat with the door wide open on the warm summer days, in the little ten-by-twelve house; with his chair tilted backward, his feet upon the desk, he chewed upon a cigar and contemplated the monotonous prospect for many hours at a time without interruption. The only periods when he displayed any activity being those rare ones when his employers—or rarer still, some customers—came upon him ; then his industry was lovely to behold. His eyes bulging out with exertion, his hat off, his coat sleeves turned up, he could be seen writing away for dear life, scarce hearing the approaching footsteps, so absorbed was he.

This delectable youth spent a very quiet summer, his only amusements being the killing of stray blue-bottle flies in his window, and insulting women who had the misfortune to pass his place unattended. At this latter he was quite an expert, being a graduate of a down-town office. He used to tell the fellows of his club, when they met evenings for the customary poker playing, that he really could'nt stand such a cursed existence much longer. With nothing to look at all day except prairie grass and those confounded white real estate signs, just like overgrown tombstones, he felt sure that the blasted monotony would drive him to suicide. Next pay-day coming round he would think better of it however, and conclude to go on a while longer, which he did until the fine weather coming to an end without any perceptible advantage accruing from the little house and tenant thereof, his employers politely dismissed him. Now followed the long, slow winter, every month of which was marked to Mrs. Ellinthorpe by an increasing weariness. Romulus told her that next summer with the road running through their land, and station completed, would cause a delightful change in their surroundings. She smiled feebly, making no reply. Remus and the young wife— they were married now—paid the mother some visits, generally contriving to get there when Romulus was absent. They cheered her with their happiness, their simple hopes and joys. They had furnished the three rooms which constituted their home. When the spring days came again Remus coaxed his mother into coming to the little nest and sharing a simple meal with them. They treated her with every deference and kindness; the truth was, their hearts ached for her.

Romulus was showing the effect of the mental strain upon him. His brown locks were thickly seamed by gray, two long wrinkles had formed across his forehead; there were crowsfeet around his eyes, a slight stoop in his shoulders, too,—his eyes retained their eager piercing light, but it was no longer that of hope.

It was October now; the station upon his land, for which he had worked so hard and from which he had hoped so much, had been standing for a year. Frequently upon a Sunday of these late autumn days he would walk out to it—it was a very long walk—and sadly contemplate the ground. The dead weeds and grasses crunched mournfully beneath his feet. Far away to the south stretched the prairie to meet the sky; all that broke the monotony of the view was the railroad raised about six feet above the surrounding level, and the station—a melancholy travesty upon his plans and schemes. It was a neat building, quite tasty in fact, upon one of the side doors of it was inscribed, "Ladies' Waiting Room." Alas! No ladies ever waited there. The trains went scurrying past it at frequent intervals, and the passengers aboard cracked jokes about the little station standing in its loneliness, with the unbuilt acres all around it. The desolate year that it had spent there had aged it more than a couple of years of use, for every pane of glass in it had been smashed to atoms—no boy passing it could resist throwing a stone.

Romulus thought bitterly, as he looked upon this devastation, that it was like ancient times, when each wayfarer along the road would throw another stone upon the heap already started to the memory of some dead friend. Surely this was *his* heap—the monument to broken aspirations. Upon its front the name of the station—all black and white—stood out pretentiously. How delighted he had been when this building was in process of construction; how sure he had been that a few more months would see a prosperous town growing up about it. Then he looked even more dolefully upon the broad graded street, with the great sewer running through it, which bounded his land on one side. He shuddered, remembering the mortgage he had raised to meet the expenses of that sewer and grading.

He would walk on half a block beyond the station on this expensive street, and look at where the big sewer emptied itself into a stream—which stream was an offshoot of the main river of the city. This offshoot had wandered some distance from the parent stream and lost itself upon the prairie. As he contemplated this, an awful fear would beset him. Some day, perhaps not so far off, the city would build a bridge across this stream and mayhap insist upon the property owners helping to pay for it. He felt that this would be the "last straw."

There was a fascination to him in looking at the land; he had sacrificed so much to it—staked and lost love, honor, every pleasure of life upon it —that covered, though it was, all over by assessments and mortgages, it seemed really all that he had left. He would walk around and on it for an hour or two, noting where the rough trenches had been ploughed through it—the indicating lines of where the streets would some day be—the big black and white signs that the real estate men had standing thickly on it. So far as *selling* the land was concerned, these signs had heretofore seemed to work upon the scarecrow principle.

Sometimes when he took these excursions, the sun would shine brightly, the air blow softly, kind nature would smile on him to soothe his forlornness, then recreant hope returned again. But the days were not always thus; at other times the gray sky frowned upon him, the heavy clouds hung lowering on the horizon, the biting wind whistled angrily around him, the lonely prospect unrolled appallingly before him, and sadness steeped his very soul. He would turn his anxious glance to where the clouds of smoke at some distance to the north, west and east of him, denoted the city with its outlying suburbs. Would these buildings never stretch to him? Must he wait for long years yet to come? Then the salt tears of disappointment would stream down his cheeks as he dejectedly retraced his steps.

It was midwinter again. The snow lay thick upon the ground, the frost snapped viciously. Poverty hurried on all the extra garments she could procure, even if patched or ragged; want walked blue-lipped and shivering along the city streets. The brothers had exchanged no words since the memorable day when Remus made his discovery. Now, under the pressure of a mutual grief, they met and spoke once more, for Mrs. Ellinthorpe was dying. Remus saw it long before Romulus gave it any serious thought.

Remus and the young wife had quietly brought to the old woman the only real joys and comforts she had ever known. An atmosphere of generous love surrounded their every action to her. In her long weeks of helplessness they waited on her with unceasing devotion. What thoughts passed through the tired brain, they knew not; the pale blue eyes were full of changing expressions, but she said little.

One stormy winter evening, just before the time when Remus and his wife generally came over to keep the night watch with the mother, Romulus, who sat beside her engaged in reading some real estate journals, saw her eyes sparkle with sudden lustre, she smiled, too, very happily and sweetly.

"Ah, mother," cried Romulus, delightedly, "you are better now, you will get well! Here have I been reading most encouraging things in real estate; you'll ride in your own carriage yet upon our land."

A gray shade passed over her face, the light was fading in her eyes, she turned them upon him with a look in which years of despondency seemed blended, gave a little sigh, and expired.

Ten years have passed since that winter afternoon. Success lingered so long upon the way that the flowers all fell from her garland, and by the time she reached Romulus she was nothing but a middle-aged matron with a strong commercial flavor about her.

He realized the truth of what Remus had foretold. One can't have everything—as we grasp in one direction something else slips by.

Remus has worked very hard, but he holds unpurchased blessings. As he returns from daily toil two fine boys rush out to greet and call him father, the face of his early love smiles benignly at him, his soul is anchored for all time in the haven of content.

Romulus looks even more sadly now upon the factories and dwellings which cover his acres than he did in those years when they were a weed-grown desolation, for he knows of a surety that he gave up the only things in life worth having, and that there are temples he cannot unlock with his golden key.

POEMS.

GRANDMA.

Take off your wraps, dear Fannie,
  'Tis good, and kind I own —
You should come and visit Granny
  When you knew she's all alone;
Not that I'm ever alone, dear,
  For thoughts companions be,
Who kindly traverse each bygone year
  Of my three-score years and three.
Still you must know I feel it sweet
  When a gay young girl like you
Will visit Grandma's dull retreat
  And bring some sunshine through.
So, give us the news, my birdling!
  How goes the world today?
What are the latest songs they sing?
  What are the things they say?

Nothing but talk of the Great " World's
    Fair " —
  Is this you tell me true?
Reports and rumors everywhere
  Of all they're going to do;
Of how Aladdin's wonder place
  By this but a midget seems;
This big " white city " of glorious grace,

This solid "dream of dreams;"
Well, well, but yet, tho' it may be true,
   I remember a *Fair* long gone
'They gave to our noble boys in blue ;
   'Twas our first, our grandest one.
Grand to those tired men who came
   Alive from those fighting years,
Grand thro' our dead in their dear-earned fame,
   Grand through our women's tears.

You talk of how nations all shall be
   In this city of pride elate,
Waving their banners bright and free
   From every shore and state.
We had banners upon *our* walls
   Torn and battered by shot and shell;
Even now the bitter tear drop falls,
   I remember it all so well!
And how, as I looked at my boys returned
   Safely again that day,
I thought of the one so vainly mourned
   Who dead at Shiloh lay.
Your uncle, dear — nay, do not weep,
   He was so strong and brave —
'Twas hard to believe him sound asleep
   In the silence of the grave ;
His eyes were blue as your own, my dear,
   His voice! how glad and free,

More plainly yet from year to year
  Its tones come back to me.

That War! it is History *now*, you say.
  Is it, then, so long ago?
Why, to me it is just like yesterday.
  But, then — all's changed I know.

But tell me all you saw and heard
  On your Dedication Day!
Ah! your mounted soldiers with spur and
    sword
  Must have shown in fine array!
Five thousand voices in your hymn!
  And your guests from every land!
Here, wipe my glasses, dear — they're dim.
  There's a shaking in my hand.
It must have been fine with fireworks too,
  Rockets both big and small.
The flag of the Union, red, white and blue,
  I'd have liked *that* best of all!

But fireworks! Ah! my mem'ry goes
  To a bright October day,
Before you were born, my budding rose.
  'Twas a sight, I've heard men say,
That its like was never seen before,
  For a city, skyward flaming,
Lighted the lake from shore to shore,
  The red of the sunset shaming.

Shall I ever forget that dreadful night
  When the streets — a sea of fire —
Raised their billows of cruel light
  Hissing and swirling higher and higher!
When we stood in the water, cold, waist deep,
  And saw our homes turn dust,
And the flames still northward creep and
    and creep
  In that terrible holocaust!

Our darling Lucy, from that time,
  Drooped and withered, a faded flower,
Killed ere she reached her woman's prime
  By the horrors of the hour!
She was our dearest, sweetest, best —
  Your mother's sister, dear —
Brighter and truer than all the rest.
  But there — I do declare —
You're crying again! Ah! dry your eyes.
  You're spoiling their pretty blue!
Now teach your grandma to be wise,
  And not to sadden you;
Enjoy to the full your great "World's
    Fair,"
  Let no troubled thoughts intrude
Of your Granny in her old arm-chair,
  With her "peopled solitude;"
For you see how 'tis, my bonny one:
  Those who have gone before —

With whom the work of my life was
    done —
  Are calling me o'er and o'er,
Calling me ever thro' sun and shade,
  Through summer, or winter hours.
Their touch is soft on my spirit laid,
  Like dew on the waiting flowers.
I scarce can think of the world that's near,
  Though the present is best, 'tis said,
For an old woman's thoughts, I sadly fear,
  Are less with the living than dead.

THE FROST UPON THE PANE.

He softly looked at her, and said,
    "I'll kiss you dear, again,
And the world outside shall never know,
    For there's frost on the window pane."

The careless footsteps hurrying by
    Struck loud the freezing air,
The sound of merry laugh and voice,
    Resounded keen and clear,

But fastened close from all beyond
    By Winter's snowy chain,
They kissed the tender kiss of love,
    For the frost was on the pane!

The snows of Winters twain since then
    Their cold white hands have spread;
Long Falls of storm and Springs of rain,
    Have passed her heedless head;

And now as Winter days draw close
    Their heavy clouds again,
She sadly sees the tracery made
    By the frost upon the pane.

She backward turns the page of life
  To one remembered day,
When sunshine glistened in her heart
  Though clouds hung ashen gray;

When hope, all earnest-eye'd, looked out
  Upon the years to come;
When restlessness, despair and doubt,
  Seemed hidden, chained or dumb.

And on that page, so worn and old,
  So blurred by useless tears,
All interlined, and undertraced
  By penciled thoughts of years,

She writes the solemn words "No more,"
  Then sighing, turns again
Her saddened eyes to where the frost
  Lies white upon the pane.

COMING HOME.

I took the book within my hand
    And thought to read it some,
But not a word could understand
    For he is "coming home."
And every distant housetop made
    Those little words to me,
They marked the afternoon's long shade,
    They framed each withered tree;
The laden wagons in the street
    Just rumbled out that tune,
And with the tread of passing feet
    Sang, "he is coming soon."
Then when the dark of evening came
    And every lighted lamp
Shone with its flickering yellow flame
    A fire-fly in the damp;
When Heaven, its patient stars hung out
    The brightest lamps of all,
Love brushed away the webs of doubt,
    And Hope "held carnival!"

There was no need to count delay
    Of joys that went before,
When certainty in bright array

Stood smiling at the door;
And with a sunny look that said,
"I stay, no more to roam,"
Bade all my heart be comforted,
For he is "coming home."

RETURNED.

A little parcel, barely spanned
   Within the compass of my hand,
Ah me! how small a thing to hold
   A wealth of hopes and dreams untold.

So take this back, each garnered thought,
   Each relic careful love had sought
To deck the lighted niche, where stood
   The idol of its tenderest mood!

Would I could give you back with these
   The mem'ry of your perjuries,
And from my wearied brain efface
   Of that past time remotest trace.

It cannot be, for memory still
   Will triumph o'er impotent will,
And cruel fires of love, now spent
   Leave blackened marks the way they went.

FOR ONE DAY.

When the spring time comes, beloved,
    When the bare-branched trees once more
Feel the thrill of life awakening
    Through them as it did of yore,
When the little violet, trembling
    To the sun's responsive ray,
Opens wide its eyes with pleasure,
    We shall meet that happy day.
Only one, and yet what rapture
    May those halcyon hours impart,
When the warmth of joy shall ripen
    Sweets transferred from heart to heart;
When we'll hear the bird's shrill whistle
    For his mate, still far away,
And we'll smile, remembering only
    We are children for one day.
We shall see the white clouds floating
    In a sky serenely blue,
And we'll say the world so large, dear,
    Holds today but me and you.
Then the wind—a music sweeter
    Than the art of man can reach—
It will play a soft adagio
    To the lovers' murmured speech;

FOR ONE DAY.

Just one day, long hoped for, dreamed of,
    In the wintry months gone by.
Jeweled promise of the season
    Borealis in love's sky.
How its rosy colors cheered us
    When the fire of hope burned low,
And pale sorrow at the ashes
    Mourned the joys of long ago;
But we'll cast each care behind us
    When that balmy morn shall rise,
And together, all unthinking,
    Walk the fields of Paradise,
Every leaf and branch a token
    In their dress of living green,
Of that other life unbroken
    With no cruel death between;
Of that other life, where anguish
    Shall no blazing sword unsheath,
Where no canker worm of sadness
    Eats the rooting hope beneath,
All the passion and forlornness,
    All the sorrow put away,
When, hand clasped in hand, like children,
    We shall spend that last sweet day.

ROSEHILL.

I.

Sleep'st thou well, dearest, where the summer blooms,
  Blend with the soft wind on the day's warm breast,
Where sings the wild bird from the grove's deep glooms,
  And nature tunes her million sounds toward rest?
Where sheds the sun his bright impartial rays,
  And gleams the pond, a silver basin, set
Close to where droop the green acacia sprays,
  And breathes the odor of the mignonette?

II.

Sleep'st thou well dearest? all the air is rife
  With gentle sounds, whose tender meanings spread
A gladd'ning influence, breathing hope and life,
  E'en o'er thy grave, who liest cold and dead,
The birdling woos his little mate once more,
  The south wind dallies with the bloss'ming trees,
And every green slope of this lake-girt shore
  Shakes out sweet perfume to the amorous breeze.

III.

Yes, well thou sleepest! all the sun's warm gold
    Lights never more thy dark and narrow bed;
The happy secrets Nature's lips have told
    Unheeded sweetness speak to thee—my dead;
For though she flaunt her glorious summer hours,
    And deck with garlands every moment 'round,
She sheds in vain the crimson of her flowers,
    And cannot call thee from thy rest profound.

FORGET ME NOT.

The walks with weeds are overgrown,
    All thick about them lie
Crisp autumn leaves of somber tone,
    To match the lowering sky;
The wind that turns them, murmurs low
    The message it has brought
From northern fields of ice and snow,
    . With heralding unsought;
The flower beds, their beauty fled
    Where weeds in jostling number,
Cross stems above the blossoms dead
    To guard their earthy slumber.
No careful hand that rest shall break,
    No kindly eye may see
The verdure that the spring shall wake
    On withered stem and tree;
All is deserted; on the wall
    The green stains thickly spread,
And ivy strives to cover all
    With curtaining leaves instead;
The fountain basin, blotched and cracked,
    Filled by decaying mosses
Where time has coursed its changeless track
    And age each mark engrosses;

The ruined dial's fallen apart,
    The sun that's true forever,
Shall brightly touch its disused heart
    With meaningless endeavor;
And there, beyond them all I see
    Solemn, and sad, and gray,
The old house seeming but to be
    The sentinel of decay;
I will not penetrate its gloom
    To see from floor to ceiling
Its dusty trace of fate and doom,
    Its storied unrevealing.
Though sad its garden, sadder far
    To tread again these floors,
And see, as some undying star,
    The memory that endures.
I'll pace once more the lonely walks
    And watch the frowning weather,
And listen to the mystic talks
    The dead leaves hold together.
A few pale blossoms still remain
    From Summer's wreath, slow falling,
All bending to the stern refrain
    The cold storm king is calling.
One slim white rose its pale cheek lays
    Against the mouldering wall,
Like a sad thought of other days
    Beyond Hope's slow recall.
And here in this lone corner, blue
    As dropped from morning skies,

A tiny flower is peeping through,
   Nature's last sweet surprise;
Ah! happy ground that gave it birth,
   Most glad, sun-favored spot!
To bear the sweetest flower on earth,
   The blue forget-me-not!
I gaze upon the tiny thing,
   The magic key that opes
That heavy door whose solemn swing
   Has hidden many hopes;
And down the long deserted hall,
   That led to happier years,
I stretch the cloth of memory's pall,
   And mark the way with tears,
And bless the grief that thus can melt
   The ice, that hardening made
A sorrow that no softening felt,
   No tenderness betrayed;
For He who made the flower and sun,
   The pleasure and the pain,
Shall come to claim them everyone
   In His good time again;
He seeks us with unresting care
   And each forsaken spot
May yet beneath His fostering care
   Bear one forget-me-not.

www.ingramcontent.com/pod-product-compliance
Lightning Source LLC
Chambersburg PA
CBHW030311240426
43673CB00040B/1135